Constructing Girlhood

Feminist Perspectives on The Past and Present Advisory Editorial Board

Constructing Girlhood:
Popular Magazines for Girls
Growing up in England, 1920–1950

Penny Tinkler

Taylor & Francis
Publishers since 1798

UK   Taylor & Francis Ltd, 4 John St., London WC1N 2ET
USA   Taylor & Francis Inc., 1900 Frost Road, Suite 101, Bristol, PA 19007

First published 1995

A Catalogue Record for this book is available from the British Library

ISBN 0 7484 0285 3
ISBN 0 7484 0286 1 (pbk)

Library of Congress Cataloging-in-Publication Data are available on request

Typeset in 10pt Times
by Solidus (Bristol) Limited

Printed by SRP Ltd, Exeter

For Muriel,
and in memory of Marjorie.

Contents

Acknowledgments

Thanks go to Penny Summerfield who supervised the PhD thesis on which this book is based, for her encouragement, also her advice and thoughtful comment on the writing of *Constructing Girlhood*. I would also like to mention members of the Centre for Women's Studies at Lancaster University during the late 1980s who persuaded me to proceed with this project, especially Lisa Adkins and Celia Lury. Special thanks go to the friends and colleagues who have given invaluable support, and also constructive feedback on the preparation of the manuscript for this book, in particular Lynn Abrams, Margaret Badley, Sally A. Branch, Bridget Cooke, David Morgan, Alison Oram and Bobbie Wells. Thanks also to Joy and Frank Tinkler, Mario Chin and Rosie Briggs who have been a constant source of support.

I would also like to express my gratitude to those people who responded to my requests for help in researching the production of girls' magazines, especially the women and men who contributed insights into editorial processes through correspondence and/or interview: Gordan Davies, Mary Grieve, James Hemming, Patricia Lamburn, Mrs Jean Lee, W.O.G. Lofts, Peggy Makins, W.D. McClelland, Marcus Morris, Lorrie Purden. I would also like to thank the staff at the following libraries and archives for their assistance: Lancaster University Library Inter-Library Loans Service, The British Library, the Institute of Practitioners in Advertising and the Mass-Observation Archive.

Finally, I would like to thank Deb Tarrant for her unstinting encouragement, wacky sense of humour and also practical support throughout the writing of this book.

Material copyright the Trustees of the Mass-Observation Archive at the University of Sussex, reproduced by permission of Curtis Brown Group Ltd, London. Magazine covers are reproduced by permission of The British Library.

Chapter 1

Introduction

Because I've been a worker like you, I know what girls like, and I'm going to give you a paper you'll enjoy.

(Editor, *Peg's Paper*, 1919)

Essentially the *School Friend* will appeal chiefly to the girl at school, the girl whose tastes have not previously been catered for.

(Editor, *School Friend*, 1919)[1]

Magazines for 'girls' proliferated during the interwar years although many became casualties of the Second World War. As the descriptions of *Peg's Paper* and *School Friend* reveal, girls' papers targeted a variety of groups including working-class and middle-class schoolgirls, and also young working women employed in factories, mills and commerce. The term 'girl', as this range suggests, was used quite broadly in periodical publishing, although it principally referred to the unmarried adolescent; wives and mothers were more usually described as 'women'.[2] Magazines for schoolgirls and young workers proved extremely popular with adolescent female readers, indeed the quantity and quality of magazines read by working-class girls was a source of anxiety throughout the first half of this century.[3] The range of magazines produced for adolescent girls between 1920 and 1950 is the focus of this book. How did magazines present girlhood and femininity to their readers? How were these representations produced? What does the form and content of these papers reveal about the cultural construction of adolescent girlhood in this historical period?

Emerging and recent research has contributed important insights into the position of women in society during the period 1920 to 1950,[4] but with the exception of research into the schooling of girls, the conditions and experiences of adolescent girlhood remain largely undocumented.[5] This neglect is particularly noticeable with regard to those girls who had left full-time school, which for most was at 14 or 15 after 1947. The cultural construction of adolescent girlhood in this period has similarly received scant attention despite a recent flourish of insightful historical studies of popular novels and magazines produced for girls and women, most notably by Gorham, Rowbotham, Cadogan and Craig, Drotner, Auchmuty, Reynolds, Fowler, Beauchamp and Wells which have followed on from White's pioneering study of 1970.[6] As with social and economic histories, studies of popular magazines have tended to obscure adolescent girlhood, focusing either on magazines for 'women' or 'schoolgirls', neglecting the range of papers produced for young working girls; indeed there has been a tendency to conflate papers for young workers with those for an older, usually married, readership thereby denying their specificity as magazines for adolescent readers.[7] There are, however, important reasons for focusing on adolescent girlhood during the period 1920 to 1950 not least because we still know very little about the configurations of gender, class, age and race for the conditions of girlhood and its cultural construction. Similarly we remain largely uninformed about the implications of social, economic and cultural change for approaches to girls growing up in this period, in particular the significance of the two world wars, the depression, demographic imbalance, the declining birth rate, interwar homophobia, and the 1920s postwar 'back to the home' pressures. However, it is not only that adolescent girlhood has been marginalised in twentieth-century social and women's history, it is also that there has been little attention to biography, age, and the processes of growing up and growing old.

Constructing Girlhood addresses aspects of biographic change through an exploration of the ways in which popular girls' magazines constructed, organised and managed age as well as social class in their production of different categories of girl readers and in their representations of age- and class-specific aspects of adolescence. In its attention to age, this book addresses change along two axes – historical and biographical – and so differs from previous historical work on magazines which has focused on social class as the major variable in the cultural construction of femininity; although age is recognised in these studies, it is not explored as a dynamic in the sense of how magazines vary according to the age of their readership. Attention to the ways in which popular literature constructed and managed age is particularly important in the context of twentieth-century preoccupation with age, age-grades, and generation. Indeed the concept of adolescence as a period of transition between child and adult was largely a product of late nineteenth and early twentieth century initiatives which institutionalised a prolonged period of dependency of young people on the family, facilitated by the extension of compulsory schooling and restrictions on child labour. This institutionalised dependency was further consolidated by changes in the legal status of young people, the introduction of the Youth Service in 1939 and attempts, following the Fisher Act of 1918 and the Education Act of 1944, to establish compulsory part-time continuation education for adolescents who were no longer in full-time education.[8] Underpinning these developments was a highly influential body of knowledge from within the new science of psychology which sought to describe, categorise and explain adolescence as a crucial but vulnerable and unstable stage in the process of maturation. Indeed this period is notable for attempts to demarcate the contours of adolescence as a period of transition between childhood and adult maturity characterised by emotional, physical, psychological and philosophical change.[9]

For girls growing up during the period 1920 to 1950, as for girls today, the years between 12 and 20 were marked by a number of changes. The most important of these were the transition from school to paid or unpaid work, and 'entrance' into heterosexual relationships on the path to marriage and motherhood. These were neither natural nor universal characteristics but widely experienced socially constructed features of female adolescence which varied along the lines of social class. Of particular import for growing up was the 'heterosexual career', that is the assumed and encouraged 'entrance' of girls into relationships with the opposite sex as a prelude to marriage and motherhood. Although many women did not marry in this period, from choice or lack of opportunity, a heterosexual identity expressed through monogamous marriage remained central to perceptions of mature womanhood; adjustment to heterosexuality was widely seen as essential to the formation of an adult woman's identity and the successful fulfilment of her 'natural' roles as wife and mother.[10] The importance attached to a heterosexual orientation and marriage was fuelled by hostility towards single, especially professional, women in the interwar years. This was rationalised by the arguments of sexologists and the new psychology which normalised heterosexuality, and pathologised celibacy and homosexuality. It also mapped out sexual development for girls culminating in monogamous marriage and motherhood.[11] Heterosexuality was central both to constructions of adolescence and the social relations which organised adolescent experience. For this reason the adolescent as historical subject and 'adolescence' as a social construct are central to the feminist project of revealing the institution of heterosexuality and uncovering the history of women's position within the relations of heterosexuality.[12]

A second transition of particular importance for girls growing up in this period was the move from full-time schooling to full-time paid or unpaid domestic work. Indeed the interwar years are notable for the extension of a pattern of school followed by paid employment for the majority of girls from all social groups. Leaving full-time schooling signalled a change in occupation, so to speak, as girls either became full-time wage earners or unpaid home-workers. This transition also heralded a shift in the girl's character as a consumer; if based in the home as unpaid domestic and care worker she often acquired responsibility for domestic budgeting and consumption, and if she entered the labour market she usually enjoyed some personal disposable income whilst she remained single

useful
for
teenage

and unhindered by dependents. Whilst most adolescent girls did not have the level of disposable income associated with girls growing up in the 1950s, young workers were nevertheless constructed and courted as consumers in the period between 1920 to 1950, not least by the periodical press.[13]

In the production of magazines for girls, the age of the intended reader was an important consideration in terms of its significance for the intended reader's position in the heterosexual career, her occupation – whether schoolgirl, unpaid home-worker or paid worker – and, linked to this, her character as a consumer. Editorial perceptions of the intended reader's social class background were also important. In her study of women's magazines, White claims that pre-1950 magazines were principally determined by the social conditions and role of women, hence changes in the magazines' format were a direct response to women's needs. Magazines, she argues, were 'trend followers' rather than 'trend setters'; 'no modification in magazine content could occur without being preceded by a corresponding change in the social conditions of women'.[14] This study of the construction of representation in girls' magazines suggests a more complex relationship between the editor and reader. Editors did not simply respond to the social conditions of adolescent girlhood. A number of other considerations were involved in the production process, namely prevalent ideologies of femininity and constructions of girlhood; publishers' objectives, directives and culture; and girls' interests, desires and needs. Editorial negotia-tion of these factors shaped magazine engagement with the varied and changing conditions and experiences of adolescent girlhood, contributing to the cultural construction and management of biographical and historical changes.

Recent research has argued that the position of women in society can best be understood in terms of the articulation of the autonomous systems of patriarchy and capitalism, where patriarchy is understood to mean 'a system of social structures, social relations and practices in which men dominate, oppress and exploit women'; and where capitalism is those relations which enable capital to expropriate wage labour.[15] In the context of the nineteenth and twentieth centuries, Walby argues that women's position in paid employment was characterised by considerable tension between these two systems.[16] Summer-field's study of the position of women workers in the Second World War similarly exposes the tensions between the interests of patriarchy and capital, drawing attention to the ways in which this constrained the state's ability to mobilise female labour in the war effort.[17] *Constructing Girlhood* explores the articulation of capitalism and patriarchy in the production of popular literature for girls and in the construction of representations of adolescent girls and girlhood. In this context, the position of girls in the relations of capital are understood in terms of their relation to wage labour, the reproduction of wage labour through child bearing, and consumption. Although there is controversy concerning what actually constitutes patriarchal relations, for the purpose of this book I shall focus on patriarchal interests in the paid workplace and those embedded in the institutions of heterosexuality, including marriage and the family, within which females were subordinate to men and provided for male sexual, emotional and domestic needs.[18]

The argument presented here is that the changing form and content of girls' magazines were largely determined by the articulation of the interests of capital and of patriarchy. Indeed, girls' magazines provide an example of how the relations of capital and of patriarchy were often in tension: they also illustrate how these different and often conflicting interests were managed, negotiated and, on occasions, harmonised within the sphere of cultural production. The key point of tension and negotiation can be summarised as follows: the form and content of magazines represented the articulation of capital's concern to exploit girls as consumers, with patriarchal interests in the heterosexual development and orientation of girls as a necessary precondition of their acceptance of unequal gender relations and a subordinate position within marriage. The segmentation of publishing for adolescent girlhood was underpinned by assumptions about the different consumer potential of school and working girls, but it also corresponded to the different positions which girls in their early, as opposed to their late, teens were expected to occupy in the heterosexual career. For example, as discussed in chapter 5, many school-aged girls were interested in boys and were avid readers of romance magazines. However, editors of schoolgirl papers deemed their readers to be too young for heterosexual associations and they denied their readers' sexual interest in boys, or indeed girls, and focused instead on girls' friendships. In contrast, editors of papers for older working girls expected their readers to be preoccupied with boys and courtship as a prelude to marriage. These papers subsequently prioritised heterosexual relationships and excluded close friendships between girls and women. Editors had to address girls' interests because girls were the main purchasers and consumers of these magazines, but this did not mean that they merely responded to their readers' wishes. The content of magazines and the representational management of girlhood were quite fundamentally shaped by perceptions of where readers were located in the heterosexual career. This overarching problem gave rise to two specific areas of negotiation.

Firstly, magazine editors needed to address their readers' desire for power, independence and excitement, without challenging patriarchal interests in male dominance and a girl's acceptance of a future role as subordinate wife, mother and home-maker. In magazines for school-aged girls, editors accommodated readers' fantasies by creating a relatively liberated period of female adolescence (discussed in chapter 3). This independence was, however, only temporarily acceptable, moreover most heroines continued to exhibit domestic and nurturant qualities which signalled their future contentment with a traditional feminine destiny. Magazines for working adolescents were more constrained in addressing girls' fantasies of power and autonomy precisely because their readers were of an age when finding and securing a marriage partner was considered of paramount importance. Nevertheless, they too could not afford to estrange their readers and they subsequently sought to address their readers' desires. This can be seen in the management of the bachelor girl, examined in chapter 5, and in the fictional representation of sexually sophisticated female characters which are discussed in chapter 6.

The second area of negotiation was between girls as wage labourers and girls as unpaid domestic, emotional and sexual servicers of men. Following the First World War there was considerable concern that girls were rejecting marriage, domesticity and maternity, and there were also fears that girls were seeking to be independent of men in both economic and sexual terms. Magazines addressed these different interests with care as they assumed that their readers wanted careers and modernity but also that they needed to work. The result of this negotiation, as we shall see in chapter 4, was a modern career girl who eventually accepted marriage and domesticity. Clues to this destiny included references to her domestic skills and attention to the ways in which the modern girl was visually different from men, indeed the feminine body, discussed in chapter 6, was a central rationalisation of unequal gender relations and the sexual division of labour. In the mid-1930s the tension between women as producers within capital and as producers within patriarchy was again played out in discussions of married women's work, examined in chapter 4. As with the 1920s modern girl, the readers' presumed need for work was an important factor in editorial negotiation of these interests. In this case, the employment of married women outside the home was accepted as enabling couples to marry and have children.

One outcome of these editorial attempts to reconcile the contradictions of gender, was the construction of the 'modern' schoolgirl or young worker, that is the production of new and updated versions of girlhood and femininity consistent with contemporary conditions and demands on girls growing up. Indeed, popular girls' magazines were involved in the production of ideals for girlhood and femininity that negotiated the demands of patriarchy and capital with readers' needs and interests. In constructing the 'modern' girl, editors faced the added problem of inheriting older notions of femininity, and therefore had to engage in yet another act of reconciliation. This resulted in the production of frameworks for moral guidance that fused the old with the new.

Commentators on popular literature have, until quite recently, been quick to draw conclusions about the influence of magazines on young female readers.[19] In the 1960s and 1970s, for example, historical and contemporary evaluations of literature were premised on socialisation theory which postulated that the media, alongside the family, was highly influential in the acquisition of gender and class identity.[20] Historical assessments of the effect of reading are, however, difficult to substantiate,[21] and socialisation theory has been the subject of severe criticism for its determinism and focus on cultural as opposed to structural influences.[22] Recent developments in the fields of cultural and media studies have also opened up the issue of the media's influence, and convincingly challenged the traditional model of the media as a manipulator of audiences. Addressing issues of meaning, reading and readers, this research draws attention to the multiplicity of meanings within a text, the heterogeneity of the 'audience', the variety of 'reading contexts', and the ways in which the reader is actively involved in the production of meaning.[23] One result of this has been a shift from attention to texts, their production and content, to the study of readers and reading practices.[24] Whilst attention to reading is more than a necessary corrective to past preoccupations with text, being concerned with processes of meaning production, studies of text and cultural production are still valid. According to Hall, '[w]hile any one cultural text offers a multiplicity of meanings to its readers, ultimately not just any meaning can or will be drawn from it': readings are 'structured in dominance', offering a pattern of preferred options in line with the 'preferred institutional, political and ideological order'.[25] In girls' magazines, these preferred readings were framed in ways which were intelligible to readers located within the same dominant culture, for example in articles, letters pages, advertisements and editorials.[26] Attention to these 'preferred meanings', in conjunction with a study of production processes (pursued in chapter 3), can contribute important insights into how different social groups construct and manage gender, along the axis of social class and age within the wider context of social, economic and cultural change (discussed in chapter 2).[27] It can also reveal some of the key meanings which many girls would have identified in their reading.

Constructing Girlhood is not concerned to explore the effect on girls of magazine messages. Such a project would necessitate a different type of enquiry. But this study does elucidate some of the lessons in femininity to which many girls growing up in this period were exposed. Research into the reading of 1980s magazines by Ballaster *et al.* suggests that women are conscious of magazines as bearers of particular discourses; the authors conclude that '[w]e may not agree with the versions of femininity offered in any particular magazine text, or in magazines in general, but our disagreement is a response to, a reaction to, these versions, rather than a reshaping or a destruction of them'.[28] It seems highly probable that girls growing up in the period 1920 to 1950 similarly recognised the preferred readings embedded in their magazines. This was partly because these readings were framed so explicitly by editorials, feature titles, illustration and techniques of repetition and reinforcement. Easy to follow, step-by-step guidance on interpretation were often employed in articles and other direct information features while fiction was formulaic and relied upon a limited range of codes.[29] These particular readings were reinforced by other cultural forms such as contemporary popular films, which were featured and discussed within many schoolgirl and working girls' papers of this period.[30]

Through reading magazines girls growing up between 1920 and 1950 did learn about girlhood and femininity but this does not mean they passively accepted or acted upon these 'preferred meanings', nor that these readings were exclusive. Girls probably produced a range of meanings and pleasures from their reading.[31] Under certain conditions, however, both the fiction and non-fiction elements of magazines were able to offer girls moral guidance. Central to this effect was some form of magazine engagement, whether direct or indirect, with the reader; this helped to secure the preferred meaning, and establish its relevance for girls and also its possible influence.[32] This was facilitated by editorial strategies, which aimed to foster the readers' loyalty, trust and identification with the magazine.[33] Perhaps most important for securing the 'preferred meaning' and the role of magazines as moral guides was the fact that magazines were one of the few mediums to specifically address girls, bestowing on them an importance that they were generally denied as females and as adolescents.[34] Moreover, these papers broached topics from the perspective of the adolescent, providing detailed and accessible information on issues of concern to girls growing up.

Evidence that at least some girls sought advice on how to manage the experiences of adolescence is provided by the numerous letters received by girls' magazines, only a few of which were actually printed in the correspondence features.[35] Girls' need for guidance on growing up is also conveyed in Pearl Jephcott's rather sad description of a working-class girl in the 1940s:

> The match-box maker of fifteen, with her boyfriend of sixteen, her two nights a week at the pictures and her most cherished possession still an old doll, searches Silver Star to see how other, rather older people cope with the problems of sex that are constantly brought to her attention now that she is a member of the adult world of workers. How can she get to know the things that older girls know?[36]

Constructing Girlhood explores the kind of knowledge with which this match-box maker, and girls in other social niches, were furnished by magazines of the period 1920–1950.

Notes

1 *Peg's Paper*, 5 May 1919, p.1; *School Friend*, May 1919, p.1.
2 There were, however, anomalies in the use of the term 'girl': it was often employed as a term of flattery to describe older women; it was used to belittle women by suggesting their child-like status; reference to being 'girls' also suggested a reclaiming of the relative freedoms of childhood and adolescence and the female

sociability that was a strong feature of girlhood experiences. Although there are problems with using the term 'girl' to describe females who clearly have adult responsibilities and competencies, it is nevertheless convenient and also appropriate, given the theme of this study, to use this term throughout.

3   For an example which is typical of this concern, see Jephcott (1942).
4   For example, Lewis (1984); Summerfield (1984); Summerfield and Braybon (1987); Glucksmann (1990); Roberts (1984); Beddoe (1989).
5   On schoolgirls, Summerfield (1987a) and (1987c). Alexander (1989) provides a rare glimpse of young female waged workers in the 1920s and 1930s.
6   On papers for schoolgirls see Gorham (1982) and (1987); Drotner (1988); Bratton (1981); Cadogan and Craig (1986); Rowbotham (1989); Reynolds (1990); Auchmuty (1992); Wells (1993). Also Tinkler (1987) and (1995b). On women's magazines see White (1970); Fowler (1991); Beauman (1983).
7   For example, White (1970). McRobbie (1991), p.83, in her study of *Jackie* in the 1970s, briefly comments on how contemporary girls'/women's magazines define age groups from early childhood to old age.
8   Gillis (1974); Springhall (1986); Tinkler (1994a) and (1994b).
9   Dyhouse (1981), ch.4; Griffin (1993), ch.1.
10   On the heterosexual expectations of Victorian and Edwardian girls, see Dyhouse (1981), Gorham (1982).
11   On psychology and the sexologists see Dyhouse (1981) ch.4; Jeffreys (1985).
12   Jeffreys (1989), p.16.
13   See Abrams (1961).
14   White (1970).
15   Walby (1987).
16   Walby (1986).
17   Summerfield (1984).
18   Walby (1990), ch.1.
19   Jephcott (1942); Alderson (1968); Hoggart (1958); Orwell (1982b).
20   For example, Cadogan and Craig (1986).
21   Bratton (1981), p.24.
22   Walby (1990), pp.91–4.
23   For overview see Ballaster *et al.* (1991) ch.1, especially pp.38–42, also ch.5; Bonner *et al.* (1992) section I.
24   Drotner (1988); Auchmuty (1992).
25   Hall (1980), p.134.
26   Craig and Cadogan (1986); Drotner (1988); Fowler (1991).
27   In order to examine preferred meanings I have used a close textual analysis of the magazines, which is attentive to the structure and presentation of magazines and the subtleties of representation. Quantitative content analysis, such as that employed by Ferguson (1983), is not sensitive to these features, moreover it tends towards generalisations, which obscure aspects of representation that are a central feature of this study, namely the tensions and negotiations which are articulated within representations of girlhood and femininity. As Ferguson explains (p.4), content analysis 'involves selecting specific categories of subject matter and counting the number of times there is reference to a topic or category of topics in a particular issue of a particular year'. For criticism of content analysis see Scott (1990), p.32.
28   Ballaster *et al.* (1991), p.131. Whether the women in this research used 'transparent'

readings, which adopted the stance of the implied reader encouraged by the text, 'mediated' readings wherein they recognised the message and reported it with neither empathy or disagreement, or 'displaced' readings which involved adopting the position of the implied reader in order to criticise it, the women recognised and could report the 'preferred reading', see ch.5.

29   Research on the child's concept of story reveals that by the age of nine, most children have developed expectations about the roles of typical fiction characters and are able to predict common patterns of action and behaviour. See Applebee (1978).

30   According to Barthes (1972) p.27, our understanding of a text is always informed and structured by our prior understanding and use of other texts; what he refers to as inter-textual reading. Reynolds (1990) argues that juvenile literature provides the lens through which other texts are perceived and filtered.

31   On possible pleasures and positive readings of schoolgirl stories see Auchmuty (1992) and Frith (1985). Frith also discovered that an attraction of schoolgirl stories for modern girls was the sense of control they experienced in reading arising from the predictability of the text and its structure. One way in which girls did reject these papers was by not purchasing or reading them. Nava (1992), p.185 reminds us of this consumer power.

32   Fowler (1991), p.52, makes an explicit link between this engagement and the ideological potential of fiction: 'sufficient realism is required for readers to suspend disbelief, that is, some correspondence must exist between their experiences and those represented in the story world.'

33   White (1970), p.96, also Leman (1980) comment on editorial recognition of the use of personal identification in interwar women's magazines. Correspondence features were particularly important for achieving this using strategies common in post-1950s magazines, see McRobbie (1991) and (1981), p.121, also Winship (1987), ch.5.

34   Dixon (1987), p.19, cited in Auchmuty (1992), pp.23–4, argues Mills and Boon 'put women first and see them as true "heroines" of the world'. As Drotner (1988), p.237 points out, magazines were also more topical and responsive to readers' needs than novels.

35   Although there has been some doubt as to the authenticity of these letters, evidence suggests that most were genuine or versions of the letters received. See Hemming (1960) for an examination of the letters sent to *Girl* magazine between 1953 and 1955; the paper's letter page was introduced due to reader demand. See also Brew (1943), p.110.

36   Jephcott (1942), p.110. Hemming (1960) similarly commented on the adolescent girls' need for information on matters concerning growing up. Contemporary studies of film also suggested that girls looked to the screen for this information, see Wall (1948), pp.109–110.

Chapter 2

Adolescent Girlhood:
A Historical Context

In her study of girlhood in late Victorian and Edwardian England, Carol Dyhouse demonstrates the significance of both social class and gender for girls' experiences of family and education.[1] Such cross-cutting of gender-specific experiences was also characteristic of the conditions of girlhood between 1920 and 1950. Some historians of the interwar period have claimed that social class differences diminished, largely as a result of the experiences of war.[2] As this chapter demonstrates, whilst experiences of girlhood were influenced by wider social and economic changes, social class remained significant for girls' experiences of home, family, education and employment throughout the period. The conditions of girlhood were also shaped by race although little is yet known about the details of 'black' girls growing up in England at this time, or indeed before. Nevertheless, the 'whiteness' of the girls discussed in this chapter was clearly significant for their experience of girlhood.[3] Age was also key to girlhood experience; indeed adolescence was a period characterised by transitions. Whilst English girlhood between 1920 and 1950 was differentiated along a number of axes it remained a specifically feminine experience; girlhood remained quite distinct in important ways from boyhood.

Before going on to look at aspects of girlhood in this period it is first appropriate to clarify what we mean by the terms 'working class' and 'middle class'. The discussion of girlhood that follows draws upon the social classification used by the 1951 Registrar General, the objective of which was to ensure that each social class category was homogeneous in relation to basic criteria of general standing in the community. Drawing upon occupational categories identified by Routh, the Registrar General's social classifications in 1951 can be translated as follows:[4]

	Social Class	**Typical Occupations**
I	upper/upper mc:	higher professional, bankers, large retailers
II	middle mc:	lower professional, managerial and administrative employers/retailers/proprietors employing at least one assistant
IIIa	lower mc:	Occupational Class 3/4, small retailers, shop assistants, nurses, telephone/telegraph operators
IIIb	upper wc:	Occupational Class 5, skilled artisans, public servants
IV/V	mid-lower wc:	Occupational Class 6 (semi-skilled), Occupational Class 7 (unskilled)

MC = middle class. WC = working class.

According to social survey criteria, £250 per annum marked the dividing line between the middle and working classes in this period although there were discrepancies. Non-manual workers in Social Class (SC) IIIa were frequently paid less than £250 p.a. but they and their families perceived themselves to be middle class.[5] Earnings in the lower professions (SCII) were often on par with those of foremen (SCIIIb) which meant that there was frequently parity of income between some sectors of the middle and working classes. A further problem with this system of classification is its failure to address the circumstances of men with large families and with irregular earnings, or those who were unemployed. As Rowntree discovered amongst the York working classes, these two factors were responsible for considerable poverty.[6] There is no reason to suggest that middle-class families did not also experience similar problems. Helen Forrester's middle-class family were thrown into dire poverty following her father's bankruptcy during the 1930s.[7]

Standard classifications of social class raise immense problems for historians of women. Formulated around male employment and income these systems do not lend themselves to the classification of women's work and standard of living.[8] Women who lived in male-headed households were denied recognition for their work and contribution to the family's standard of living. This was simply read off from male employment. Moreover, such classifications did not consider the distribution of income and resources within the household which was generally highly differentiated by gender and age. It has been estimated that only 5–15 per cent of men in industrial England handed over their pay packet intact to their wife[9] and that women were often ignorant about how much their husbands earned.[10] Rowntree was aware of this when researching *Poverty and Progress*: 'most of the interviews were with women, and frequently a woman only knows what money her husband gives her, not how much he actually receives.'[11] These classifications also naturalise the heterosexual couple. How can the experiences of young women be articulated within a classification system constructed around male occupation and/or income, especially when they live independent of men, be it a father or husband?

The social differences of the family contexts in which most girls grew up, differentiated otherwise common experiences of being 'white' girls. These social differences have been systematised as class differences on male-biased occupation or status criteria which, in themselves, tell us little about their significance for the organisation and conditions of girlhood. This chapter addresses this invisibility and explores the impact of these social differences on girls' experiences of home, health, schooling, employment and the transitions of adolescence. Constructing a set of typical features for each social class is, however, complicated by the diversity of family contexts. Nevertheless, this approach does contribute an important, if somewhat generalised, dimension to these social class labels, which engages with the conditions of girlhood. This approach also produces social categories that correspond with the sorts of information available in, and about, girls' magazines and, as we shall see in chapter 3, it thereby provides a useful context in which to set a discussion of the intended and actual readership of girls' magazines in this period.

Returning to the matter in hand, what characterised the conditions of girlhood for different social groups? More specifically, how did girls fare in home and health in this period?

Home and Health

Numerous factors determined home conditions and it is difficult to be precise about the characteristics of middle-class as opposed to working-class homes and how these affected the lives of girls. As we have seen, there was no clear division between the occupational income of the upper working class and the lower middle class, and social-class labels obscure the effects of irregular earnings, unemployment and family size, which all worked to determine standards within the home.

Housing provision, which was of key importance to domestic standards, varied enormously during this period. Middle-class girls tended to live in large old Victorian dwellings or in new semi-detached houses clustered in suburban housing estates. Modern houses were supplied with gas, electric fires and running hot water but not all middle-class housing had such modern amenities. In Birmingham, for example, a 1946 survey revealed that 14 per cent of middle-class families had no indoor sanitation.[12] More generally, pre-1914 houses were 'drafty, expensive to heat and maintain and involved long distance carrying of coal and water' and, as Beddoe explains, 'The efficient running of these houses depended wholly upon a plentiful supply of domestic servants — a supply that was not forthcoming in the interwar years.'[13]

Prior to the First World War, the brunt of domestic management fell to the hierarchy of domestic servants that middle-class families typically employed. After the war few women were keen to take on this type of employment. Labour Exchange policies subsequently forced many girls into this work, but a shortage remained particularly of resident domestic servants.[14] The unwillingness of young women to enter domestic service was not the only reason for the interwar decline of this occupation. Families from SC II and IIIa experienced a fall in their standard of living during the twenties as their incomes remained static in relation to the general rise in prices.[15] A move towards domestic self-sufficiency was one outcome of this change in fortunes. Upper-class and upper-middle-class families were less drastically affected although in the interwar years their once extensive crew of servants was pruned down to include a cook, housemaid, parlour maid and child's nurse. The implications of this shortage of servants was that middle-class women and their daughters became increasingly responsible for the organisation and also the practical business of maintaining the home and family. The growth of magazines for 'new poor' middle-class women offering practical advice on domestic matters reflected this change in the middle-class home.[16] Evidence suggests that in these homes daughters often shared responsibility for domestic conditions continuing a pre-war tradition in lower-middle-class households of girls helping out when servants were not around.[17] During the thirties, surveys suggested that the middle classes generally experienced a rise in living standards. According to Glynn, conspicuous consumption was the most prominent feature of middle-class life during the interwar years; after food and mortgage or rent, families in SC I and II had 48.3 per cent of their income available for unessential items.[18] Whilst this over-generalises the economic status of middle-class families, many of which did suffer during the depression, most middle-class households did have more disposable income, some of which was spent on labour-saving domestic appliances. In 1938 families where the man was earning £400–500 per annum could afford a fridge, vacuum and a gas or electric cooker.[19] Whilst this may have eased domestic work, the increased professionalisation of housekeeping in the interwar years raised domestic standards to new heights of excellence thereby continuing to tie women and their daughters closely to the care of the home.[20]

Housing available for working-class girls was highly variable although poor housing conditions predominated. The Women's Health Enquiry Committee of the 1930s revealed that only 6.9 per cent of their sample of working-class mothers lived in good quality accommodation with electricity, a toilet, hot and cold water, and access to a children's playground.[21] Similar findings emerged from Rowntree's survey of York residents, which revealed that less than 12 per cent were living in good quality housing in 1938.[22] Following the Wheatley Housing Act of 1924, which subsidised slum clearance and rebuilding until 1932, a rash of 'dormitory' council housing estates emerged on town outskirts.[23]

This type of housing, which featured front and back gardens, a parlour, kitchen with an electric oven, bathroom, sitting/living room and two or three bedrooms, accommodated 24.9 per cent of York working-class families in 1938.[24] The main beneficiaries of these new houses were, according to Glynn, the upper working class;[25] certainly the rent would have been too high for families solely reliant on the income of a man in occupations typical of SC IV and V. However in York, Rowntree noted that of the 3297 houses in this category, nearly a thousand were occupied by families dispossessed by slum clearance schemes, some of whom were sufficiently poor to qualify for rent rebates.[26] It would be wrong to assume that girls who lived in these homes were more comfortable than those who lived in older housing. The high rents in council property often exacerbated a family's poverty with implications for the health of children: 'The fact that school MOs have remarked upon the deterioration in physical fitness of children who have moved from bad to good housing conditions is a proof that the lower standard of diet necessitated by a higher rent is not offset by the healthier home environment.'[27]

The majority of Rowntree's sample, representing 63.2 per cent of the local working-class populace, lived in slums or poor quality housing.[28] The Women's Health Enquiry Committee discovered that almost a third of its sample of 1250 women lived in comparable housing conditions.[29] 'Mrs R' of Llanelly lived in two rooms in a four room house which she described as 'damp, dark and low': due to the location of a drain in the house, her home was infested with rats and, in the summer, with bugs.[30] Even by 1940 many of the worst deficiencies of working-class housing remained. In Clerkenwell, for example, up to eight families in furnished sub-lets often shared one w.c., while in north Battersea 60–70 per cent of closets were used by more than one family.[31] The prevalence of such housing conditions was accentuated during the forties by the destruction caused by war-time bombing. In 1951 the Census General Report for England and Wales proudly announced that over half the households in England and Wales had exclusive use of piped water, a cooking stove, kitchen, sink, and fixed bath. The report failed to comment on the lack of amenities available for the remaining 50 per cent of the population despite the fact that it estimated that 1.4 million households did not have exclusive use of kitchen sink and toilet.[32]

The housing conditions in which many working-class girls lived required a considerable effort to maintain and labour-saving devices were not generally available. Hire purchase enabled many families to acquire some modern amenities, but by the late thirties one fifth of households still did not possess an electric or gas cooker.[33] The brunt of these conditions fell on women and their daughters, indeed working-class girls assumed considerable responsibility for domestic work in the home from an early age. This was commented upon by the 1931 Report on the Primary School: 'the heavy domestic duties especially those carried out by young girls in the home, often make for listlessness and fatigue.'[34]

Such observations were repeated in numerous interwar and wartime studies.[35]

Overcrowding remained a problem for working-class girls throughout the period. A survey of 200 people from a poor area of Shoreditch in 1938 discovered that only 25 per cent of 11 year olds and 33 per cent of 15 year olds had their own bed. In a group of 315 children, 33 per cent slept four or more to a bed, 13 slept six or more to a bed, and 10 per cent slept in a room with both their parents.[36] The problem seems to have eased by 1951, but 650 000 households of two or more persons still lived in overcrowded conditions.[37] Cramped and insanitary housing must have affected health; indeed, a Glasgow survey of the period discovered a correlation between the number of rooms in a house and the weight and height of children living within it.[38] Due to the sexual division of labour, which located women mainly in the home, it seems likely that girls and women suffered most from the increased burden of living and working in such conditions.

Tension often arose within the family as a result of continued disturbance and lack of privacy. In *Road To Wigan Pier*, Orwell described a house where 'three grown up girls shared the same bed and all went to work at different hours, each disturbing the others when she got up or came in'.[39] Rose Gamble remembers how her family of six ate, lived and slept in one room partitioned by a rag curtain.[40] Similar experiences were noted by the Women's Health Enquiry Committee.[41] The lack of privacy these conditions permitted posed a problem for the adolescent girl, especially as she was expected to keep the fact that she menstruated hidden from view. Sanitary towels were not widely used by working-class women until the Second World War and most girls who menstruated in the interwar period used rags to soak up the blood which, after use, were left to soak overnight in a bucket.[42]

Clearly, the majority of working-class girls lived in households that were unaffected by interwar attempts at housing improvement. In contrast, middle-class and upper-working-class girls generally had access to superior homes. It would be misleading, however, to read off health from housing conditions. Whilst it is tempting to assume that in middle-class households, with less than four dependent children, girls experienced a high standard of living and good health, the unequal income distribution within the family and low nutritional standards may have resulted in poor health. There has been much work on income distribution but largely in relation to working-class families. It is therefore difficult to gauge the effects of this on girls from the middle classes. However in lower-middle-class and upper-working-class families additional income was often tight as a result of attempts to maintain a resemblance of respectability to outside observers and, as we have seen, girls were often expected to provide domestic assistance. In these households it seems likely that girls experienced a lower standard of living than their brothers, arising from the assumption that males deserved preferential treatment in terms of food and leisure.

In working-class homes where the male breadwinner was dead, unemployed or in irregular or low paid work (mainly SC IV, V and SCIIIa/b), home conditions were greatly affected. Interwar social surveys were unanimous in pointing to the continued, if localised, existence of poverty arising from these factors.[43] Several surveys indicate that the main sufferers were school children under 15. Rowntree, for example, estimated that approximately half those in poverty in York in the 1930s were children.[44] A Bristol survey carried out by Tout in 1938 calculated 44.3 per cent.[45] A high incidence of rickets and the slow decline in mortality rates from tuberculosis were just two of the child health problems attributed to poverty.[46] Another health issue was what was officially known as 'mental retardation'. In 1931 the Report on the Primary School noted a London survey which claimed that 10 per cent of the city's school population were 'mentally retarded'. The problem was particularly acute in poor and overcrowded areas such as Lambeth, Southwark and Rotherhithe, where 20 per cent of the children were 'retarded'; in more prosperous Dulwich, Lewisham and Hampstead barely one per cent of school children were afflicted.[47] A piece of research strongly suggestive of the idea that this 'retardation' was a matter of nutrition was published in 1938. This showed that young children who ate a good breakfast high in 'protective' foods performed significantly better in intelligence tests than those who did not.[48]

It seems likely, arising from the assumption that males required more food than females, that schoolgirls were affected more than their brothers by the generally poor diet available in most working-class homes.[49] Certainly men did have preferential treatment concerning food. Rose Gamble remembers that 'nobody but dad ever had fish. It never occurred to us to expect to be included in his little luxuries.'[50] The tendency to control the leisure of girls to a greater extent than boys may have heightened this disparity as boys could acquire money and food outside the home. The effects of an inadequate diet were probably accentuated by what George Orwell describes as 'cheap palliatives' and the 'fish and chip standard'.[51]

The persistence of child malnutrition throughout the interwar period indicates that the provision of free school meals and milk to school children had only a limited effect. In order to qualify for free school meals and milk a child had to be recommended by a school health inspector. Health inspections were not, however, universally available. According to a 1930s investigation, only 57.7 per cent of schoolchildren received one.[52] These tests, which lasted two minutes, were based on highly subjective criteria such as the colour of the skin, lustre of the hair and appearance of the eyes.[53] The results of these inspections were not always consistent with the experience of teachers. Middlesborough LEA, for example, claimed that there was no evidence of malnutrition amongst local school children despite the fact that teachers asserted that 9.5 per cent of their pupils were undernourished.[54] Eventually the local authority acknowledged they were mistaken and provided free meals for 3 per cent of the children. As a Save The Children Report concluded: 'The provision of meals or milk in only one area does not necessarily mean that all the children in that area whose standard of nutrition calls for extra nourishment in fact receives it.'[55] Indeed it would appear that school inspectors noticed only as much malnutrition as the government public health officials were prepared to recognise.[56] By 1939 only 4 per cent of all school children received free school meals, 55 per cent school milk and of course neither were provided at weekends or during school holidays.[57] Wartime fears about national efficiency did push authorities to address the extent of child malnutrition and extend provision of free school meals and milk. By 1945, 40 per cent of school children received free school meals and 70 per cent free school milk.[58] The extension of school provision together with increases in household income and diet control through rationing and subsidies, probably contributed to a considerable improvement in child health.

Aside from poor nutrition, it is likely that health standards for schoolgirls, especially in working-class homes, were also affected by the double burden of school and domestic work. As we have seen, the 1931 Report on the Primary School made specific reference to this. Secondary school mistresses and Board of Education officials similarly noted that this double burden posed a health risk for older girls. For example, the 1923 report on curriculum differentiation drew attention to the difference in physique of day, compared to boarding school, pupils which it attributed to the effects of travelling to and from school, lack of nourishment and domestic responsibilities.[59] As late as 1938, headmistresses expressed concern that girls from poor homes frequently suffered 'breakdowns' which 'may be attributed to the combined effects of under-nutrition or unsuitable nutrition, of home duties performed out of school hours, and the lack of adequate facilities for private study and recreation'.[60] Johansson has argued that in the late nineteenth century mortality rates were high amongst rural girls who did not have access to paid work because of the low status attached to the non-earning female, whereas girls who lived in towns where there were chances of earning, fared better in health terms. She further suggests that the extension of compulsory schooling and girls' prolonged financial dependence on their families around 1870 may have contributed to higher death rates amongst girls than their brothers.[61] It seems likely that working-class girls who stayed on at school past 14 years of age during the interwar period may also have been adversely affected by their inability to earn, and therefore similarly regarded as a drain on the family's resources.

Conditions were also hard for those girls who were compelled to assume full-time responsibility for home and family after leaving school. Autobiographies indicate that this was a common practice during the interwar period. Helen Forrester, for instance, describes how she was forced to leave school prematurely (and illegally) to care for her younger brothers and sisters so that her mother would be free to undertake paid work.[62] In cases where the mother was ill or died the eldest daughter was often expected to take her place. Grace Foakes became a substitute mother in the twenties; as she explained, 'mother now rarely left her bed and so it was decided that I should give up work and stay at home to look after her and the rest of the family.'[63] The appearance of this theme in contemporary novels suggests that it was perceived as a normal and expected duty for a daughter. In Winifred Holtby's *South Riding* Lydia Holly takes on full responsibility for her family after her mother dies during childbirth:

> She [Lydia] was not a religious child, and did not try to tell herself that it would be all right, that her mother would get better, and she would return to school; she was not an irresponsible child and did not dream of escaping from her obligations.[64]

Girls who assumed full-time responsibility for the home once they left school were highly likely to experience a deterioration of health due, in part, to the low priority attached to their maintenance. As Helen Forrester complained: 'The daughter who did not have to go to school or to work would be the one to be clothed and fed last.'[65] It would also seem that the home-based girl would adopt the common practice amongst mothers of stinting herself to provide for the family. The long hours and constant demands of domestic and care work accentuated fatigue particularly if she was tied to a small, overcrowded home and trying to manage on a limited budget. It also seems probable that the girl would have had little time for relaxation and 'leisure'. In most cases she would be compelled to withdraw from childhood street activities but, unlike her peers in paid employment, she would not have had either the pocket money or the time to engage in other forms of public leisure.

It is tempting to believe that once a working-class girl left school and started earning she experienced an improved standard of living and health. Elizabeth Roberts has suggested that when a girl started working she expected an improved home life, in particular, better and more food.[66] The 'keep' which young workers handed over to their mothers may well have resulted in more, and better quality, food. Pearl Jephcott's study of working girls in the 1940s supports this view.[67] Whether a young worker earned exemption from domestic duties is another matter. Interviews with young workers between the ages of 14 and 18 during wartime certainly revealed that girls experienced a quite considerable domestic burden, the girls who Jephcott studied helped with domestic tasks such as ironing, cleaning, shopping and child care.[68] Irrespective of home conditions, the transition from school to paid work often exacerbated girls' health problems.

Throughout the thirties there was much concern about the health and fitness of adolescents, the 'physically illiterate'; a 1934 speech by the Chief Medical

Officer to the Ministry of Health referred specifically to the incidence of sickness among girls, also TB and bad posture.[69] Concerns about the health of young workers lay behind the emergence of industrial welfare initiatives in the 1920s and 1930s and, in wartime, the establishment of the Service of Youth scheme, under the Board of Education, which assumed direct responsibility for the physical well-being of adolescent girls and boys who were no longer in full-time education. Prior to the war, however, it was the health of working boys, in particular their vulnerability to tuberculosis, which aroused most anxiety in official circles. In 1934 the Ministry of Health, for example, described how there was particular cause for anxiety about the state of nutrition of boys between the ages of 14 and 18.[70] Demographic figures provide evidence of the Ministry's fears. In 1921 boys outnumbered girls in the 5–10 age cohort by 15000, but by the time these children reached their late teens, girls outnumbered boys by 15000.[71] The high mortality rate amongst boys arising from illnesses related to malnutrition and poor housing, should not obscure the fact that for most working-class girls and many of their middle-class peers, health standards were also extremely poor arising from bad housing conditions, poor diet and the gender-specific burdens of domestic responsibilities.

Education Provision and Policy

The extension of education provision following the 1870 Education Act contributed significantly to the institutionalisation and universalisation of childhood and adolescence for all social groups. Education provision was, however, highly variable and differentiated along the lines of both social class and gender. The Hadow Report in 1926 described post-primary education as consisting of 'traditional and overlapping categories of elementary education for nearly all children up to the age of fourteen and secondary for a small minority of children from the age of eleven'.[72] Hadow suggested that the education system be reorganised to provide primary schooling for all children between the ages of 5–11 and secondary education for all children over 11 in either secondary modern, secondary grammar, or secondary technical schools. These reforms were not fully implemented until after the 1944 Education Act. Given the diversity of provision and school environments it is impossible to present a typical picture of schoolgirl experiences, although an overview of some key features is nevertheless useful for pointing to the significance of social class.

In the twenties, following the Fisher Act of 1918, the public post-primary system of education was already being reorganised and consisted of a confusing variety of schools, often developed to suit local needs and circumstances. Within this sector there were elementary schools catering for children aged 5–14 which offered girls a curriculum of reading, writing, arithmetic, physical exercise, and also compulsory domestic subjects such as needlework and cookery; senior elementary schoolgirls in one London school in the 1930s spent two afternoons a week learning cookery for two years.[73] There were also a range of post-primary schools that catered for girls between the ages of 11 and 14–15 years including selective and non-selective central schools, Higher Grade Schools and Higher Elementary schools that had not been absorbed or changed in to Central or Secondary schools. Even within central schools, conditions varied according to tradition although the girls' curriculum usually consisted of subjects taken in elementary school combined with commercial training in shorthand, book-keeping, typing and office practice, or industrial training, namely needlework and domestic subjects.[74]

The secondary school that existed in 1920 was defined by the Hadow Report as 'a day or boarding school offering to each of its scholars up to and beyond the age of sixteen, a general education ... of wider scope and more advanced degree than that given in Elementary schools'.[75] The classification of girls' secondary schools attempted by the Board of Education in 1923 reveals at least three types of secondary schooling. The first group consists of County and Municipal schools, that is public secondary schools, which recruited most of their pupils from public elementary schools at 11 years of age. The second group consisted of High Schools, Endowed schools and large Boarding schools whose pupils came from diverse backgrounds including private schools and home education under a governess. Due to the variation in the ages at which girls were accepted into these schools and the different types and standards of their primary education, the proficiency of these schools varied greatly. The last group identified in the Hadow report included Aided schools and partly or wholly municipalised Grammar schools, once again entrance age and backgrounds varied greatly because they offered free places to girls from public elementary schools. Grant-Aided schools, for example, offered a liberal curriculum of wide scope which included English language and literature, history, geography, mathematics, drawing, natural science, languages, games, singing and domestic subjects. Although the teaching of domestic subjects was compulsory for all girls, secondary school teachers often regarded such studies as only appropriate for their less academic pupils.[76]

Girls whose education consisted solely of elementary schooling left at 14: these girls were invariably working class. Post-14 schooling was restricted to the secondary school sector. Board of Education statistics indicate that, in 1933, 76.4 per cent of secondary school intake was from the public elementary sector.[77] This figure obscures the limited opportunity for elementary schoolgirls to gain a secondary school education. Tawney estimated that only 5–9 per cent of all primary school pupils gained access to a secondary education in 1922.[78] There has been a tendency amongst historians to label secondary schools as 'middle class', however recent research shows that social composition varied between schools. Felicity

Hunt's study of two girls' secondary schools in Bedford shows that 60 per cent of the girls' fathers were from Social Economic Groups (SEG) I or II (equivalent to Social Class groups I and II).[79] Penny Summerfield's analysis of the composition of eight girls' secondary schools in Lancaster, Morecambe, Preston and Blackburn reveals a different picture (although there were wide variations between individual schools) with 37 per cent of pupils from SEG IIIa, 27 per cent SEG IIIb, and only 13 per cent SEG I and 19 per cent SEG II.[80]

Throughout the interwar period this parallel education system was severely criticised for wasting potential. In 1922 Tawney described public elementary education for children over 11 as inferior to the secondary/grammar-type schooling available to most middle-class adolescents. He argued that they were 'cheap substitutes' that the Board of Education did not regard as equal, more as an 'annex to the primary school', which was reflected in the inferior facilities of these schools, their semi-vocational curriculum, and the low pay of teachers relative to those in secondary schools. Tawney complained that there were insufficient places and provisions to allow bright working-class children to achieve their potential.[81] Kenneth Lindsay similarly criticised the lack of opportunities for bright working-class children in his book *Social Progress and Educational Waste* (1926) which highlighted the regional inequalities of access to secondary education.[82] Concern about waste re-emerged with force during the Second World War. In *Girls Growing Up* (1942) Pearl Jephcott lamented the fact 'that more than three-quarters of the able children of the manual labourer, who have brains to profit by a secondary education, do not receive this.'[83] Like Tawney, Jephcott regarded a secondary school education as far superior to an elementary one; it 'is of utmost value to them because it not only helps their own development so enormously but opens a whole range of careers which are closed to the children who only have an elementary education'.[84] Although the Education Act of 1944 reorganised education into one system of primary followed by secondary schooling, there remained a distinct difference in the quality and status of Secondary Modern and Secondary Grammar schools.

Clearly only a minority of elementary schoolgirls gained a secondary education, but one must be wary of assuming that all secondary school pupils from an elementary school background were working class and generalising about the opportunities for working-class girls. Penny Summerfield's study of 15 Lancashire secondary schools in 1921 revealed that local elementary schools were not totally the preserve of working-class children. Summerfield argues that local elementary schools were being used by parents of SEG I, II and III although their patronage depended on the neighbourhood and reputation of the school.[85] Of those working-class children who gained access to secondary school the vast majority would be from SEG IIIb. This is further supported by the high percentage of the elementary school intake who paid fees, 67 per cent in 1921 and 55 per cent in 1930.[86]

Competition from middle-class girls for the limited number of secondary school places clearly affected a working-class girl's chances of acquiring a secondary education. There were other factors which also impaired her prospects. Standards of primary schooling were obviously significant and these were tied to available resources. Overcrowded classes had a particularly marked effect on the type of schooling a child received. Kathleen Betterton describes her Junior School where there were 60 pupils, consequently 'the only method with a class of such size was regimentation. Accordingly, they set a small group of us to work on our own while they drilled their unwieldy classes in arithmetic and spelling and basic knowledge.'[87] Another common practice noted by the Primary School Report involved 'devoting over much attention to the clever children who give promise of winning free places and scholarships, with the result that insufficient care and thought are given to the problem of making adequate provision for the average and retarded children in the school.'[88]

Autobiographies clearly reveal how the tone of instruction varied according to the local conditions and traditions. Kathleen Betterton, who attended a London County Council elementary school, recalls that after the age of eight life became more serious as 'we had entered upon the race for survival'; 'By the time we were half way up the school the likely scholarship winners had been marked down, and from then on they received a quite different degree of attention.'[89] In contrast, Winifred Foley's early education in the Forest of Dean was amazingly casual:

> as long as the pupils scraped through the low standards of learning required by the school inspector, he [the head master] was not much concerned with our education. When he required the labour, the older pupils were sent to gather kindling wood for his home fires, sacks of bracken for his pigs' bedding, leaf mould for his garden, and black-berries for his wife's preserves. These activities passed as nature study.[90]

This laxity can be largely attributed to the local tradition whereby a child left school as soon as possible, girls entered domestic service while boys went down the mines. In other schools it was the bright pupils who were often offered 'privileges', which frequently meant exemption from lessons. The disastrous effects that this had on academic progress can be seen from the experience of 'Mary Smith' whose potted autobiography appeared in Pearl Jephcott's 1940s study *Girls Growing Up*:

> the teacher thought I was alright as far as History and Geography were concerned and when we used to go for these lessons she used to give me (along with three other girls) cupboards to clean, books to bind or

back, her private writing to do, her lunch to make, and to go errands, the result was I got behind with my History and Geography while the rest of the class went ahead.[91]

As these autobiographical accounts suggest, school traditions did affect scholarship prospects. These traditions were, however, closely correlated to social class, and success in scholarship exams depended on a child's social and economic environment. As Lindsay discovered, one school in Lewisham won as many places as the whole of Bermondsey; seven boroughs in London's poorer areas won an average of 1.3 places per thousand pupils, in seven better off boroughs the comparable figure was 5.3 per thousand. Similar variations existed in Bradford where only 34 per cent of schools in poor areas compared to 75 per cent in wealthy areas won scholarships.[92]

Working-class girls were not only handicapped by prevailing school provision – they were also restricted by the conditions of home and health already described. Fatigue often impaired a girl's chances of attaining the necessary academic standard, so too did absenteeism and late school attendance. Oral histories and autobiographies provide numerous examples of girls staying away from school to nurse the sick or to help with domestic work. The effect which this could have on academic performance is conveyed in this girl's answer to the question 'did you ever think of going to Grammar school?' – 'No. I had to do the work at home. They wouldn't let me sit for an exam. I don't think I would have passed anyway because I had so little time at school. I was always off when mother was ill or she was away, nursing a new baby. I got no opportunity to learn.'[93]

Winning a scholarship did not necessarily mean that a working-class girl would be able to continue her education past 14. As we have seen, parents often assumed that if necessary one of their daughters would leave school to help in the home. Financial constraints also prevented many working-class girls, especially from SC IV/V, from accepting a secondary school place. Although the Free Place System was introduced in 1907 so that 'no child should be debarred from receiving the benefits of any form of education by which they are capable of profiting through inability to pay fees', the financial sacrifices required of secondary schooling militated against this.[94] There do not appear to be any figures that show the number of girls who refused a free place on financial grounds although specific case studies do offer some indication of its prevalence. For example, a number of free scholarships to a Bradford secondary school were turned down because of the inadequacy of maintenance grants.[95] Secondary schooling incurred many expenses, parents had to pay for their daughter's uniform, equipment, travel and so-called trivial items like a hymn book and donations to the Church Mission.[96] The expense of providing just the uniform can be gauged to some extent by the list of clothes that some secondary schoolgirls were required to wear: in the 1920s Kathleen Betterton's public boarding school expected girls to wear:

tickly woollen combinations with sleeves and buttons at the neck; liberty bodices with buttons all over; white calico under-knickers, always discreetly known as 'garments'; navy blue bloomers; a button-up blouse; a tie; a blue calico 'pocket' that tied (eighteenth century fashion) round the waist; a navy blue box-pleated tunic; ribbed black woollen stockings . . . tie and suspenders.[97]

As Lindsay concluded in 1926, it was mainly the skilled artisans of the working classes who could afford to allow their daughters to accept free places at secondary schools.[98]

The importance of maintenance grants had been recognised in 1895, but only 40 per cent of free place pupils received this assistance in 1919 and the value of it varied between local authorities and according to the character of the individual application.[99] In 1920, for example, London County Council insisted that students requiring maintenance grants had to reach a higher intellectual level than other qualifying pupils in their entrance examination.[100] Although the 1944 Act abolished secondary school fees it did not make any changes to existing practices regarding maintenance grants, and it seems likely that the financial expenses of a post-15 schooling continued to blight the education opportunities of many working-class girls from SC IV and V.

Those working-class girls who were able to accept a place at secondary school often did so at considerable cost to themselves and their families. As we have seen, the double burden of domestic and academic work, combined with an inadequate diet, often resulted in ill health amongst scholarship girls. The cultural tension which many girls experienced also took its toll. Rose Gamble recalls that as a 'Special Placer' she 'had three lives to live, one in the yard, one at home, and one at school'.[101] Cultural conflict was often manifest within the school in the form of acute snobbery towards the scholarship girl: 'Outwardly there was nothing to distinguish us. We wore the same clothes, plaited our hair in the same tight pigtails, blew our noses on the same outsize handkerchiefs. But there was a difference and we all knew it. One of the first questions put to new girls by the rest was always – "Are you a scholarship girl?".'[102] As Rose Gamble explained, 'there was a gap a mile wide between me and the clique I so desperately wanted to be a part of'.[103] While scholarship girls were often ostracised by other secondary schoolgirls, they also became increasingly alienated from their elementary school friends, particularly once they left school at 15 to start work. Once girls started work their relation to the street and other children changed. The scholarship girl, dressed in her uniform and preoccupied with homework, was estranged from this.

Statistics for the period 1927–1930 show that 32.2 per cent of annual secondary school intake left before their sixteenth birthday and presumably without a School Certificate.[104] Oral history and autobiography suggest that these 15-year-old girls came from families who found it a financial and domestic strain or impossibility to keep their daughter at school after 14. Only a small proportion of secondary schoolgirls stayed on past sixteen. In three York secondary schools surveyed by Rowntree, only 84 out of 1274 students remained in school after their sixteenth birthday; 21 of these held scholarships to enable them to take an advanced course (16–18 years) for the Higher School Certificate.[105] It is likely that a few very academic pupils from an upper-working-class background managed to stay on at school after 16. Most of these would have been destined to leave at 17 for Teacher Training that lasted two years and for which the Board of Education provided a bursary and exemption from fees.

A university education was available to a minority of girls who stayed on at secondary school until 18 or 19 and acquired the necessary Higher School Certificates. The standard BA/BSC degrees lasted three to four years and provided a gateway into the professions where opportunities for girls were limited almost entirely to secondary school teaching. Subsidies for this form of higher education were hard to come by. A few leaving scholarships for university were available from schools, universities and, after 1921, the Board of Education. Lancashire 'leaving scholarships' were worth approximately £50 (1910–1930) at a time when annual university fees amounted to at least £100.[106] This, according to Summerfield, worked to reinforce the middle-class character of university entrants, and in turn of secondary school mistresses.[107] Five major scholarships of £65 were available for university students in York; in 1938 all 16 holders of these had attended an elementary school.[108] This does not necessarily contradict Summerfield's findings given that some ex-elementary pupils came from middle-class backgrounds although I am inclined to believe that this group were primarily upper working class and lower middle class.

Throughout the period 1920–1950, post-primary education provision remained polarised. Numerous commentators pointed to the different and inferior education afforded by elementary schools compared to secondary schools. Whilst in theory the secondary sector was open to the bright working-class girl, in actual fact it remained the preserve of the middle-classes. For the majority of working-class girls schooling ended at 14, 15 after 1947. Those working-class girls who accepted places at secondary schools invariably left before their seventeenth birthday.

Education provision was clearly stratified by social class. It was also gender differentiated and promoted a domestic curriculum for all girls throughout the period 1920–1950.[109] After the two world wars, which could be seen as periods when patriarchy was consolidated, this orientation was more directly and powerfully expressed than in other periods of relative stability when a domestic curriculum was nevertheless present, though given less emphasis. Individual schools could, however, adapt their curriculum to suit their needs; some secondary schools viewed domestic subjects as only suitable for non-academic pupils, while others took more advantage of domestic concessions. Irrespective of curricula differentiation, oral history clearly shows that schools successfully conveyed a range of informal lessons about social class and gender through the 'hidden curriculum'.[110]

Girls and the Labour Market

Education policy suggests that girls were primarily defined as future wives and mothers. This was the destiny of most, but not all, girls. Young women also had a role in the economy as paid workers. Indeed one of the most noticeable features of the period 1920–1950 is the increased proportion of adolescent girls of all social classes in the labour market. Despite attempts to extend education provision most working-class girls entered full-time paid work at 14, and 15 after 1947. Many of these girls had part-time jobs such as street trading, harvesting and paper rounds before they left school. Work after leaving school also became more acceptable for secondary or grammar schoolgirls. The 1923 report on curricula differentiation noted that while the ideal of the leisured young lady still survived, most families could not afford to financially support dependent adult daughters; although school life did not finish until between 16 and 18 years, most girls did not marry until their twenties and an increasing number did not marry at all, partly as a result of the demographic imbalance but also out of choice. The percentage of women who had never been married increased over the period; in 1921, 36.8 per cent of females over the age of 15 had never been married, in 1931 35.4 per cent and in 1951 40 per cent.[111] The changed fortunes of middle-class daughters contributed to the universalisation of adolescence as a period marked by a transition from school to paid work.

Census figures show that 44.8 per cent of girls aged 14 to 15 years were in full-time employment in 1921.[112] Girls of 12 and 13 years of age were also noted as full-time workers; in Preston 30 per cent of local girls aged between 12 and 13 years were in employment.[113] In 1931, 1 680 283 girls aged 14 to 20 were in full-time work, that is 75.1 per cent of this age group. Following the raising of the school leaving age in 1947 the proportion of girls aged 15–19 in full-time work rose to 78.7 per cent in 1951.[114] Although the trend was towards the increased employment of young women it is important to recognise that these figures hide wide regional variations. For example, in 1921 50.8 per cent of Barrow girls aged 15 to 19 were in full-time work, whereas in Preston 86.7 per cent were in paid employment.[115] The percentage of young wives in the labour market also increased in this period suggesting an increased tolerance of young married women in the labour market. Whereas only 21.2 per cent of adolescent wives (aged 14–19) were in paid work in 1921, this had risen to 19.4 per cent (aged 15–20) in 1931 and 39.3 per cent (aged 15–19) in 1951.[116] While the participation rate for girls in England and Wales rose during the period it nevertheless remained lower than that for boys. In 1931, 89.9 per cent of boys aged 15–20 were in full-time work, by 1951 this had risen to 98 per cent of 15–19 year olds.[117] The most likely explanation for this difference is that girls were often kept at home after leaving school to help in the home. Unfortunately Census tables do not provide statistical evidence to support this as they offer no breakdown of the category of girls listed as 'Not Gainfully Employed, Or Retired', which included figures for students, the unemployed, and girls who stayed at home.[118]

So, what kinds of jobs did girls enter after leaving school? In 1921 a third of girls aged 14–19 went into the major industries, in particular the textile and clothing industries. Domestic service was the next largest employer accounting for a quarter of girls' employment. Offices employed 11 per cent of girls in general clerical work, while wholesale and retail sales accounted for 9 per cent of girls' employment.[119]

The proportion of girls in domestic service actually increased between 1921 and 1931. This was largely the result of Labour Exchange policies which forced many girls to accept domestic work by withdrawing their entitlement to unemployment benefit.[120] This pressure on girls to enter domestic service was partly a response to the demand for servants by the middle classes; it also reflected the conventional assumption that service was the most fitting employment for girls, a view embodied in moves by local authorities to establish training courses or reconditioning centres to attempt to alleviate female unemployment by providing training in domestic and needle trades.[121] In other occupations the Census also shows signs of change by 1931. The proportion of girls employed in industry fell from 32.9 per cent in 1921 to 23.8 per cent; this decline corresponded with the continued contraction of the traditional industries, which was accentuated during the thirties. As industry contracted, white-blouse work in office and shops became increasingly significant as a source of young women's employment; office work, mainly clerical but also typing, accounted for nearly 12 per cent of girls by 1931 while the proportion of girls employed as shop assistants rose to 10.5 per cent partly as a result of the expansion of department stores and the increased consumerism of the middle classes.[122]

By 1951 the structure of girls' employment had changed radically. The most noticeable feature was the shift away from domestic service towards white-blouse work, in particular retailing and office work, and also teaching and nursing. Personal service accounted for only 3.6 per cent of girls in 1951 compared to 23 per cent in 1921. Office work, in contrast, became the major employer of girls by 1951 accounting for over a quarter of adolescent female workers. Reflecting this development, employment in this sector became increasingly specialised offering posts for typists, shorthand typists, secretaries, office machine operators, costing and estimating clerks. The proportion of girls in sales work had also risen accounting for 14 per cent of working girls. The increased significance of other areas of service work such as beauty and waitressing jobs and, in communications, the rise of the telephone operator, also reflected increased consumer demand. However, industries still absorbed a large proportion of girls, roughly 20 per cent, the major single employer being the clothing industry, followed by the rayon and light engineering industries.[123]

The expansion of white-blouse work can be seen as a new form of service work reflecting the shift away from heavy industry and private forms of domestic service towards public servicing jobs in offices, shops and communications. The expansion of the non-manual sector for girls and women occurred at a much faster rate than for boys and men during this period.[124] Although the structure of employment for young women workers changed drastically during the period 1920 to 1950, girls' options remained concentrated at the bottom of the occupational hierarchy in a narrow range of jobs and, more specifically, servicing work.

As we have seen, domestic service was a major area of employment for girls during the twenties when roughly a quarter of domestic servants were taken on straight from school at 14 or 15 years of age. The importance of service varied between local employment structures. In mining areas domestic service was the usual employment for elementary schoolgirls.[125] In localities where light engineering and textiles factories were established domestic service was often less significant. The fact that service only accounted for 10 per cent of the Preston female workforce in 1921 and 13 per cent in 1931, for instance, can be explained by the predominance of the textiles industries as an employer of females.[126] Generally, however, domestic service became increasingly unpopular during the interwar period largely due to unsatisfactory conditions of work. Three features that girls found particularly objectionable deserve to be mentioned. Firstly servants often had to pay for their own uniforms, which was perceived by girls as a real mark of subservience and was despised by many. Another feature that was particularly disliked was the tendency of employers to restrict all areas of their employee's life including her leisure, friends and her religious behaviour. Related to this, domestic servants were extremely vulnerable to sexual harassment as evident in the number of letters which girls' magazines received on this subject.[127]

Retail, clerical and factory work were often viewed by girls as favourable alternatives to domestic work because they appeared to offer more personal freedom, and in the case of factory work, better pay. Conditions and prospects in these areas were, however, far from ideal. Industrial employment provided a major, if declining, source of work for ex-elementary schoolgirls during this period. Indeed, ex-elementary schoolgirls, usually recruited straight from school at 14 or 15 years of age, represented a quarter of adolescent employment in industry between 1921 and 1931 and roughly a sixth by 1951.

Conditions in industry varied, but with the exception of certain enlightened employers such as Cadburys, pre-1939 factories were characterised by poor working conditions. Modern factories were healthier than the old, but canteens and adequate washing facilities remained luxuries for most manual workers between the wars, and long hours were not uncommon. Beauchamp cites the example of a firm where women and young persons worked up to 22 hours a stretch on night shift.[128] The Factory Act of 1937 established a 48 hour week as the norm for girl workers. But, as Lewenhak points out, 17 out of the 31 sections of the Act dealing with women and young persons were devoted to permissible exceptions and many girls continued to work a 60 hour week in non-textile factories and longer hours in certain seasonal trades.[129] Small workshops and laundries often evaded protective legislation while big industrial factories introduced conveyor belts often with serious consequences for the health of their female workers. As Beauchamp noted, 'the girls found that under the Bedaux system the speeding-up was terrific; many of them collapsed from the strain as soon as the rate fixers left them; extra money earned was cancelled out by loss of time due to illness.'[130]

Industrial work was increasingly deskilled during this period and women in particular were relegated to the bottom of the skill hierarchy. Between 1921 and 1951, according to Lewis, the number of skilled female workers decreased by 34 per cent compared to 11 per cent for men.[131] This, Lewis argues, was the result of the decline of traditional areas of skilled women's work, such as textiles, and the move towards unskilled work in new industries such as electrical engineering. Even where girls and women were employed doing skilled work it was often redefined as semi-skilled: this was a common practice in engineering during the 1939–1945 war.[132] As Lewis concludes, 'It appears that skilled work had become, by definition, work that is not performed by women.'[133] The shift in occupational structure towards service work also facilitated this deskilling as women's ability to service was seen as *natural* and as therefore not entailing any skill. Irrespective of how much skill their work involved, girls and women consistently earned less than their male counterparts. In 1938, girls aged 14–20 earned on average 18s 6d per week compared to 21s 1d for boys.[134] While girls' rates of pay increased during the forties they remained low relative to male earnings. Prospects were poor and few girls were ever promoted to forewoman or overseer because employers often found it cheaper to lay off girls once they reached 17 or 18 and to replace them with 14- and 15-year-old school leavers.[135]

Apprenticeships were one way of working through the industrial system but these were few and far between. Small factories and trades did offer girls informal apprenticeships. In the tailoring industry, for example, girls entered at 14 or 15 years of age as 'runners' (they ran for the threads for the machines) and gradually progressed to machining: Phyllis, interviewed by Jephcott in 1942, recalled working as a runner from 8am to 5pm with two 15 minute breaks and 30 minutes for lunch. By 16 she had progressed to making 400 'pants' a day and at 17½ she was making utility coats.[136] Unofficial apprenticeships, like the above, often led to exploitation as girls taken on at learner rates were kept at these even though they were often doing skilled work; when they finally qualified for the full piece-rate on their work they were often dismissed. Formal apprenticeships were not necessarily any better and often demanded considerable physical and financial commitment. Mrs Austen who entered the confectionary trade as an apprentice in 1921 worked a 12 hour day from 6am to 6pm for five shillings a week.[137] Even after completing an apprenticeship girls were not guaranteed employment.

Sales work, whether retail or wholesale, was a growing area of employment for adolescent girls from working-class and middle-class backgrounds, in fact 42 per cent of shop staff were under 21 in 1935.[138] Retail work was insecure, particularly as many shops preferred to employ young and cheap staff: the proportion of 14–15 year olds who worked in sales increased over the period from 8.3 per cent in 1921 to 19.5 per cent in 1951.[139] Young workers suffered least from unemployment in this area. Indeed, according to some contemporaries, shop work was increasingly becoming a 'blind alley' occupation, especially for girls who generally remained at the bottom of the staff hierarchy.[140] In 1922 shop girls earned on average £120 per annum compared to the male average of £169, in 1935 wages had risen to £123 and £180 per annum respectively.[141]

Conditions of work in shops varied and were often very poor. The interwar period witnessed the growth of large stores but a large proportion of girls were employed in small, local shops. In many trades shop assistants worked 48–60 hours a week but it was common for girls to work over 60 hours.[142] It is tempting to think that such excesses were restricted to small retail establishments but in 1925 Woolworths were taken to court for sending girls under 18 to work from 7.45am to 12 noon and then seven hours in the afternoon.[143] One of the features which sales assistants in small shops found most objectionable was the extent to which the employer could control their activities both during and outside work hours. Mrs Windsor who was employed as a sales assistant in Lancaster between 1924 and 1934 poignantly described how on one occasion she had planned to go to a party after work:

> We were working late, we used to weigh all the currants. Nothing came ready packed. He (the boss) decided after tea that we would start packing currants, and he set me off filling the top shelves, and I tried not to let him see me, but I was actually crying. The dance finished at ten o'clock and I arrived at quarter to ten. The shop officially closed at seven but he didn't think I should go.[144]

It is difficult to discover what type of retail outlet girls from secondary as opposed to elementary schools entered. Although conditions in small, local shops were probably worse in terms of promotion, pay and conditions than in the big stores, as Mrs Windsor describes, the local shop often had more status:

> Woolworths had just come into the town before I left school, but on principle I wouldn't work in Woolworths. I could have been getting a lot more money than I was getting in the grocer's shop, but because it was a privately owned firm it was a little better.[145]

Office work as a source of female employment increased in significance throughout the period but it implied different things for girls who entered at 14 as opposed to 16. Elementary schoolgirls were employed as general office workers. Helen Forrester earned 10 shillings a week at 14 when she was employed as an office girl in the thirties. Forrester's duties included making tea, indexing, filing, purchasing food for committee meetings, and at the end of day delivering the 'Presence's' mail by hand.[146] Helen's situation in the 1930s was very similar to that of Madge described by Beauchamp in 1937, who did 'all the office filing, but has also to pack heavy and bulky parcels, carry them a long way, keep card indexes and petty cash records, dust the office, polish desks and so on.'[147] This type of work was invariably dead-end. A number of girls sought to enhance their job prospects through evening classes but these did not combine well with long working hours: Beauchamp describes how Hilda, aged fourteen and a half, worked in a shop from 8am to 6pm, she arrived home at 6.45pm and then rushed off to attend evening classes which started at 7.30pm. Her friend worked 8.30am to 6pm in an office but was frequently required to stay late after work – 'As she is usually home from work too late to go to evening classes she has no chance of qualifying for a permanent job.'[148] However, it was not just the difficulty of obtaining skills and promotion that contributed to the subordination of the young girl, it was also the rigid gender hierarchy of office organisation in which girls worked. Working-class girls who acquired commercial training at one of the popular central schools entered the office at 15 or 16 equipped with shorthand, typing and office skills and were therefore better placed than their sisters who started work at 14 with no such skills. Specialised office jobs such as shorthand typist and secretary did offer better rates of pay than general office work, although girls' training did not improve their prospects. Commercial training for boys, on the other hand, prepared them for an 'avenue of opportunity'.[149] Secondary schoolgirls who left school at 16 or 17 were also attracted into clerical work; 'The one word "business" sums up the prospect of life for the typical secondary schoolgirl'.[150] Although it is unlikely that these girls would have undertaken the type of work which Forrester described, equipped with perhaps a six month secretarial course, their options were restricted to rather mundane work with few prospects. It is not surprising that Secondary school headmistresses were so opposed to this career choice for their girls.[151]

Despite the Sex Disqualification (Removal) Act of 1919 the only professions that were readily accessible to girls between 1920 and 1950 were teaching and nursing.[152] After 1907 the Board of Education phased out the pupil-teacher system that had provided access for the bright working-class girl to the post of elementary school teacher. This route had been inexpensive as girls started earning at 18 years and no costly training was required. Raising the academic standards of the elementary school teacher resulted in the proportion of uncertified teachers falling from 31 per cent in 1911 to 18 per cent by 1931.[153] Whilst it could be argued that the expansion of the secondary school sector and provision of free places allowed working-class girls easy access to an appropriate training for elementary school teaching, the prolonged loss of income and the inadequacy of maintenance grants acted as a disincentive to many working-class girls.

Opportunities to enter secondary school teaching were limited to mainly middle-class girls who could afford to stay on at school until 18 and go on to university. In the 1930s only three girls a year went to university from Park School in Preston, 6–12 went to teacher training college; two out of a 100 pupils at Blackburn High School went on to university, eight to teacher training.[154] Wages and conditions for school teachers differed according to whether they were in a private school or one recognised and aided by the Board of Education – the former was the less desirable offering lower wages and no pensions. Governesses experienced the poorest job conditions, and were often treated with less respect than a cook.[155] Throughout the period women teachers earned less than men. In 1928, a female elementary teacher started on £150 per annum compared to the male rate of £168; graduate secondary school teachers in London started on £264 and £276 respectively.[156]

Nursing, the other major female profession, accepted girls at 16 for a four year probationary course. While nursing was open to elementary schoolgirls, autobiographies suggest there was a lot of snobbery surrounding recruitment, that 'sheltered' girls were preferred to ex-domestic servants or factory workers.[157] As with school teaching, work conditions varied according to the type of hospital in which the girl was employed. In London County Council hospitals where treatment of nurses was markedly better than in voluntary hospitals, nurses earned £30 in their first year, £35 in their second year, £45 in their third year and £50 in the fourth year out of which they had to pay their exam and registration fees (uniforms, lodging, food and laundry were inclusive). Lectures had to be attended in their free time outside of the 50–60 hour week.[158] Even when qualified a nurse might expect only £65 per annum (1937) rising by £5 per annum to a maximum of £80, which represented 75 per cent of male nurse earnings.[159] Promotion opportunities were limited to a few sister's posts or hospital administration jobs in which case the salary rose to £125 per annum, but many first rate nurses never reached these and their salary remained only slightly higher than that of a clerk.[160] Nurses in all types of hospitals had to contend with vexatious rules; as Monica Dickens describes 'the etiquette of the cuffs took a probationer at least a week to learn'.[161] Matron supervised life in and outside of work hours; in some hospitals nurses were not allowed out after duty or only with the matron's permission and they were reprimanded for the slightest indiscretion such as sitting in the hospital grounds without wearing stockings.[162]

Although the Second World War has been described by some contemporaries and also historians as a period of wider occupational opportunities for women,[163] feminist historians suggest that this is an optimistic assessment. Although new types of work were available, women were often denied access to skilled work and were frequently channelled into domestic and servicing jobs especially within the Services; moreover it was in traditional areas of 'women's work' that most of the post-war prospects lay.[164] Conditions of work also deteriorated in some respects during the war; the hours worked in ordnance factories combined with the time taken travelling to and from work often meant an extremely long day.[165] In line with the pre-war employment pattern, Summerfield demonstrates that war work continued to be differentiated by social class. In factories this emerged as a division between shop floor and office work as managers tended to avoid giving 'nicely brought up' girls jobs on the factory floor; in the women's Services social class distinctions were apparent between Services and also within them.[166]

This overview of girls' employment suggests that those girls who left school at 14 or 15 from an elementary school entered jobs with poor prospects and pay. In fact the evidence shows that the types of work open to 14 and 15 year olds were often dead-end and also short term. One option open to girls who wished to improve their job prospects was to attend evening classes; this was not easy. The division of work opportunities for elementary as compared to secondary schoolgirls became more pronounced over the period. On the one hand there was an expansion of jobs which required some form of training. On the other hand, much industrial and office work became increasingly deskilled, a tendency which aroused concern amongst youth workers and observers who claimed that modern working conditions led to mental, physical and moral deterioration.[167] Secondary schoolgirls who entered the labour market at 16 or 17 years of age usually for clerical or retail work were generally not much better off than their peers from elementary schools although their jobs offered better pay and security. Only a few, mainly middle-class girls, acquired the education and training necessary for entrance to the professions where they still ranked second to their male peers.

The monotony of much of the semi-skilled and unskilled work available to ex-elementary schoolgirls and, indeed, to the majority of secondary schoolgirls was often reflected in high mobility between jobs. Mrs Raphael's study in Leeds in 1938 found that 9 per cent of men, 26 per cent of boys, 30 per cent of women and 48 per cent of girls (under 18) were mobile; labour turnover for girls was particularly high in factories.[168] The most important aspects of work for these young people were the wages it offered and the company it afforded: 'A girl writing of a change of job will generally speak of two points only, of her wages, and of the friendliness or otherwise of the people with whom she works: and will make no reference at all as to what she does in the new work . . . lack of interest in the actual work and lack of any opportunities for the girl to express her real interests through her job, make the people in whose immediate company she works all important.'[169]

Marriage, An Alternative Career?

Surveys and oral history indicate that the majority of girls from all social classes saw marriage as a major feature of their adult life, and for many it was their primary ambition alongside having a family. For instance, a Pilgrim Trust's study of mainly ex-elementary schoolgirls at a juvenile Instruction Centre in 1938, observed that most girls wanted to marry.[170] In 1949 a Mass-Observation survey of girls from grammar, secondary modern and technical schools confirmed the continued strength of this ambition, while 68 per cent of the sample looked forward to marriage, 40 per cent of the girls over 16 wanted nothing more than marriage.[171] This survey did not specify whether the 32 per cent of girls who were not preoccupied with marriage were from elementary or secondary schools although they were probably from the latter, signifying the broader expectations girls were encouraged to foster by secondary school teachers.

Some critics have argued that women took boring jobs with low pay and no prospects because they saw their work as a stop gap before marriage, and having this attitude they did not campaign to improve their conditions of employment.[172] This looks at the issue from the wrong angle. Girls from all backgrounds were steeped in the expectation that they would marry but it seems probable that girls in boring, monotonous jobs, which offered no prospect of more challenging and better paid work would have been keener to leave the labour market than girls in more demanding jobs. However, as we have seen, the number of jobs open to elementary and secondary schoolgirls which offered varied and stimulating work, good work conditions, good pay and prospects were few. The prospect of improving work conditions through trade unions was extremely limited. In 1948 only a quarter of women workers were unionised.[173] This was partly because girls were disproportionately concentrated in occupations which it was hard to organise. More importantly perhaps, as feminist historians have shown, in areas of successful male trade unionism male members were often hostile or showed disinterest towards their female colleagues. Where there was conflict between the interests of male and female members, trade unions gave priority to those of men.[174] There was also a lot of ageism in male trade unionist sexism as is clear from the move by the Amalgamated Engineering Union in 1943 to prevent girls, defined as under 21, being shop stewards.[175] This was apparently done to protect the dignity of trade union negotiations but it seems likely that it was also an attempt to protect the status of male shop stewards. It is not surprising that girls were suspicious of the Unions and perhaps cynical of their value. Certainly the organisation of many trade unions did not facilitate their active involvement, for example meetings were often held in pubs, which were not generally considered suitable places for girls to be seen. Given the prevailing conditions of women's work and the limited opportunities to change them it is not, perhaps, surprising that marriage, running a home, caring for husband and children may have seemed a humane and satisfying alternative.

Those, mainly secondary schoolgirls, who anticipated challenging post-school prospects frequently believed marriage and career to be compatible. Edith Mercer's study of secondary schoolgirls in 1940 discovered that all wanted to have a career and 77 per cent thought they would also like to marry.[176] According to Gertrude Williams a desire to combine marriage and employment had become increasingly prevalent amongst middle-class women.[177] This belief was not shared by most elementary schoolgirls particularly if they did not envisage, or already occupy, exciting jobs: 'In almost all working homes marriage is looked on as having a primary claim and other forms of employment are viewed in relation to it. The working girl who plans her future in terms of a possible independent career is an exception.'[178] This attitude demonstrates their recognition of the difficulties of combining paid work and marraige, it also conveys the view that the home and family should be a girl's chief responsibility, a belief that was often reinforced by employment practices, in particular the implementation of marriage bars.[179] While secondary schoolgirls increasingly believed that a professional career and marriage could, and should, be compatible, marraige bars also persisted in the professions.[180] Acute labour shortages during and after the Second World War did lead to the lifting of marriage bars in professions such as teaching. This prompted considerable optimism from some observers,[181] but this was misplaced; according to Elizabeth Wilson, the graduate wife in postwar Britain 'seemed an embarassment rather than a welcome addition to society, even when there was an acute shortage of teachers and nurses'.[182] The image of the career women, teachers in particular, as 'frustrated spinsters' strengthened the view that a career was pursued at the expense of marriage.[183]

Transitions

For most girls growing up between 1920 and 1950 adolescence was a period of transitions. Although a minority of middle-class girls continued their education and training throughout their adolescent years into university or an equivalent establishment, most middle-class girls and virtually all working-class girls left school during their teens and usually before their seventeenth birthday. For some girls this meant a return to the home either as 'young ladies of leisure' or more often as mother's helper or substitute. In both cases leaving school represented a significant turning point in their girlhood experiences. The majority of girls in this period, however, entered the labour market on leaving full-time schooling. Girls like Winifred Foley who went into resident domestic service experienced a dramatic transformation both in terms of the organisation of their lives which were structured by the needs of their employer, and in terms of their new status within their families as wage earners. One's fourteenth birthday, Foley explains, was very important: 'This birthday meant for a daughter that she was old enough to get her feet under someone else's table...'[184] As Gamble recalls of her experience of growing up in the 1920s:

> [t]here was nothing gradual about growing up. As long as you were at school you looked like a child in short trousers and frocks, and you were treated like one, but when you left school at the end of term after your fourteenth birthday, childhood ended. It was abrupt and final, and your life changed overnight.[185]

Starting full-time work was personally significant for most girls. One way in which girls reinforced their new status was by distancing themselves from all things childish including street games and physical exercise. Dress was another important signifier of their new status as was the ability to purchase cosmetics and magazines with what remained of their wages after they had paid their 'keep'.[186] Girls also expected to be treated differently within the home in terms of their entitlement to food although, as we have seen, girls were not so successful in avoiding domestic chores. A study by James and Moore of young people's leisure in Manchester during the late 1930s which was based on day diaries produced by a group of working-class adolescents, some at school and some at work, suggests that girls' domestic responsibilities did not drastically decrease on leaving full-time education. Indeed it was only when girls reached their sixteenth birthday that domestic duties significantly declined. This the authors attributed to parental recognition of their daughter's interest in the opposite sex. This study suggests that in the case of girls' domestic and leisure experiences, their position in the heterosexual career was as significant, if not more so, than their entrance into full-time work. James and Moore discovered that boys experienced an abrupt change in life style on commencing paid work largely as a result of the removal of all domestic duties and a complete change in leisure activities.[187]

Although 'going steady' was for working girls, even schoolgirls often had boyfriends. According to Jephcott, by the time most working-class girls were 16 they were quite preoccupied with boys, boyfriends and their marriage prospects.[188] Other contemporary studies also point to this interest and leisure practices geared increasingly around mixed-sex activities.[189] Middle-class girls tended to lag behind their working-class sisters in this respect largely because of their extended schooling and the demands of homework although this did not stop some girls from clandestine meetings with boys.[190]

Pressures to get a boyfriend started early. As with girls today the assumption of heterosexual coupling underpinned much of adolescent leisure practice.[191] On the one hand, girls' friendships fragmented as friends started courting. On the other, leisure activities were increasingly geared around having a boyfriend and once a girl started 'going steady' leisure almost exclusively revolved around the couple's respective homes. Pressures to have a boyfriend had an immediate dimension in terms of girls' leisure and friendships but they were also deemed of longer-term significance. Girls from all social groups were bombarded with messages about the desirability of marriage and motherhood. Although middle-class girls could pursue a career if they did not marry, their 'lot' was not generally portrayed as a happy one. Indeed what is particularly striking about the interwar years is the naturalisation of heterosexuality and attacks on women, whether celibate or lesbians, who did not marry.[192] The suspicion and hostility which women attracted when they remained outside heterosexual relations were fuelled by the media interest in lesbians during and after the First World War, most notably the failed libel action of dancer Maude Allan to counter the charge that she was a lesbian (1918) and the prosecution in 1928 of Radclyffe Hall's novel *The Well Of Loneliness*. The obscenity trial around this novel aroused huge publicity and led to further suspicion being cast on single women.

While this period was notable for its overt promotion of heterosexuality it was also characterised by the pursuit of a scientific understanding of sexuality which was bound up with the construction, mapping and management of heterosexuality. One outcome of this was the sexualisation of adolescence and increased attempts, by the medical and psychology professions, also educationalists and youth workers, to institutionalise and manage adolescent sexuality in line with the prescribed heterosexual career which culminated in marriage and motherhood. Following the work of G. Stanley Hall on adolescence and Freud on sexuality an extensive range of books appeared offering advice to teachers and others who worked with girls about the developmental needs of their adolescent charges; needs which were explicitly tied to heterosexual development as the necessary prelude to their womanly fulfilment as wives and mothers.[193] The interwar and war years also saw the Board of Education introducing measures to guide the heterosexual development of girls and also boys through sex education.[194] The increased support for co-education and, in youth work, mixed-sex activities, can also be read as attempts to manage heterosexual development. Popular girls' magazines, as we shall see, contributed to these tendencies.

Not all girls went on to marry, and many were to discover that they were not heterosexual, but most were exposed to pressures to get married. The option of professional spinsterhood which was promoted by some secondary school mistresses, if not usually by parents, was only available to a few. Most girls growing up in this period did not have access to, or the means to attain, this relatively positive spinster identity. As autobiographies of lesbians who grew up in this period suggests, in the absence of positive, or indeed any, images of same-sex relationships it was extremely difficult to avoid pressures to find a boy and get married although many subsequently left these relationships and came out as lesbians.[195]

Girls growing up in the period confronted a number of changes. For most there were two significant transitions associated with age, leaving school for full-time domestic or paid work and entrance into heterosexual relationships. Experiences of these transitions was shaped by a number of factors, which more generally structured the conditions of girlhood, namely gender, social class, race and age. These factors were also central to the production of popular magazines for girls in this period. The following chapter looks at this range of girls' magazines drawing on this overview of the characteristics of different social groups of girls to explore their intended and actual readership and also the processes by which these papers were produced for an audience of adolescent girls.

Notes

1 Dyhouse (1981).

2 Marwick (1991), pp.340–5.

3 On 'whiteness' see charles (Helen) (1992). Women's history is increasingly uncovering evidence of the significance of race for women's experience in Britain especially in the nineteenth century and in relation to Empire. See, for example, Ware (1992).

4 Routh (1965), pp.156–7. For points of discrepancy see Armstrong (1972), pp.209–11.

5 Glynn and Oxborrow (1976), p.47.

6 Rowntree (1941), p.ll0.

7 Forrester (1981).

8 Phillips (1987), ch.2.

9 Cited in Owen (1974), p.235.
10 Madge (1943).
11 Rowntree (1941), p.25.
12 Glynn and Oxborrow (1976), p.237.
13 Beddoe (1989), p.92.
14 For contemporary concern about shortage see Myers (1939).
15 Branson (1977), p.94. See also Glynn and Oxborrow (1976), p.49.
16 White (1970), pp.93–6.
17 Dyhouse (1981), p.17; see also comment in *Girls' Own Annual* Vol. 6, p.405 concerning the scarcity of servants making it increasingly necessary for girls to do housework; also Vol. 8 on 'facing a maidless condition'.
18 Glynn and Oxborrow (1976), p.48.
19 Ibid., p.49.
20 White (1970), p.103; Lewis (1984), p.116.
21 Spring Rice (1981), p.131.
22 Rowntree (1941), p.226.
23 Branson (1977), p.113.
24 Rowntree (1941), p.231.
25 Glynn and Oxborrow (1976), p.238.
26 Rowntree (1941), p.239.
27 Cited in Spring Rice (1981), p.153.
28 Rowntree (1941), pp.245, 251
29 Spring Rice (1981), p.140, ch.vi.
30 Ibid., p.145.
31 Women's Group on Public Welfare (1943), p.88.
32 *Census of England and Wales* (1951) General Report, p.123.
33 Davidson (1982), pp.68, 71.
34 Board of Education (1931), p.55.
35 See Mrs Eleanor Baton in Beveridge (1932); James and Moore (1940/1944); Roberts (1984) pp.23–4 the cases of J1P and P2P; Jephcott (1942), p.14 example of a girl who had done the housework since she was 8 years of age.
36 Cited in Women's Group on Public Welfare (1943), p.27.
37 *Census of England and Wales* (1951) General Report, p.122. Frequent reference was made to poor and overcrowded housing conditions in surveys and government reports of the 1940s and 1950s. For example, Board of Education (1943b), p.5; Ministry of Education (1947), pp.11–12.
38 Save The Children Fund (1933), p.35.
39 Orwell (1982a), p.51.
40 Gamble (1982) , p.16.
41 For example, Spring Rice (1981), p.132.
42 Roberts (1984), p.17.
43 Constantine (1980), p.26.
44 Rowntree (1941) p.156.
45 Cited in MacNicol (1980), p.49.
46 Cited in MacNicol (1980), p.54.
47 Board of Education (1931), p.54.
48 Cited in MacNicol (1980), p.47.
49 Spring Rice (1981),ch.vii.

50 Gamble (1982), p.l0. Jephcott (1942) p.67: 'Girls are still inferior creatures in many homes. The best food, the seat by the fire and all that this implies are often the boys' prerogative in 1942, as they were a hundred years ago before the emancipation of women was seriously considered.'
51 Orwell (1982a), p.80.
52 Save The Children Fund (1933), p.l28.
53 MacNicol (1980), pp.53–4.
54 Save The Children Fund (1933), Appendix iii, p.105.
55 Ibid., p.64.
56 Oddy (1982), p.132.
57 Women's Group on Public Welfare (1943), p.31.
58 Oddy (1982), p.132.
59 Board of Education (1923), pp.73–4.
60 Board of Education (1938), p.119, see also pp.112, 118.
61 Ryan Johansson (1980), p.159.
62 Forrester (1981), pp.67–8.
63 Foakes (1972), p.72. See also Last (1983), p.236.
64 Holtby (1983), p.195.
65 Forrester (1981), pp.67–8. Johansson (1980) p.174 suggests that the low priority attached by families to the non-earning daughter was quite established prior to 1910.
66 Roberts (1984), pp.40–1.
67 Jephcott (1948), pp.142–3.
68 Jephcott (1942), pp.126–7 suggests child-care responsibilities of young workers may have increased during wartime; Jephcott (1948) pp.10, 142–4 on domestic work; Mass Observation, *File Report 1422* Appendix IV; Mass Observation (1943) *File Report 1567*, 12 January, pp.3–4; James and Moore (1940/1944). Wartime youth registration interviews revealed extent of domestic responsibilities amongst girls see, Tinkler (1994a), pp.396–9; Ministry of Education (1947), p.21.
69 Cited in Rooff (1935), p.91.
70 P.R.O. M.H. 791337, Note of Meeting, 12 July 1934, cited in MacNicol (1980), p.59.
71 *Census of England and Wales*, General Report, 1921 and 1931.
72 Board of Education (1926).
73 Beddoe (1989), p.38.
74 King (1990).
75 Board of Education (1926).
76 Summerfield (1987a).
77 Board of Education (1933).
78 Tawney (1922), p.48.
79 Hunt (1985).
80 Summerfield (1988).
81 Tawney (1922), p.l9.
82 Lindsay (1926).
83 Jephcott (1942), p.52.
84 Ibid., p.52.
85 Summerfield (1988).
86 Branson (1977), p.l20.

87 Betterton (1982), p.207. See also Lindsay (1926), p.ll9.
88 Board of Education (1931), p.79.
89 Betterton (1982), p.206.
90 Foley (1977), p.48.
91 Jephcott (1942), p.l6.
92 Lindsay (1926), p.8.
93 Roberts (1984), p.24.
94 Board of Education (1926).
95 Lindsay (1926), p.ll.
96 Gamble (1982), p.l70.
97 Betterton (1982), p.208.
98 Lindsay (1926), p.21.
99 Lindsay (1926), p.37.
100 Ibid., p.39.
101 Gamble (1982), p.l70. See also Humphreys (1981), p.56; Hemming (1960), pp.64–6.
102 Betterton (1982), p.208.
103 Gamble (1982), p.l88.
104 Ministry of Education (1954), p.5.
105 Rowntree (1941), pp.311, 320.
106 Summerfield (1987b), p.41.
107 Ibid., p.41.
108 Rowntree (1941), p.311.
109 Dyhouse (1978), pp. 291–311.
110 Summerfield (1987a) and (1987c).
111 *Census of England and Wales* (1951) General Report, Table 59, p.130.
112 *Census of England and Wales* (1921) Occupation Tables, table 4.
113 Roberts (1984), p.35.
114 *Census of England and Wales* (1951) General Report, Table 60, p.l31.
115 Roberts (1984), p.39.
116 *Census of England and Wales* (1921) Occupation Tables, table 4, p.54 and *Census of England and Wales* (1951) Occupation Tables, table 6, p.131.
117 *Census of England and Wales* (1951) General Report, Table 60, p.l31.
118 Garside (1980).
119 *Census of England and Wales* (1921) Occupation Tables.
120 Lewis (1984), p.213.
121 Pilgrim Trust (1938), pp.246, 256–7.
122 *Census of England and Wales* (1931) Occupation Tables.
123 *Census of England and Wales*, Occupation Tables, 1921 and 1951.
124 Lewis (1984), p.l58.
125 Foley (1977).
126 Roberts (1984), p.205.
127 On letters to magazines see ch.6. Further details on conditions of domestic service see Noakes (1980); Foley (1977); Beauchamp (1937), pp.73–6.
128 Beauchamp (1937), p.37.
129 Lewenhak (1977), p.234.
130 Beauchamp (1937), p.23; See also p.29.
131 Lewis (1984), pp.171, 182.

132 Summerfield (1984).
133 Lewis (1984), p.171.
134 Branson and Heinemann (1971), p.146; Routh (1965), p.105.
135 Brittain (1928), p.4.
136 Jephcott (1948), pp.12–13.
137 Roberts (1984), p.65.
138 Beauchamp (1937), p.46.
139 Calculated from *Census of England and Wales*, Occupation Tables, 1921 and 1951.
140 Beauchamp (1937), p.46. Beauchamp also cites concerns expressed in *The Shop Assistant*, August 24, 31 1935.
141 Routh (1965), p.95.
142 Beauchamp (1937), p.47.
143 Lewenhak (1977), p.211.
144 Roberts (1984), p.64.
145 Ibid, p.64.
146 Forrester (1981), ch.19, 20.
147 Beauchamp (1937), p.52.
148 Ibid, p.52.
149 King (1990), p.85.
150 Pratt (1934), pp.288–9. See also Ministry of Education (1954) , p.53.
151 Summerfield (1987a), pp.158–61 on attitudes towards girls' post-school destinations.
152 In 1921 there were 348 461 women in the professions of which 203 802 were teachers and 94,381 nurses. 'Physicians, surgeons, registered medical practitioners' were a growing category of women professionals numbering 1253 in 1921 (0.34 per cent of all women professionals), rising to 2810 in 1931 (0.72 per cent of all women professionals). Figures from Darcy (1984), cited in Beddoe (1989), p.77.
153 Summerfield (1987b), p.42.
154 Summerfield (1987a), p.159.
155 Beauchamp (1937), p.67.
156 Brittain (1928), p.64.
157 Hall (1977), p.28.
158 Beauchamp (1937), pp.62–72.
159 Routh (1965), p.69.
160 Ibid.
161 Dickens (1980), p.84.
162 Ibid.
163 For example, Williams (1945); Douie (1949).
164 Summerfield (1984), p.187; Braybon and Summerfield (1987), pp.259–67.
165 Summerfield and Braybon (1987), p.220.
166 Ibid., pp.197–8.
167 Durant (1938), p.90.
168 Raphael et al. (1938), p.259.
169 Jephcott (1948), p.121.
170 Pilgrim Trust (1938), p.254.
171 Mass Observation (1949) *File Report 3150*, p.12.
172 Williams (1945).
173 Cited in Pelling (1976), p.205.

174 Lewenhak (1977): Braybon (1981), ch.3, 8; Summerfield (1984).
175 Summerfield (1984), p.157.
176 Mercer (1940), pp.19–20.
177 Williams (1945), p.89; Lewis (1984), p.153 claims that 3 out of 4 married women wanted to combine marriage and a career in the 1940s.
178 Pilgrim Trust (1938), p.230.
179 For example, Crook (1982), p.43.
180 Martindale (1938), p.149.
181 Bloom (1944), pp.31–2.
182 Wilson (1980), p.19.
183 Jeffreys (1985); Oram (1989).
184 Foley (1977), p.141.
185 Gamble (1982), p.122. See also Jephcott (1948), p.10; Roberts (1984), p.10.
186 Although levels of pocket money varied, Joan Harley's 1930s research, cited in Davies (1992), p.84, on mainly working-class Manchester girls aged 14–19 years revealed that pocket money ranged from 6d to 6s 6d. On average girls received 2s 6d in 'spends'. See also Jephcott (1948), p.138 and Reed (1950), p.38 table XX.
187 James and Moore (1940/1944).
188 Jephcott (1948), pp.11, 17, 67–8, 76, 103–4; Jephcott (1942), pp.132–3.
189 Mass Observation (1949) *File Report 3150*, p.9: Of 200 London girls, 14 per cent of 14–16 year olds spent Saturdays with a boy or boys whilst 80 per cent of girls aged 16–19 spent Saturdays in male company.
190 On attempts by secondary schoolmistresses to prevent girls associating with boys and girls' subsequent clandestine meetings see Summerfield (1987a), pp.164–5. The restrictions imposed on secondary schoolgirls 1930–1955 by the hours of their schooling and demands of homework are conveyed in James and Moore (1940/1944) and Hemming (1960), pp.122–3.
191 Griffin (1985).
192 Jeffreys (1985); Oram (1989).
193 Dyhouse (1981), ch.4.
194 Board of Education (1943a). See also Tinkler (1995a).
195 For example, the experiences of Diana Chapman and Shirley McLean in Hall Carpenter Archives Lesbian Oral History Group (1989).

Chapter 3

Magazines, Readers and Editors

Following the launch of the first girls' periodical in 1869, magazines aimed at a young female readership proliferated and diversified. By 1920 magazines catered for adolescent girls of all ages and social classes. Schoolgirl fiction magazines, typified by *School Friend*, *Schoolgirls' Own* and *Girls' Crystal*, are perhaps the most famous of these girls' magazines. Another, and very different type of schoolgirl paper sought to provide both instruction and information alongside light fiction entertainment. These papers, in particular the highly successful *Girls' Own Paper*, and also *School-Days* and the *Schoolgirls' Pictorial*, were welcomed by teachers and even stocked in libraries. While both the *Girls' Own Paper* and the *School Friend* targeted schoolgirls of this period, an extensive range of other magazines addressed the young and single working girl. These magazines built on markets identified by the successful late Victorian and Edwardian papers such as *Girls' Realm* (1898–1915), *Girls' Friend* (1899–1931) and *Girls' Weekly* (1912–1922). Although *Girls' Friend* and *Girls' Weekly* did survive the war they emerged into a post-war world of heightened competition, taking their place alongside an extensive list of titles aimed at working girls including *Girls' Favourite* (1922–1927), *Peg's Paper* (1919–1940) and, somewhat later, *Miss Modern* (1930–1940). Although marked by significant differences, these working girls' papers shared a preoccupation with romantic fiction.

Despite the range of papers produced for girls in this period it would be wrong to assume that they attracted the readers they ostensibly targeted; the intended and actual readership of these papers was not always synonymous. One possible reason for this is that magazines were unable to respond to, or reflect, the range of their readers' needs and desires. This was partly because girls were not homogeneous even within specific age and social-class groupings. The inability to satisfy readers also stemmed from the necessary selectivity editors were compelled to employ in producing magazines for different groups of

Table 3.1. Interwar Girls' Magazines examined in this study[7]

Schoolgirl Papers

Elementary Schoolgirl Papers:
School Friend, Amalgamated Press (AP) 1919–29, relaunched in 1950
Schoolgirls' Own, AP, 1921–36
Schoolgirls' Weekly, AP, 1929–39 (incorporated into Girls' Crystal)
Schoolgirl, AP, 1929–40
(Girls') Crystal, AP, 1935–63

Secondary Schoolgirl Papers:
Schoolgirls' Pictorial, AP, 1924–25
School-Days, AP, 1928–29
Girls' Own Paper (GOP), Religious Tract Society (RTS), (GOP and Woman's Magazine,
    1908–27; Woman's Magazine and GOP, 1928–30; GOP, 1931–47, also issued as
    Girls' Own Annual 1931–41; GOP and Heiress, 1947–50; incorporated into Heiress
    1950–56)
Girl, Hulton Press, 1951–64

Romance Magazines

Working Girls' Magazines:

a) Business Girls' Papers
Girls' (Best) Friend, AP, 1899–1931 (incorporated with Poppy's Paper)
Girls' Weekly, Thompson, 1912–22 (incorporated with My Weekly)
Girls' Favourite, AP, 1922–27 (incorporated with Eve's Own)
Girls' World, Shureys, 1927

b) Millgirl Papers
Peg's Paper, Newnes & Pearson, 1919–40 (incorporated with Glamour)
Polly's Paper, Shureys, 1919–24 (incorporated with Every Girls' Paper, then Girls'
    Mirror)
Poppy's Paper, AP, 1924–34 (continued as Fortune 1934–36, then incorporated with
    Oracle)
Betty's Paper, Allied Newspapers, 1922–41
Pam's Paper, Allied Newspapers, 1923–27
Every Girls' Paper, 1923–24.

c) Miss Modern, George Newnes, 1930–40

Mother-daughter Magazines:
Red Star Weekly, 1929–
The Oracle, AP, 1933–
Lucky Star, Newnes & Pearson, 1935–57
Miracle, 1935–58
Silver Star, Newnes & Pearson, 1937–40; then Silver Star and Golden Star, 1940–60
Fortune, AP, 1934–36

---

readers, a process shaped by a number of factors. Before looking at aspects of the production process this chapter introduces the range of magazines which addressed girls during the period 1920 to 1950 (see table 3.1), their form, content, tone and the type of reader they primarily addressed, it also looks at the actual readership these different papers attracted.

Magazines for 'Girls'

Although it is a relatively straightforward exercise to discover whether papers targeted school or working girls it is more difficult to be precise about the social class of the intended audience. Magazines did not employ class labels and there is little information which conveys editorial intentions in these terms. One way of exploring the social class of the intended reader is to examine the congruence between magazine content and the characteristics of different social groups, which we examined in chapter 2. It is important however to bear in mind the composite character of most magazines which contained articles, adverts, editorials, fiction and pictures. Whereas editorials, adverts and articles were usually intended to explicitly address the concerns and conditions of girlhood, and subsequently communicated information about the intended reader, fiction was often designed to transcend experience and was therefore less informative about the reader's identity. For this reason, fiction magazines are particularly difficult to assess. The main criteria that I have used to categorise the intended readership of magazines relates to the occupation of the reader, whether at school or in paid or unpaid work, and her place in the heterosexual career. These are the characteristics which emerged as important features of age and social class in our overview of adolescent girlhood during the period 1920–1950.

Schoolgirl papers roughly divide into two types, elementary schoolgirl papers and secondary schoolgirl papers. As the titles of most of the elementary schoolgirl papers indicate, readers were expected to be in full-time schooling; indeed the school theme was a recurrent and dominant feature of fiction and articles. *Schoolgirls' Weekly*, for example, featured an editor's page entitled 'Notes in Class' and *Schoolgirl* had a regular article 'Out of School Hours'. The schoolgirl identity of the intended reader was also reinforced by the near absence of advertising.[1] The particular type of schooling most often depicted in these papers tells us little about the social class of the intended readers. Fiction did not feature the kinds of schools which most girls attended, instead stories were set in expensive boarding schools where scholarship girls from impoverished backgrounds were depicted rubbing shoulders with the daughters of wealthy parents. These magazines usually featured a few articles which were primarily concerned with domestic skills such as needlework and cookery. In the case of *School Friend*, articles were presented within the fictional magazine 'Cliff

House Weekly', edited by the popular schoolgirl character Barbara 'Babs' Redfern, and were consistent with the fictional school and its pupils, thereby providing few clues as to the identity of the intended reader. However, the range and tone of the articles give the impression that readers were perceived to have few home resources for leisure; articles discussing domestic crafts were described as offering useful contributions to personal maintenance or the care of younger siblings. Film and film stars were a major topic. Given that contemporary surveys reveal that cinema-going was a major pastime of elementary schoolgirls, it seems plausible that those schoolgirl papers which concentrated on cinema to the exclusion of other leisure interests were largely catering to this audience.[2] Girls' clubs which attracted a moderate following amongst elementary schoolgirls in the interwar period, were also featured in the few articles.[3] The *Schoolgirls' Own*, for example, presented its readers with a regular 'Girl Guide Corner'.

Although elementary and secondary schoolgirl papers differ in content suggesting different perceptions of the reader's background, education and interests, this did not mean that magazines were aimed at mutually exclusive sets of readers. Elementary schoolgirl papers did present images of the types of reader which secondary schoolgirl magazines appear to have addressed. In view of the changing conditions within the class structure during the interwar years, it is likely that identifying working-class and lower-middle-class families would be difficult and, in terms of the intended audience, perhaps such a differentiation was unnecessary. Indeed, in view of the publishers' commercial objectives, it is probable that elementary schoolgirl papers were intent upon attracting as wide an audience as possible. Although this would have embraced middle-class girls who were avid readers of these papers, sales would have been dependent upon the greater purchasing power of working-class schoolgirls. Frank Richards, founder of *Schoolgirls' Friend* and the earlier schoolboys' magazines *Gem* and *Magnet*, clearly appreciated the immense significance of the working-class readership;[4] apart from its potential size, contemporary surveys also suggest that girls as well as boys from 'poorer districts' had more pocket-money than their peers from more affluent homes.[5]

The content of secondary schoolgirl papers such as *Girls' Own Paper*, *School-Days* and *Schoolgirls' Pictorial*, was more diverse than that of their elementary counterparts and clearly imbued with the educational ideals of the professional middle classes. The *Girls' Own Paper* in particular was very much in tune with the views of secondary school headmistresses and with the objectives and ethos of the girls' club movement.[6] Editors of secondary schoolgirl papers set out to entertain and instruct. The *Girls' Own Paper* featured many of the most popular contemporary writers including Angela Brazil, Elsie Jeanette Oxenham and Elinor Brent Dyer, as well as W.E. Johns of 'Biggles' fame, and it also devoted over 50 per cent of its content to articles on living

Figure 3.1 *The School Friend*, 12 July 1924, magazine cover, reproduced by permission of The British Library.

abroad, nature, religion, foreign languages, crafts, sports, girls' clubs, books and careers. Similarly *School-Days* incorporated articles on crafts, cookery, dress-making, tennis and hockey. It also provided two pages of letter puzzles and quizzes, articles on nature, films and poetry plus the 'School-Days Circle Club' which promoted pen-friendships. The content of these papers indicates that readers were expected to possess a wide range of interests and have access to leisure facilities both inside and outside the home.

    School-Days and *Schoolgirl Pictorial* were both short-lived publishing ventures although the *Girls' Own Paper* survived in one form or another from 1880 to 1950. In the 1920s the *Girls' Own Paper* was incorporated with *Woman's Magazine*; the combined paper addressed girls and women, 'girls' being defined as single young women in their late teens and early twenties. The inclusion of exotic recipes and references to the management and care of domestic servants in articles such as 'Furnishing the Maid's Room' suggests that the intended reader was from the upper and middle classes. Leisure features aimed at younger readers included tips for motorists, this was at a time when only the upper and upper-middle classes could afford cars.[8] Features also suggested that girls had prolonged education and access to finishing school: in 'Miss Hope' (1927) the reader was introduced to a young woman with a degree in Domestic Science. The *Girls' Own Paper* was also attentive to the needs of the post-war 'new poor' middle classes. Domestic articles suggested that many readers had very practical responsibilities, mothers had to rear and supervise their own children and run their homes, albeit with the help of a maid; they also had to renovate rather than replace their furnishings. This sort of domestic coverage has been seen by Cynthia White as an indication of the drop in living standards experienced by the pre-war aristocracy and upper middle classes.[9]

    With the liberation of the *Girls' Own Paper* from *Woman's Magazine* in 1931, the paper became more clearly identified with schoolgirls aged between 12 and 18 years; working girls attracted very little comment or coverage. The full colour covers, which featured healthy and lively girls engaged in outdoor pursuits, provide a clear image of middle-class adolescent girlhood. Issues of the *Girls' Own Paper* in the 1940s portrayed readers as preparing for, or as having just completed, their School Certificate. This age range was reflected in the fiction and in the types of interests and activities presented, from stamp collecting to boyfriends. During the Second World War, the *Girl's Own Paper*'s intended readership embraced the breadth of adolescence with recruitment articles for the war industries, the women's Services and pre-Service training corps like the Campaigners, which was open to girls and boys aged between 12 and 21 years. At this time, however, the *Girls' Own Paper* acknowledged that a number of its readers would be entering paid work before their nineteenth birthday and more attention was directed to matters of employment. This could also have been a reaction to editorial assumptions that girls from a wider range of backgrounds would be reading the paper, partly because of the lack of alternative reading and also as a result of the social-class mixing which the *Girls' Own Paper* repeatedly referred to (whether this was a reality is nevertheless open to question).[10]

The editors of the *Girls' Own Paper*, inspired by missionary zeal, aimed to incorporate readers from all backgrounds but it was quite clearly middle-class in tone, content and in its expectations of readers. One clear indication of whom the *Girls' Own Paper* was not intended for is provided in the story 'Other People's Ways' (1940) in which Joan Verney described how Lady Joan was safe from 'dirty children with fleas' being billetted on her during the war.[11] Commenting on this, Cadogan and Craig argue that the *Girls' Own Paper* did not envisage such children reading the paper.[12] One could argue that no magazine encompassed such readers; it is significant, however, that only the *Girls' Own Paper* directly snubbed them. Most of its readers were assumed to attend secondary school as indicated by articles on the School Certificate, Higher School Certificate and professional training. Whilst a small proportion of elementary schoolgirls did have access to a secondary school education, as we saw in chapter 2, most working-class girls would have been unable to remain at school past their fourteenth birthday. Fiction that featured heroines from affluent backgrounds reinforced this middle-class tone throughout the period. The regular adventures of the Lockton family (1941) featured four children living in Cairo due to their father's work as a wing commander. In the absence of Mrs Lockton who worked as a volunteer in an Anglo-American hospital, the children were supervised by a governess-cum-companion. Families in straitened circumstances were also featured but their upper and middle-class origins were clearly conveyed. In 'Such a Quiet Place' (1941) Mrs Stacey, a widow with adolescent daughters, inherited a country house called 'Little Thatches', which she subsequently ran as a guest house.

In 1948 the *Girls' Own Paper* joined with *Heiress* and was heralded as a 'teen-age' magazine. From the outset it addressed older working girls and young married women aged between 16 and 25 years with articles on beauty and housekeeping alongside many of the standard *Girls' Own Paper* features. Adverts proliferated suggesting that readers were earning. An illuminating feature on 'Your First Job' (1948) described the reader as having just left school at 17, presumably with a School Certificate, and looking for work in business or factories, or alternatively seeking professional training.[13] The merging of these papers in 1948 heralded a general broadening of class appeal and a more specific focus on working and courting girls at the expense of schoolgirls. This shift also clearly represented the demise of a very particular approach to girls' literature, one which was more in tune with the aims of secondary school mistresses and Girl Guide leaders than with commercial publishing.

Romance magazines proliferated in the interwar years and can be roughly

Romance mags

divided into four types, three of which specifically addressed working girls in their teens – business girls' magazines, millgirl papers and *Miss Modern*. The business girls' papers, *Girls' World*, *Girls' Favourite*, *Girls' Friend* were, as their titles suggest, intended for 'girls'. Although this manner of address was ambiguous, the content and tone of these magazines indicates that readers were assumed to be both working and courting. Articles on beauty and clothes were introduced as valuable to the 'business girl', *Girls' World* described how 'the girl who works long hours each day in office or factory often finds that her skin is sallow, and eyes lustreless and dull.'[14] Numerous features offered advice on love and relationship matters – 'Ten Golden Rules for the Engaged Girl', 'Should a Girl Make Love?', 'Your Best Boy', 'Don'ts for the Engaged Girl'. Letter pages similarly articulated these interests; readers of the *Girls' Friend* (1930) had their 'Love Knots untied', *Girls' World* (1927) provided a correspondence feature to cater for the 'difficulties in daily life. It may be love trouble, business worries, home frets.' Joyce in *Every Girls' Paper* offered advice on love, health, business and daily life while Zenaide in *Girls' Weekly* (1920) employed the stars to illuminate 'all matters about love, business or marriage' (clearly Zenaide did not think that marriage and a career were compatible). This image of the reader as a working and courting girl was also carried over into the fiction which focused on the romantic adventures and encounters of the working girl in her late teens. Explicit references to the age of the reader were rare, but the fact that the intended reader was assumed to be courting, even engaged, suggests that the magazine's main priority was with girls in their late teens. The free gift of a coloured plate of 'Miss Seventeen' offered in *Girls' Favourite* supports this impression. Young wives were occasionally mentioned, *Girls' World* for example offered advice 'For the Girl who is wed' (1927). It is clear however, that the young wife was not the central concern. While marriage and domesticity were presented as the modern girl's ambition, they were not portrayed as the reader's present reality. In fact the editor of *Girls' Favourite* (1927) went to great pains to stress that his readers were not yet ready to settle down:

> there was once a terribly efficient, brogued and horn-rimmed spectacled person who paid me daily visits for a week armed with 'A Hundred Steps Towards Home-Making'. It took me about ten thousand words . . . to convince her that Girls' Favourite readers did not, as a general rule, want to know about how to make homes, not yet awhile, at any rate.[15]

Depictions of girls in white-blouse work and occasional references to factory girls, suggest that the intended reader was from the working classes and lower-middle class. The *Girls' Favourite* was unusual in that it focused almost exclusively on office girls. A letter from 'Two Factory Lasses' to the editor of *Girls' Favourite* (1922) suggested that these girls felt excluded. Belying the

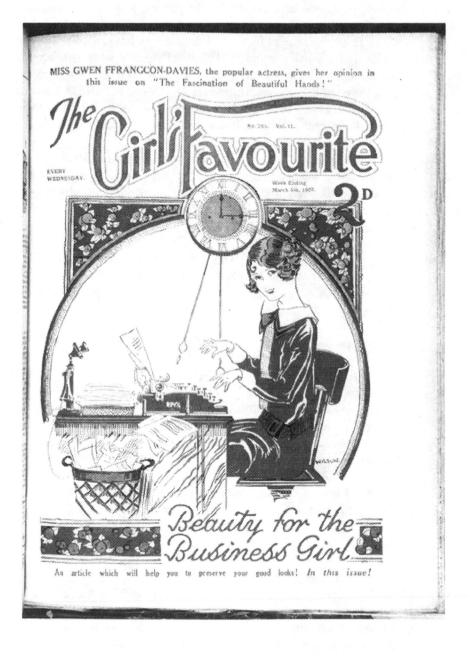

Figure 3.2 *The Girls' Favourite*, 5 March 1927, magazine cover, reproduced by permission of The British Library.

actual focus of the paper, the editor replied: 'The paper is intended for all types of girls, and the articles and stories are chosen from that point of view.'[16] As we saw in chapter 2, girls who entered factory work probably left school at 14 with no formal qualifications, usually from social classes IV and V, while office work and hairdressing attracted many working-class girls as well as girls from, or destined for, the lower middle classes. Business girls' magazines also recognised that a number of girls would be compelled to remain at home forfeiting paid work in order to assist with domestic tasks and child care and they featured advice on how to earn 'pocket money' by working from home.[17]

The original millgirl magazine, *Peg's Paper*, was launched in 1919 by Nell Kennedy with the clear intention of catering for girls working in mills and factories, that is jobs that required no formal qualifications and which were available to girls of 14 straight from school. This was clearly conveyed in the editor's attempt at rapport with her readers:

> lets be pals, ... Not so long ago I was a millgirl, too, and my clogs clattered with yours down the cobbled street ... Because I've been a worker like you I know what girls like, and I'm going to give you a paper you'll enjoy.[18]

As if to consolidate this identity, millgirl papers were given distinctively working-class names – Peg, Poppy, Betty, Pam. While readers were assumed to be in low-paid jobs, some articles grossly inflated the average working-class girls' income. Some features, for example, suggested that readers could afford expensive bridal gowns at a time when most young working-class couples settled for a smart reusable costume and a tea party rather than a honeymoon.[19] Fiction, as George Orwell pointed out, also inflated living standards in ways that were not consistent with the economic reality of readers:

> Ostensibly the characters are working class people, ... [but they] are all living at several pound a week above their income ... Not only is 5–6 pounds a week standard set up as the ideal, but it is tacitly assumed that is how working-class people really do live.[20]

There were inconsistencies, however, as some fiction depicted considerable economic hardship even if it was rather romanticised. As with the business girls' magazines, the centrality of the romance theme shifted attention from work to courtship and placed the intended reader firmly in her late teens and early twenties. Articles on marriage and home-making did appear but these were peripheral. Introductions to the regular correspondence features which proliferated during the 1930s confirm the significance of romance and courtship. *Poppy's Paper*, for instance, had two such features by 1936 – 'Mrs Nell

Newman's Page for Lovers' and 'Problems I Put Right For My Girls' by Nurse Elizabeth.

Miss Modern, a monthly magazine launched in 1930, similarly addressed the unmarried working girl:

> I may be a woman in years, but I am still a girl at heart. Girlhood interests me intensely. I am only one step away from it, and that pleases me, for if I were older I might be too far removed from you to sympathise with you and, if I were younger, I could sympathise but I couldn't advise, not having the necessary experience.[21]

Once again the term 'girl' was ambiguous, but *Miss Modern*'s articles, fiction and its numerous adverts were clearly targeted at the working and courting girl in her late teens and early twenties. Although primarily concerned with the single woman, house-keeping articles and adverts concerned with the care of babies suggests that some readers were assumed to be married with young children. In marked contrast to other romance magazines, *Miss Modern* initially addressed a quite affluent middle-class reader; in 'Meeting His People' Lady Vincent offered advice on social etiquette including tips on how to treat the servants of one's prospective in-laws.[22] By 1935 the tone and content had shifted to embrace white-blouse workers of the upper-working class and lower-middle class. Nevertheless, vocational options which required extensive training and the assumption that girls had received a secondary school education, confirm the largely middle-class identity of the intended reader. This is not to say that these readers were seen as affluent. *Miss Modern*, like its schoolgirl counterpart the *Girls' Own Paper*, recognised the financial constraints which characterised the lives of many interwar middle-class families and in 'Look Ahead and Make Yourself Independent' (1935) it directly addressed the middle-class girl who had lived a leisured life prior to the First World War but who had more recently fallen on hard times.[23] In its promotion of endowment policies to prepare girls for their future this paper suggested that a good standard of life could not be taken for granted, a girl could not depend on her parents nor assume a future husband would support her in adult life. Fiction similarly explored problems of financial hardship faced by girls growing up in these social groups.

During the 1930s most of the working girls' papers disappeared as production was rationalised. This was probably due to the effects of the Depression and also the assumption that readers could be addressed by other types of papers. At this time there emerged a new range of romance magazines – *Glamour, Lucky Star, Red Star Weekly* – which, although similar in terms of their social-class tone, were dominated by racy fiction. There has been a tendency for critics and historians of popular literature to conflate these papers with millgirl magazines such as *Peg's Paper*.[24] While there was an overlap in

Figure 3.3 *Miss Modern*, October 1930, magazine cover, reproduced by permission of The British Library.

terms of intended and actual readership, close attention to the form and content clearly designates the readers of *Peg's Paper* and the like as 'girls' in their teen years, while magazines such as *Silver Star* introduced in the 1930s were aimed at a wider audience of 'women' and also girls. In contrast to the magazines we have discussed so far, the introductory descriptions of these magazines explicitly identified their readers as 'women' whose primary interests were in the home; both the *Red Star Weekly* and *Lucky Star* introduced themselves as 'The New Home Story Paper', *Oracle* described itself as 'A New Thrilling Story Paper For Women'. Letter pages reinforced this focus; Mrs Mann, the correspondence editor of *Silver Star*, was introduced as a wife and mother, while *Miracle* featured 'Mrs Maitland's Confidence Corner' which catered for wives, mothers, sweethearts and lonely women (presumably the unmarried and widowed). Articles addressed brides and newly weds, also married women and mothers in their twenties and thirties. The prominence of advice on the home, the introduction of toddler features such as *Silver Star*'s 'Sparkle', and the inclusion of soppy poetry depicting the trials of taken-for-granted middle-aged mothers reinforced the domestic and familial tone of these papers.

Although adolescent girls were rarely mentioned explicitly it would be misleading to assume that they were not part of the intended readership, particularly as a number of these papers actively sought to inherit the audience of the working girls' magazines, hence my classification of these as mother-daughter magazines. Moreover some of these magazines were edited by Nell Kennedy and her team, which moved from producing *Peg's Paper* and its sisters to producing *Glamour*, *Silver Star* and *Lucky Star*. A number of working girls' papers were even amalgamated into the new fiction magazines: *Girls' Weekly* was merged with *My Weekly* (1922), *Poppy's Paper* became *Fortune* and was then amalgamated with *Oracle* (1937), *Peg's Paper* was combined with *Glamour* then *Lucky Star* (1940). Editorial statements also indicate that while these new magazines were intended to collar a previously neglected market of married women who wanted a bit of escapism, they were also expected to adopt and cater for the readers of working girls' papers:

> All the charm of the *Girls' Weekly* will be retained in the new paper, and added to it will be the splendid attractions of *My Weekly*... All things which have made *Girls' Weekly* your favourite paper will be there, together with very special *My Weekly* attractions.[25]

One of the reasons why this amalgamation was possible was that working-class girls in their late teens were seen to share an interest in marriage and domestic matters with older women. This assumption was probably predicated on the fact that many working-class girls were married before they reached 25; according to Gittens, during the interwar period the average age at marriage for service

Figure 3.4 *Lucky Star*, 7 September 1935, magazine cover, reproduced by permission of The British Library.

girls was 20.8 years, 22.4 years for office and shop girls and 24.7 years for factory workers.[26] Given the expectation that girls would marry in their early twenties, most girls showed an early interest in securing a marriage suitor.[27]

Establishing the intended readership is confused by the inconsistencies within magazines and, related to this, the attempts by publishers to maximise appeal and sales. In spite of these difficulties it is nevertheless possible to construct quite a clear image of the primary intended reader in terms of occupation and their place in the heterosexual career. These features tell us much about the age and social-class background of different sets of intended readers. But what about the actual readership? The readership groups which magazines targeted and the audiences they actually attracted were not necessarily synonymous. In order to appreciate which girls, if any, were exposed to different kinds of feminine lessons, it is useful to investigate the characteristics of the actual readership of these different papers.

Readers

Oral history would seem to offer one of the most fruitful sources for the study of magazine readership but recollections of popular magazines tend to be rather vague.[28] This can be partly attributed to women confusing the magazines which they read as girls with those popular with their own children; a confusion amplified by the similarity of magazine titles and the vast number of issues that many girls, particularly elementary schoolgirls, seem to have consumed in their youth. In isolation, oral history sources would seem to suggest that magazines were of marginal significance for girls growing up between 1920 and 1950; however circulation surveys and contemporary studies present a different picture pointing to their wide and avid readership during this period, an impression also conveyed through contemporary commentary and autobiographies.

Spurred by their desire to identify the consumer potential of different social groups and the advertising power of popular magazines, a number of readership and circulation surveys were undertaken between 1928 and 1948.[29] Perhaps because school children were assumed to have only limited purchasing power, these studies did not address the reading of schoolgirls nor the papers produced for them. Pre-1939 surveys also failed to analyse readership by age so there is no way of gauging the popularity of magazines with a specifically adolescent audience. Surveys produced from 1939 did identify an adolescent cohort, either 14–24 years or 16–24 years, but as we saw in chapter 2, this age range included girls in very different circumstances – at school, in full-time paid work, full-time care of the family and home, marriage (perhaps combined with work), even motherhood. A more general problem with readership surveys stems from their sampling and methodology which obscured many magazines known from other sources to have been popular with adolescent girls.[30]

Motivated by concerns about the use of leisure and the influences of the media, the 1940s witnessed the emergence of a number of studies concerned with reading practices. For insight into the reading of schoolgirls the most useful source is Jenkinson's contemporary survey of girls' reading published in 1940. Drawing upon the results of 1330 questionnaires distributed to girls from secondary and senior schools, Jenkinson identified and described the most popular magazines by the age and schooling of reader. With the exception of business girls' papers, which did not survive into the 1930s, this survey mentions most of the widely read magazines of the interwar period. Whilst less ambiguous than class labels, the classification 'secondary schoolgirls' may have hidden wide variations in the social background of pupils, however it is safe to assume that the majority of secondary schoolgirls in Jenkinson's survey would have been middle class. Other useful studies which emerged in this period include Fenwick's 1953 study of schoolgirl reading and Jephcott's two 1940s studies of the lives and experiences of young working girls. So what did girls read?

Schoolgirl's Own and other papers of this ilk were, according to Jenkinson, widely read by senior (elementary) schoolgirls of 12 to 14 years of age and their secondary school sisters. Indeed secondary schoolgirls tended to read slightly more of these papers than their senior school counterparts.[31] Amongst 12 year olds, Jenkinson discovered that *Schoolgirls' Own* was read by 34 per cent of the secondary schoolgirls and 32 per cent of senior schoolgirls, at 13 years it was read by 36 and 38 per cent of girls respectively, and at 14 years by 21 and 47 per cent.[32] The popularity of these schoolgirl papers was also noted by Fenwick who recorded that 81 per cent of his sample of 500 girls aged between 14 and 15 at a Select Technical School read schoolgirl papers, 62 per cent of girls aged over 15.[33] *School Friend* emerged as the most popular magazine in Fenwick's study, being read by almost 60 per cent of 14–15 year olds and 52 per cent of girls over 15.[34] In 1950 *School Friend* was purported to enjoy a circulation of a million copies per week.[35] While statistics reveal that secondary schoolgirls continued to read these magazines into their fifteenth year there are no clear indicators of the extent of this reading amongst schoolgirls over 16 years of age, although Trease claimed that older schoolgirls quickly tired of school stories.[36] Schoolgirl papers did remain popular with young working girls although they took their place alongside an increasingly large number of romance magazines. Jephcott's study, *Girls Growing Up* (1942), focused on the experiences, including the reading practices, of working-class working girls. These girls, aged 14 to 18 years, had all attended local elementary schools which they left at 14 to work in factories, warehouses, shops, offices and in domestic service. Jephcott's study of their reading suggested that working girls continued to read schoolgirl papers throughout their teens: 'What child bound all day by an elementary school classroom or the walls of a factory does not long to be cruising, skating, riding or giving a garden party in an Emir's palace?'[37] Trease similarly recorded that schoolgirl magazines were avidly read by a fifth of the shop girls, and one tenth of the office and factory workers who frequented his local youth club.[38]

Letters to schoolgirl papers offer few clues as to the identity of the readers. Most papers only acknowledged the letters they received. Where correspondence was encouraged and printed it reveals little about the readers' identity. Letters to *School Friend*, for example, adopted a tone more akin to the magazine's fantasy world than the readers' real lives; as George Orwell anxiously noted, 'It is clear that many of the boys and girls who write these letters are living a complete fantasy life'.[39] Robert Roberts, writing of his working-class childhood in Salford, recalls how his friends adopted the language of the magazines; 'self-consciously we incorporated weird slang into our oath sprinkled banter – Yarooh! My Sainted Aunt! Leggo! and a dozen others.'[40] This pattern can be seen in the letters sent to the girls' magazines in which readers adopted the slang of the paper probably because it enhanced their sense of belonging to this privileged world of adolescence.

Cadogan and Craig claim that the *Girls' Own Paper* was popular with middle-class parents who wanted 'good' literature for their daughters; they also assert that working-class girls dismissed this paper as 'prissy', resenting its educational overtones.[41] Although they present no evidence to support these assertions, readership studies do show that the *Girls' Own Paper* was not greatly popular compared to the elementary schoolgirl papers, and that secondary schoolgirls constituted its principal audience. According to Jenkinson, amongst the 12, 13, 14 and 15 plus cohorts of secondary schoolgirls the *Girls' Own Paper* was mentioned by 13, 7, 13 and 5 per cent respectively. In contrast, only 4 per cent of senior schoolgirls, all of them aged between 13 and 14 years, read this paper.[42] In fact by 1940 its circulation was roughly 30000 copies per month compared to that of schoolgirl fiction weeklies which averaged 350000 per week.[43] As the *Girls' Own Paper* was frequently stocked by libraries, schools, youth clubs and churches, it is likely that readership exceeded this level, particularly during the Second World War when girls were encouraged to circulate their magazines because of the general shortage of periodicals.[44] Specific information about the readership of the *Girls' Own Paper* prior to Jenkinson's 1930s survey, also the shortlived *School-Days* and *Schoolgirls' Pictorial*, does not appear to be available. Letters to the *Girls' Own Paper* offer few clues. During the 1920s when it was combined with *Woman's Magazine*, few letters from adolescent girls were acknowledged in 'Editor's Answers'. By 1940 when the *Girls' Own* had established itself as a specifically girls' paper, its postbag was similar to those in other schoolgirl papers and consisted of editorial comment on readers' letters, which rarely offered any precise information about the reader. A regular correspondence feature by Reverend Wigley was also introduced in the 1940s but aside from confirming the Christian faith of *Girls' Own Paper* readers, questions such as 'Is it Christian to dance?' and 'Why should I marry a Christian?' reveal little except that these perplexed readers were in their late teens and early twenties.

Information on the readership of working girls' magazines of the 1920s, 1930s and 1940s is more forthcoming from contemporary readership surveys, although little is known about the business girls' papers which folded in the twenties. Another magazine which slipped through the net of readership studies was *Miss Modern*. Its letter page reveals that readers were in their late teens and early twenties but information with which to ascertain social class is difficult to discern; queries regarding courtship and love tended to obscure the reader's background and with the exception of a few letters from office girls, references to work were scarce. However, the frequency with which *Peg's Paper* was mentioned in studies and commentaries of the period is witness to its extensive popularity with both working-class working girls and also schoolgirls between 1919 and 1940; it is also evidence of the anxiety which romance papers generated.[45] Letters to these papers, which were primarily concerned with boys, romance, appearance, work and parents, were sent by young working-class and lower-middle-class girls employed in domestic service, factories, mills, offices, shops and restaurants.

Millgirl and mother-daughter magazines were remarkably similar in their preoccupation with romance and it is not surprising that they were often lumped together in contemporary studies; Jenkinson describes them as 'erotic bloods'. Readership surveys were unanimous in pointing to the popularity of these 'erotic bloods' amongst elementary schoolgirls and ex-elementary working girls although these papers constituted only a small component of the reading of secondary schoolgirls.[46]

This class difference in reading practices is also evident in Jephcott's description of the interests of young wartime evacuees;

> A fourteen year old secondary schoolgirl says that *Crystal* is the popular magazine with her friends, but when she was evacuated and went to a village elementary school the girls were all reading *Red Star Weekly*, a more sentimental type of magazine.[48]

Fenwick's 1953 study similarly showed that mother-daughter magazines were popular with schoolgirls, in fact a quarter of 14–15 year olds and a third of girls over 15 read these magazines.[49] Periodicals such as *Red Letter*, *Glamour* and *Red Star* were, he rather condescendingly noted, 'more popular with girls from poorer cultural backgrounds', by which he meant the lower strata of the working classes.[50] Older girls were also vociferous readers of mother-daughter magazines.

Although the age range used in table 3.3 obscures the representation of specifically adolescent reading in 1939, it is clear that mother-daughter

Table 3.2. 'Erotic Bloods' Read by Schoolgirls in 1939 (expressed as a percentage of the total number read by the age group)[47]

Age in years	Secondary schoolgirls	Senior schoolgirls
12+	2.3	27.1
13+	3.4	23.9
14+	3.2	30.6
15+	3.3	–

magazines were more popular with working-class than middle-class schoolgirls and young workers; the most popular magazine, *Red Letter*, constituted roughly 9 per cent of working-class reading. Hulton's survey of 1947 recorded that 15 per cent of 16–24 year olds from social classes IV and V read *Red Letter*, 9 per cent *Miracle* , and 6 per cent *My Weekly*.[52] Letters to these magazines confirm their popularity with adolescent girls.

In spite of the limitations of available sources it is evident that girls' magazines constituted an important aspect of the leisure of many girls growing up in England between 1920 and 1950. While there was some overlap in terms of the intended readership of different sets of magazines, for the most part they targeted specific age and social-class groupings. As we shall see in subsequent chapters, these magazines offered their readers different kinds of feminine lessons. In general terms, the social-class tone of magazines closely correlated with the groups of readers these different types of magazines actually attracted. Concerning age however, there was a distinct disjuncture beween the magazine's intended readership and actual audience. This was most noticeable with regard to the range of romance papers which, although aimed at working and courting girls, also wives and mothers, actually attracted a considerable following

Table 3.3. Readership of Mother-Daughter magazines by class for girls aged 14–24 years in 1939 (as percentage of girls who read each magazine by class).[51]

Magazine	Social Class			
	IV	III	II	I
Red Letter	10.97	7.48	2.1	–
Red Star	8.07	5.07	1.4	2.0
My Weekly	4.41	4.12	1.8	2.0
Miracle	8.45	4.21	0.9	2.0
Oracle	5.74	3.26	0.5	2.0

amongst elementary schoolgirls. This suggests that magazines for working-class schoolgirls did not meet all the needs of their intended readership. What did schoolgirls want, and why didn't schoolgirl papers cater to this need? What factors did structure the form and content of magazines, and contribute to the construction of the intended reader?

Producing Magazines for Girls

Research into magazine production processes has been a much neglected aspect of historical work on popular magazines. In some respects this is not surprising given the paucity of information on this topic. Few records of editorial policy survive from the interwar period, most have been destroyed or lost and, in many cases, publishers and editors avoided written policy statements. Oral history sources are also scarce as few editors survive from this period of magazine publishing. A few contacts have emerged from my enquiries which have provided invaluable insights into general aspects of magazine production for girls and women as well as details specific to millgirl and mother-daughter magazines.[53] These have been augmented by various autobiographies and secondary sources.[54] Personal recollections of editorial policy are, however, often hazy and incomplete, which is not surprising given that 50 or more years had elapsed since the production of these magazines. Respondents, as is now well recognised, also redefine and recreate their history in the light of contemporary knowledge, attitudes and sensitivities. Key questions concerning gender relations, for example, were clearly addressed by interviewees with modern sensibilities in mind. Although in isolation these sources are unable to offer a precise account of magazine production they do suggest the outline of these processes, the key contributors and factors. They also reveal the central role of the editor in the production of magazines for adolescent girls between 1920 and 1950. As we shall see in subsequent chapters, in conjunction with a close reading of the magazine text, these sources flesh out an understanding of the cultural production of girlhood.

Editors were in an extremely powerful position and had considerable control within their respective magazines, which included commissioning the fiction and dictating its plot; Nell Kennedy, editor of *Peg's Paper*, has been described as 'authoritarian', and Marcus Morris, the founder editor of *Girl*, 'oversaw everything'.[55] In spite of this, editors were constrained by their publishers, readers and prevalent ideas and interests concerning the position, responsibilities and behaviour of girls in society. In her analysis of post-1950s women's magazines, Ferguson describes the role of the editor as an 'agenda-setter to the female world': 'They are able to confer status upon – or withhold it from – individuals, issues and events by rendering them, or refusing to render them, visible in their pages'.[56] Ferguson criticises the classic interpretation of editors as gatekeepers pointing to the complex, active and prescriptive work which they undertake.[57] Research into the production of magazines for an adolescent readership between 1920 and 1950 also suggests that the passive model of gate-keeper is inappropriate for understanding the role of editor in the production process. Editors assumed an active and creative role mediating between the interests and needs of various groups, in particular those of publishers, readers and, during the 1940s, the government; in educational magazines, the opinions of teachers and even parents were also significant.[58] More specifically, editors strove to reconcile a number of key factors in shaping the form, content and tone of their magazines, most notably: publisher's objectives, directives and culture; reader interests as articulated by girls; editorial perceptions of the reader shaped by their own experience, prevalent ideologies of femininity and girlhood, also discourses on adolescence. Together these constituted the lens through which magazine content was chosen and representationally managed.

During the period 1920 to 1950, two particular models of publishing dominated the production of magazines for adolescent girls. Most popular by the twentieth century was the commercial and entertainment model typified by the Amalgamated Press, which published most of the elementary schoolgirl papers. According to Trease, Amalgamated Press were against trying to educate their readers through their stories for schoolgirls. On the basis of interviews with two Amalgamated Press representatives, Trease claimed that he found 'no fumbling, well-meaning experiments in education. A frank admission of purely commercial motive is coupled with a quite sincere pride in the tradition of the house for providing "clean, healthy reading".'[59] Trease was assured that there were never any ideological directives from above, but as he himself reveals, there was a house style, a particular set of values and codes of conduct that editors and authors were expected to adhere to in the production of magazines. Craig and Cadogan claim that Northcliffe, the publisher of the Amalgamated Press schoolgirl papers, imposed a censorship on swear words and that R.T. Eves, editor of *School Friend*, issued quite specific moral guidelines to his fiction writers: 'Cheats, liars and spiteful girls were not allowed to prosper: smoking, swearing, drinking and tale-telling were beyond the Pale.'[60] Whether directives were passed down, or whether the publisher, editor and authors shared a similar set of values, did not matter as far as content was concerned. A glance through any Amalgamated Press schoolgirl paper clearly reveals the moral values and standards of the social milieu from which the editors came. In some instances the publisher's ideas and values were imposed on the magazine's form and content by direct intervention from the publisher,[61] more often their views were impressed on the magazine by the editors who were socialised into the publisher's culture.[62]

In contrast to the commercial papers, the *Girls' Own Paper* was, quite literally, missionary in its objective. Published by Lutterworth Press for the Religious Tract Society (RTS), which was founded in 1799, its aim was to provide wholesome and instructive reading for girls. Reflecting on its publishing policy in 1941 the RTS noted that

> the increasing stress being placed on Christian education, the vital need for providing sound, wholesome literature for the young people who will have to mould the future, the importance of presenting the case for evangelical Christianity before thoughtful men and women, give the Society an opportunity every whit as urgent as any that have arisen in the past 142 years of our history.[63]

Although by the interwar period commercial viability had become of increased significance for the *Girls' Own Paper*, especially since it subsidised the *Boys' Own*, the magazine remained missionary in intent and was distributed through youth organisations, schools and churches and exported for use in missions in India and elsewhere.[64] In 1940, despite its modern look, the *Girls' Own Paper* remained determined to inculcate Christian values; Reverend Wigley's letter page provided readers with a Christian spiritual perspective on their problems. Mrs Goodall, editor in 1945 of the *Girl's Own Paper* as well as *Woman's Magazine* and *Playways*, clearly articulated this role in her address to the RTS executive committee:

> She felt the sponsoring of the magazine was a most valuable piece of missionary work and mentioned a letter from a Baptist minister in Wales congratulating them on the way in which they were reaching girls through the articles in the magazine; and also the numerous enquiries received from the readers by Mr Wigley.[65]

Mrs Goodall ended her speech by asking the members of the committee to pray with her for all those associated with the production of the *Girls' Own Paper* 'that they might be given wisdom and grace'.[66] In its concern to reach young minds, parental and school approval were matters of concern to the *Girls' Own Paper*. How editors gained information on these matters is not clear. In the case of *Girl*, which shared a similar Christian objective to the *Girls' Own Paper* but which was not published until 1951, a dummy paper was taken into schools and teachers' organisations for feedback prior to its launch.[67]

Magazines, whether motivated primarily by profit or missionary zeal, had to appeal to their readers and take their interests and needs into account. This was particularly true of commercial papers that targeted a mainly working-class readership, as it was the girl rather than her parents who was most likely to have purchased these papers; Fenwick's study revealed that girls generally bought their own schoolgirl and romance papers or acquired them second hand.[68] The editors of the Amalgamated Press elementary schoolgirl papers also thought that it was important to produce a paper that girls would want to read and spend their pocket-money on; the aim of every 'blood publisher' was 'to produce papers which will be bought by the child, not for him[sic]; or, if they are bought for him, then at his own insistence.'[69] The missionary *Girls' Own Paper* also had to take account of its readers although less for commercial reasons. Given its concern to provide girls with education and guidance the *Girls' Own Paper* was, by definition, required to engage with aspects of its readers' lives and linked to this, its influence depended on fostering the interest of its audience.

One of the ways in which magazines fostered engagement was by addressing the conditions of girlhood in their articles and letter features. The missionary *Girls' Own Paper* was more closely tied to the changing detail of girlhood than those commercial papers preoccupied with entertainment, and it was vocal on matters of social and economic change including the declining economic standards of many middle-class families, the demographic imbalance and women's work. At the same time, however, this paper was also out of touch with the interests of many middle-class girls in its preoccupation with sexually innocent and scholarly schoolgirls. In the case of successful commercial schoolgirl papers, editors devoted little attention to the everyday world of girlhood preferring to concentrate on meeting their reader's fantasies through fiction. Commercially orientated magazines for older working readers fostered a different relationship. Whilst preoccupied with meeting girls' interests and fantasies, editors also felt compelled to offer direct engagement with the lives of their readers on matters of work and also relationships, and to offer readers guidance in these rather precarious but important areas of adolescent experience. A number of strategies were employed to make this content as palatable and pleasurable as possible; fictional autobiographies were just one of the devices used to deliver advice on work and related matters.

Realism within fiction was also regarded by many editors as important. *Girls' World*, for example, described its fiction in the following terms: 'these stories will be full of human interest and tell of incidents that have happened to other girls. They will be love stories of men and girls, who lead just such lives as your own, and so each story will bear the stamp of reality, that will make it doubly appealing to you.' (Note reference to men and girls.)[70] *Girls' World* may have been referring to a material realism, but it is also probable that this realism was 'psychological'. In her study of women's viewing of the soap 'Dallas', Ien Ang reveals that many fans of this series contend that the pleasure of 'Dallas' comes from the 'lifelike' character of the serial. This realism, she argues, is produced by the 'construction of a psychological reality, and is not related to its (illusory) fit to an externally perceptible (social) reality.'[71] Consequently girls' magazines, even fiction papers, could be closely engaged with their readers whilst exhibiting little regard for the material conditions of girlhood. No matter how closely magazines sought to identify with their readers, they did not simply respond to, or reflect, what their readers wanted. The content of magazines was the product of editorial negotiation and compromise of different sets of interests including their own culturally located views on their readers' needs.

Editorial assessments of their readers' interests were often based more on assumptions about their readers than market research, although sales figures provided some feedback. In romance magazines with the emphasis on sales, it was remarkable that editors managed to develop a successful formula. Nell Kennedy was the only editor of a romance paper who seems to have spent time getting to know her intended readership; admittedly she was the founder editor of a large number of magazines so many benefited from her research. Her daughter recalls how Nell Kennedy

> went up to Wigan churchyard and she stayed, I remember vividly, in Wigan for six weeks, and she used to go into the churchyard every day and sit and listen to the millgirls whilst they ate their sandwiches ... And she listened to them endlessly to find out what their dreams were, what their aspirations were, and what they would want in a magazine.[72]

Generally, despite the need to meet their readers' interests, editors did not pay much attention to market research; interviews suggest that it was only used when it supported the editor's views.[73] Although market research was neglected as a guide to reader interests, letters to the editor and, more importantly, sales figures were used as reliable indicators of popularity. In making decisions about the form and content of magazines, editors relied heavily on their 'intuition'.[74]

Histories of popular culture have tended to focus on the class dimensions of cultural production; the gender dimensions of this process have been overlooked.[75] This is an important omission. In the context of girls' magazines we need to employ a framework which recognises the intersection of class and gender in cultural production. This type of magazine analysis begs more questions than it is possible to answer with available resources.[76] It is important, nevertheless, to acknowledge some of the class and gender dimensions of the editor's relationship with her, or indeed his, intended audience. In what ways did female editors empathise with their readers? How did a middle-class editor relate to a working-class audience of millgirls and with what implications for magazine form and content? How did women in male positions of cultural authority relate to their readers in traditionally feminine roles? How did men relate to a female audience?

The importance attached to intuition in magazine production would seem to suggest that, arising from their shared gender, women were best suited to edit and write for female readers. There is little doubt that female editors such as Nell

Kennedy, Biddy Johnson (*Woman's Weekly*) and Mary Grieve (*Woman*) were well aware of the gender dimensions and inequalities of contemporary life. In her autobiography, Mary Grieve quite clearly recalls the prejudice and gender specific obstacles she encountered in pursuing her career as a journalist.[77] It is also likely that the position and status of men and women in the media would probably have been very different. This was certainly the case in other professions in which both men and women worked.[78] Examining the success of these editors shows that they negotiated a path between conventional domestic expectations of women and the typically masculine characteristics of a successful career in journalism and business, a practice common amongst professional women in positions of authority.[79] Nell Kennedy for instance, occupied a very public position but at the same time she remained anonymous in her magazines and generally a very private woman. She was clearly an extremely capable business woman but also a devoted and accessible mother to her two daughters. While Kennedy had complete control over both her female staff and her magazines, such outright authoritarianism was not appropriate when she interacted with male colleagues. In negotiations with men, Kennedy utilised a characteristically 'feminine' device; as she confided to her daughter, 'Never be afraid of tears': this, as Lamburn explains, amounted to a 'sort of blackmail in the boardroom'.[80] While Kennedy was determined, clever and authoritative, she nevertheless realised that the characteristics which made for success in her profession were not necessarily compatible with feminine norms and they would not earn her either respect or support from her male colleagues. Indeed such traits would probably have earned her the labels 'unfeminine', 'masculine' or 'bitch'; women who took on the mantle of authority were, and still are, extremely vulnerable to attacks from the male establishment.[81]

Editors usually came from different class backgrounds to their readers and lived different lives. Nell Kennedy, for instance, who was the founder-editor of *Peg's Paper* and *Lucky Star*, grew up in an Oxfordshire village where she worked as a teacher. She moved to London and started work as a journalist, married the Editing Director of Pearsons and was subsequently invited to edit magazines for working-class young women. Women such as Kennedy were nevertheless acutely aware of the implications of social class on a girl's life options. This perhaps explains much of their conservatism, especially when writing for working-class girls and older women. If they had addressed members of their own social groups, an editor like Kennedy may well have been more progressive.

Unlike the shared knowledge and empathy that one can imagine existing between a female editor and her readers, one could be forgiven for thinking that men were ill-equipped for the task of producing magazines for girls. Amalgamated Press schoolgirl papers were, however, produced exclusively by men. The *Girls' Own Paper* was also edited by a man during the 1930s. These editors had no qualms about writing and editing for girls; according to Lofts, editors with the Amalgamated Press firmly believed that men knew what girls wanted, what they were like and what they aspired to be.[82] Moreover, they were convinced that men were more sympathetic and understanding in their dealings with schoolgirls than most women who, they argued, were inclined to 'mother' and restrict the exuberant youngster. Given the success of Angela Brazil's novels for school-girls, also the popular adventure fiction for girls and boys written by women using male pseudonyms, this is an unconvincing rationalisation of male control of schoolgirl papers.[83] Lofts' claim that men wrote girls' fiction because there were very few women journalists and writers is similarly unconvincing and tackles the issue from the wrong end. The lack of women journalists was an outcome of male practices which curbed women's entrance to this profession. Editors like Eves had considerable difficulty working with women writers and were, quite likely, reluctant to concede this area of journalism to them.

Amalgamated Press felt so confident that men could write for schoolgirls that they also appointed a male editor to the 1920s business girls' paper, *Girls' Favourite*.[84] Although it is unclear whether other business girls' papers were edited by men, it is significant that, with the exception of the *Girls' Favourite*, these papers presented an image of a female editor suggesting that a feminine touch was more appropriate for older readers and most likely to foster reader identification. Millgirl papers and mother-daughter magazines all seem to have had a female editor, someone whom readers could relate to and who would also have experience and knowledge with which to advise girls on how to achieve feminine and heterosexual objectives. Fictional male friends of the editor were, however, featured in these magazines as arbiters of feminine standards and as advisers on the conduct of gender relations. Romance magazines, for example, delivered advice on courtship through male personalities; 'My Pal Peter' meted out advice to girls on their relationships with men in *Poppy's Paper*, and 'The Lonely Batchelor' shared his wisdom concerning what men looked for in a girl through his regular article in *Girls' Weekly*.

So what sorts of ideas and expectations did these different editorial teams have of their intended readership and from where did these derive? While in some respects they came from personal experience and observation this is insufficient to account for the production of the magazine reader. Prevalent ideologies of femininity and girlhood were also at play in the editor's 'intuition', in particular Victorian ideals of girlhood. Central to the Victorian glorification of the home and cult of domesticity was an image of woman as 'angel in the house' characterised by innocence, purity and gentleness, capable of continual self-sacrifice and dedicated to the spiritual as well as physical care of the home. As this suggests, the idealised view of womanhood was remarkably childlike; this, Gorham argues, signified her removal from the vicissitudes of public life which was man's sphere.[85] This imagery affected girls as well as women as it was the Victorian daughter, the 'sunbeam', who most comfortably fitted with this ideal of feminine dependence, childlike simplicity and sexual purity; indeed there was an inherent contradiction between this ideal and the demands on women as wives and bearers of children.[86] Social and economic changes in late Victorian and Edwardian England prompted a recognition of 'the widening sphere' and the emergence of new positive images of girlhood in literature, notably the 'modern girl' and the schoolgirl heroine. Although these images embodied change, they also stressed continuities: 'The ideal modern girl represents an adaption, not a repudiation, of the older values'.[87] As Gorham points out, the fact that characteristics such as domesticity, self-sacrifice and innocence remained at the core of more modern ideals of girlhood is testimony to the power of Victorian conceptions of femininity.

Editors faced with producing magazines for girls in the period between 1920 and 1950 found their work similarly constrained by these incredibly resistant strains of Victorian domestic femininity. As with their predecessors, magazine editors strove to accommodate, rather than challenge, this idealisation even as they sought to entertain readers and address social and economic changes in the lives of adolescent girls. Popular girls' magazines were, in fact, one of the cultural agencies which contributed to the updating of feminine norms consistent with contemporary conditions and demands on girls growing up. Early twentieth century discourses on female adolescence, which mapped out feminine subjectivity and heterosexual development, served to consolidate and rationalise aspects of this Victorian idealisation of girlhood at the same time as they marked out a possible intermediary stage between child and adult.[88] Whilst subsequent chapters will flesh out the above outline of magazine production, the remainder of this chapter will briefly introduce three key variables in the construction of the female reader and her magazines, that is gender, age and social class.

Editors believed that girls and boys had different needs and interests; indeed this underpinned the introduction of magazines specifically targeted at a female audience many of which, like the working girls' papers, did not have a male equivalent. The editors of schoolgirl papers were of the view that their male and female readers required quite different fiction and features; this is evident in the blatant contrast between Amalgamated Press' schoolgirl and schoolboy papers. On occasions the same story would appear in both types of paper but in these cases significant differences were always introduced. Arthur Ransome, an editor with Amalgamated Press, recalls a story of a car race featured in a boys' magazine in which an animal is killed. This story was reproduced within a parallel girls' paper, but it was retold with a subtle difference. In the feminine version the driver stopped her car in order to attend to the animal thereby relinquishing her lead; in the male equivalent the driver carried on to win.[89] An ideology of innate gender difference underpinned all aspects of girls' magazines supported by traditional ideals of femininity as domestic and nurturant, but it was inflected in particular ways by age and social class.

The age of the intended reader was an important factor in editorial constructions of the reader. At one level the relevance of age was tied to the reader's occupation, whether at school, in paid work, or in unpaid domestic work within the home. In fiction magazines the reader's occupation was important in terms of her assumed consumer power and, in schoolgirl papers, it was central to the construction of the intended reader's identity. Working girls' magazines clearly distinguished their readers as having left full-time education, but courting and heterosexual interest constituted the primary aspect of the reader's identity. At another level, age was significant for whether girls were perceived and presented as potential wives, mothers and domestics or as young people enjoying a distinct adolescence. However, adolescence, defined as a specific stage between childhood and adulthood and characterised in popular and psychological discourses as a period of discovery, vitality and also instability, was essentially a masculine construct.[90] Girls were, for the most part, described as natural servicers of others and defined and characterised in terms associated with their potential adult status and roles. In contrast to their brothers, they were not perceived as experiencing a distinct adolescent stage; 'adolescent' behaviour was regarded as abnormal in girls. This, as Dyhouse points out, was especially the case for working-class girls; middle-class girls, due to the extensions of full-time education were more easily accommodated within this model.[91] According to the writings of contemporary theorists of adolescence, a girl's position within patriarchal relations as a future wife, mother and home-maker was incompatible with the freedoms expressed in the term 'adolescence'. Edith Saywell (1928) described the teen years as a period of conflict during which girls learnt to surrender themselves: 'Surrender may appear to her to involve the merging of her personality in that of her mate, and the loss of an essential freedom. She may need help in her thinking before she can realise that woman reaches her full stature along the lines of self-sacrifice, that, whether married or unmarried, her attitude to life should be one of free and willing service.'[92] Saywell's ideal girl learnt to forfeit her individuality and freedom for devoted service to men and, more generally, the race. In her analysis of female adolescent development, Saywell listed the problems which could occur for girls; interestingly these 'problems' constituted signs of healthy male development by other authors. This double standard is most clearly seen in a comparison of two essays that appeared in a volume edited by Mary Scarlieb in 1925; the first by Miss Helena Powell entitled 'The problem of the adolescent girl' and the other by Rev. Elliott, which discussed 'The care of the adolescent boy'.[93] Even the titles were quite explicit about the double standard; what was healthy and normal behaviour for boys was described by Miss Powell as unnatural, unhealthy and even dangerous for girls, hence girls required careful guidance during their adolescent years. This exclusion of girls from adolescence and youth or alternatively the pathologising of this stage for girls were dominant themes. In *The Revolt of Modern Youth* published in Britain in 1928, the American writer Judge Lindsey clearly associated adolescence with youth:

> A young boy is quite a different animal from anything else in the world on two legs or four. He is unique, both in his independence of mind and in his rather hostile sensitiveness to whatever comes his way. Young girls, by comparison, are immensely more stable and complaisant in matters of social conduct. A girl who is twelve, for instance, is a social being, already living in outward, tactful, skillful conformity to the world around her. She acquires social skills readily. She can talk with grown women with something of a grown woman's glibness and volubility.[94]

Lindsey's comments illustrate how girls were expected to move towards their adult roles of wife and mother at a very early age. It is also probable that this expectation prevented Lindsey, and others like him, from interpreting female behaviour in alternative ways. For example, Lindsey did not register that the behaviour of girls which he described could easily be explained in terms of the enforced close association of girls with women.

Editors seem to have recognised the restrictive nature of such expectations for their heroines and their readers, and the monotony of storyline that ensued. The sacrifice and surrender about which Saywell wrote were acknowledged by magazines as key features of femininity. Personal sacrifice and servicing responsibilities were also, as we saw in chapter 2, expectations which many girls, especially from the working-classes, encountered in their experiences of home and family life. However, as Saywell emphasised, such characteristics were totally incompatible with a lively and independent adolescent identity and this posed a problem for editors. How could they offer their young readers positive, youthful and attractive identities and at the same time avoid challenging patriarchal expectations of girls which defined them in terms of domestic and servicing roles and responsibilities within the family and, potentially, marriage and motherhood?

Representation of schoolgirls in 1920s magazines did manage to break with Victorian representations of young girls as 'angels within the home'. This was partly achieved by removing the heroine from the family in which patriarchal expectations of girls as emotional and domestic servicers were quite commonly oppressive. It was also accomplished by locating girls in an all-female environment in which they could escape the restrictive nature of the roles they were expected to assume in platonic and sexual relations with the opposite sex. Juvenile magazines, produced for a readership of boys as well as girls, illustrate the extremely restrictive nature of femininity and girlhood which was permissable for girls depicted in mixed-sex environments. Although the 1920s schoolgirl heroine was depicted as lively and youthful, references to the heroine as self-sacrificing, loyal and modest also conveyed continuity with the Victorian characterisation of the daughter in the home. The depiction of the scholarship girl with domestic responsibilities, or the representation of the 'substitute mother', also communicated the caring and domestic nature of femininity. Illustrations of 1920s heroines were also very similar to heroines portrayed in late Victorian literature, even if 1920s girls donned school uniforms.[95]

The 1930s fiction schoolgirl represented a more distinct break with Victorian representations of girlhood and somewhat restrictive constructions of female adolescence. These newly introduced hoydens, tomboys and madcaps offer a good illustration of the further development and extension of an adolescent identity for girls, one which was unrestricted by the spectre of domestic and maternal responsibilities. However, the often wild representations of the 1930s schoolgirl continued to work a compromise between the fundamental patriarchal concern for girls as servicers of men and as potential wives and mothers and the freedom, challenge and excitement of 'adolescence'. Magazines avoided challenging patriarchal interests by retaining latent vestiges of nurturant and domestic qualities in their female characters which signalled their future contentment with the roles of wife and mother; although not paraded, these characteristics were most visible when girls were depicted in male company. Most importantly, as the age of the schoolgirl heroines indicated (always fourth formers of 13–14 years of age), independent adolescence was merely a temporary and middle-class phenomenon. As Craig and Cadogan have argued, the introduction of female adolescence into schoolgirl magazines was purely a commercial device;

> The author's purpose is simply to crystallise the ten-year-old's image of herself at twenty; the author, if not the reader, is fully aware of certain 'socialising' pressures which will alter the child's view of herself as she gets older. Thus, fantasies of rounding up a gang of thieves or a herd of cattle, or becoming an aerial photographer, are likely to give way gradually to the more limited, but more sensible and socially approved fantasy of 'getting married' – but by this time the girl will have shifted to reading papers of another type.[96]

Schoolgirl magazines removed girls from the family and mixed-sex environments and in this way they facilitated the construction of a relatively autonomous, lively and empowering 'adolescence' for their heroines. They also side-stepped, albeit temporarily, patriarchal expectations of girls. In contrast to schoolgirl magazines, working girls' papers focused almost exclusively on characteristics and activities consistent with patriarchal ideals; these magazines actively encouraged readers to identify with, and emulate, the femininity of their heroines, and to follow the prescriptions of femininity which they presented. This focus stemmed from the fact that readers were considered to be at the age when ambitions of marriage, motherhood and domesticity should be uppermost in their minds; femininity for these girls was clearly equated with patriarchal interests. As in magazines for younger readers, editors still had a problem in that these expectations were not always appealing to girls and certainly not the stuff of a good read. Like their younger sisters, working girls had desires for power and independence. However, magazines for courting girls had considerably less leeway than those for schoolgirls in seeking alternatives to subordinate and domestic female roles. The reason for this lay in the significance of their age for their position in the heterosexual career. Girls in the late teens were at a crucial age for patriarchal relations because it was at this point that they were expected to develop a strong motivation towards heterosexual coupling, monogamous marriage and home-making. As Griffin has argued in relation to girls growing up in the 1990s, young women's transition to heterosexuality marks a crucial point for patriarchal control.[97] This constituted a dilemma for editors; how could they address their readers' fantasies and at the same time avoid posing a challenge to gender relations. Attempts to resolve this dilemma can be seen in the management, by working girls' magazines, of the 'modern girl' discussed in chapter 4 and the introduction of the sexually autonomous evil woman into mother-daughter magazines during the 1930s.

As the working girls' magazines suggest, the significance of age was inextricably linked to the reader's anticipated position in the heterosexual career. In fact, this appears to have been a primary determinant of the extent to which magazines engaged with aspects of girlhood and the way in which this was representationally managed. Where a publisher targeted a readership deemed to be entering heterosexual relationships, heterosexuality was a central consideration in the construction of magazines. It not only determined what was represented, but also how. So, for example, a major preoccupation of working girls' magazines was to provide encouragement and guidance in relationships with the opposite sex. In line with this, these magazines marginalised friendships between girls and women and even attacked women who did not hanker after a heterosexual adult identity. These magazines also engaged noticeably with aspects of the conditions of girlhood and social change which were significant for heterosexual relations such as the social and economic implications of women's paid work. In the case of schoolgirl magazines, which were produced for readers deemed to be too young to enter heterosexual relations, heterosexuality acted as a 'structuring absence'.[98] That is, although these magazines did not represent readers as involved in relationships with boys, this denial greatly determined what actually did appear in the text. Hence the preoccupation with friendships between girls, the marginalisation of boys, and the ban on sexual or romantic relations between the sexes and between women.

The heterosexual significance of age was, however, variable by social class and this had implications for the form and content of magazines targeted at girls from different social groups. The middle-class *Girls' Own Paper*, for example, discouraged its readers from thinking about boys (at least until the late 1940s) because its readers married later than their working-class counterparts and because it was committed to the promotion of professional careers for women. The social class of the intended reader was an important consideration in other ways. For example, the economic status of readers was influential because of its relevance for the successful targeting of advertising, a matter of growing interest as indicated by the proliferation of readership surveys. Another way, as we saw earlier, in which the readers' background was important was in terms of the magazine's ability to establish the relevance of its features for contemporary girls; this was particularly the case in educational magazines and many working girls' papers which felt compelled to offer advice to their readers on matters of importance.[99] This is not to say that magazines accurately represented the experiences of their readers, rather that editors tried to remain true to what they perceived as their readers' social background and the options it afforded. This can be clearly seen in magazine representations of women's work. Nell Kennedy who was founder editor of many romance papers combined a successful career with raising two daughters whom she 'brought up to do a job of work . . . [Kennedy] slightly looked down upon young women who didn't set out to do a job of work and have a goal and objective outside the home and family.'[100] This did not apply to the mill and factory girls for whom she produced weekly magazines. Kennedy assumed that her readers had neither the education nor the opportunities to pursue a career and that the majority were motivated by dreams of marriage, maternity and domesticity. As this illustrates, editors did not merely impose their standards on to their readers, instead they attempted to respond, whether rightly or wrongly, to what they perceived their readers expected and could realistically achieve. In contrast, those magazines motivated purely by profit and dominated by fiction, such as the elementary schoolgirl papers, were under no compulsion to actually address what they perceived to be their readers' backgrounds.

Conclusion

A wide range of magazines catered to adolescent female readers in the period 1920 to 1950. For the most part these magazines successfully reached their intended readership. This is not to say that magazines responded to their readers' interests or that they reflected the lives of girls. The production of magazines involved a number of factors negotiated by the editor. It is this rather complex process that accounts for the specific content of magazines, the variations between different types of magazine and also changes over time. It is also this which, for example, explains the failure of elementary schoolgirl papers to address successfully the range of interests of their schoolgirl readers. The production of the intended reader by editors was dependent partly on the publisher's objectives and also involved sets of ideas about gender, social class and age. The importance of age derived from its significance in terms of occupation, whether girls were at school or in waged or unpaid work and, linked to this, their power as consumers; it also derived from patriarchal expectations of girls, in particular it hinged on the position of girls in the heterosexual career.

The processes outlined here contributed to the modernisation of notions of girlhood and the updating of feminine ideals. They also contributed to the production of differences between magazines. The following chapters provide detailed illustration of these processes. They also examine and attempt to explain the ways in which magazines engaged with and constructed aspects of adolescent girlhood – differences between girls, the transitions of adolescence and the changing conditions of girlhood – and the ways in which these were representationally managed in fiction and non-fiction features. Magazine representations of school and work, discussed in the following chapter, show how magazines constructed differences between girls, by age and social class, and how they managed historical and biographical change.

Notes

1 These magazines sometimes advertised other periodicals and also cheap novelettes.
2 Ward (1948), p.5.
3 Rooff (1935); Jephcott (1942); Ward (1948), p.25 discovered that 32 per cent of grammar schoolgirls and 6 per cent of elementary schoolgirls were members of girls' clubs.
4 Richards (1982), p.536.
5 Women's Group on Public Welfare (1943), p.22.
6 On secondary school teachers see Summerfield (1987a). On the girls' club movement, see Dyhouse (1981), pp.104–114.
7 This is not a complete list of girls' periodicals from this period, although it does include most of the popular papers. *Every Girls' Paper* cited here is not the paper of the same title produced by the RTS between 1928–1930.
8 Branson (1977), p.222. In 1919 cars were a luxury and the preserve of the upper- and upper-middle classes. The cheapest motor in the 1920s was the Citroen at £320, which cost more than a skilled engineer earned in a year.
9 White (1970), pp.93–6.
10 See Summerfield and Braybon (1987), pp.197–203.
11 Cited in Cadogan and Craig (1986), p.270.
12 Ibid.
13 *Girls' Own Paper and Heiress*, January 1948, pp.18–19, 66.

14 *Girls' World*, 21 March 1927, p.2.

15 *Girls' Favourite*, 26 March 1927, p.192.

16 *Girls' Favourite*, 1 February 1922, p.506.

17 *Girls' Favourite*, 19 February 1927, p.55: 'There are many girls whose mothers, though they have to keep their grown-up daughters to help at home, cannot afford to give them enough pocket-money to dress fairly well, or to pay for those little pleasures which every girl who works, either at home or outside, is entitled to have.'

18 *Peg's Paper*, 5 May 1919, p.1.

19 Roberts (1984), p.82.

20 Orwell (1982b), p.199.

21 *Miss Modern*, October 1930.

22 Ibid.

23 *Miss Modern*, June 1935.

24 Orwell (1982b), p.199; White (1970), pp.97–8; Hoggart (1958), p.101.

25 *Girls' Weekly*, 4 March 1922.

26 Gittens (1982), p.73.

27 Jephcott (1948), ch.4.

28 This problem arose from some interviews which I conducted with women of various ages and from an overview of transcripts in the Oral History of Girlhood Project, University of Lancaster. Clearer recollections might have been elicited by specifically targeting (via present day women's papers) avid readers of girls' magazines from the period 1920 to 1950. This approach was successfully used in research on recollections of Hollywood stars from the 1940s and 1950s examined by Stacey (1993).

29 The earliest readership survey was conducted in 1928 by the London Research Bureau (LRB), *Press Circulations Analysed*, followed in 1934 by a similar study conducted by the Institute of Incorporated Practitioners in Advertising (IIPA). The IIPA went on to produce further surveys in 1939 and 1947. Attwoods the publisher compiled a similar report in 1947 as did Hulton Press, *Hulton Readership Survey* in 1947 and 1948.

30 The London Research Bureau (LRB) report of 1928 did not investigate the reading habits of people from slum areas or 'poor neighbourhoods', which suggests that the sample was heavily biased against readers in social classes IV and V. The disproportionately large number of middle-class households included (25 per cent of the sample but only 8 per cent of the population) led to the under-representation or invisibility of magazines read by working-class females. The report's reliance on information gleaned from interviewing housewives who, it was assumed, 'knew more about what was being read in the home than any other individual member of the family' (p.v), may also have resulted in an underestimation of the magazines read by girls who often shared papers amongst themselves. (See Jephcott (1942), p.100.) The 1934 survey by the Institute of Incorporated Practitioners in Advertising (IIPA) was even more unfavourable to small circulation magazines as it excluded those not mentioned more than 20 times per area sampled in areas as small as 2600 households. Although it did not sample households in relation to the national distribution of social class, it did represent the smaller income groups more favourably than the LRB; 78.3 per cent of the interviews were conducted with families whose income was less than £5 per week (p.ix). Later surveys by the IIPA and Hulton (1947) did allocate interviews in proportion to the class composition of

the population and were more likely to highlight the range of magazines read by working-class girls. Where specific class labels were employed, especially in the pre-1939 surveys, they were ambiguous and impressionistic. As the LRB report explained: 'By middle-class we mean the well to do and comfortably off. By lower-middle-class we mean people whose buying capacity is much more limited than the middle class, but whose social outlook and buying habits are somewhat similar to those of people in that class. By working class we mean the steadier type of workers. Slum areas and very poor neighbourhoods were not touched by the investigation.' (p.v)

31 In an earlier discussion of girls' magazines, Tinkler (1987) p.62, I state that Jenkinson (1940) found that 14 year old senior schoolgirls read four times as many schoolgirl papers as their secondary schoolgirl counterparts. In fact, Jenkinson's calculations combine comics and schoolgirl papers. Taking his figures for schoolgirl papers only, it is clear that secondary schoolgirls read slightly more schoolgirl papers than senior schoolgirls.

32 Jenkinson (1940), pp.214–5.

33 Fenwick (1953), Table 2, p.29.

34 Ibid., Table 4, p.30.

35 Correspondence with Lofts. This may well have been an underestimate given the recycling of magazines which commonly occurred.

36 Trease (1948), p.128.

37 Jephcott (1942), p.101.

38 Trease (1948), p.128.

39 Orwell (1982b), p.184.

40 Roberts (1980), p.160.

41 Cadogan and Craig (1986), p.263.

42 Jenkinson (1940), pp.214–5.

43 Correspondence with Lofts.

44 Letters to the *Girls' Own Paper* referred to it being circulated, see 'Doreen' March 1943, 'Margaret ATS' December 1942.

45 See comments on *Peg's Paper* in Orwell (1982b); Hoggart (1958); Jephcott (1942).

46 Given that most working girls' papers folded on, or before, 1940, references to romance magazines in most studies 1940–1950s refer almost exclusively to mother-daughter magazines such as *Glamour*, *Red Letter* and *Lucky Star*.

47 Jenkinson (1940) p.218.

48 Jephcott (1942), p.101.

49 Fenwick (1953), Table 2, p.29.

50 Ibid., p.35.

51 IIPA (1939) Vol 1, Table 5, p.45.

52 Hulton (1947), Table 9, p.5.

53 Past editors are difficult to locate, as the publisher D.C Thomson explained to me: 'I'm afraid there aren't any surviving editors who could help with your project.' I did locate some people who worked in periodical publishing during this period who have provided useful contacts and also insights, through interview and/or corre-spondence, into the production of girls' magazines. See acknowledgements.

54 The following sources have been useful: Grieve (1960); Drawbell (1968); Trease (1948); Orwell (1982b); Cadogan and Craig (1986); White (1970).

55 Interviews with Pat Lamburn and Lorrie Purden. The central role of the editor was

also commented on by White (1977). Grieve (1960) refers to her responsibility as editor for choosing and moulding fiction; Cadogan and Craig (1986) indicate that R.T. Eves, editor of *School Friend*, also oversaw the fiction.

56 Ferguson (1983), p.131.

57 Ibid., p.132.

58 Ferguson (1983) describes how there was a liason officer between the government and women's magazines during the Second World War; in 1948 magazines were given the role of explaining to women National Insurance, the National Health Service, National Assistance, Industrial Injuries and the Children's Act. Although Ferguson cites no evidence relevant to girls' magazines, the inclusion of a feature by R.S. Butler explaining the Education Act of 1944 to schoolgirls suggests that the *Girls' Own Paper* was also used in this way.

59 Trease (1948), p.83. Although Amalgamated Press did produce an educational secondary schoolgirl paper, *School-Days* 1928–1929, this was clearly an unsuccessful experiment.

60 Cadogan and Craig (1986), p.231.

61 Very little information is available on the production of girls' magazines even in studies and biographies of contemporary publishers; it would seem that girls' papers were not seen to be worthy of comment. A rare reference to girls' magazines appears in Pound and Harmsworth (1959), p.419, which describes an incident of direct intervention by the publisher Alfred Harmsworth, later Sir Northcliffe, in the production of a working girls' magazine.

62 Work-place culture and on-the-job socialisation would appear to have been the common ways in which the publisher's ethos was promoted. See Ferguson (1983) pp.123–5 on socialisation processes in post-1945 women's magazines.

63 USCL Chairman in USCL/RTS Minutes of Executive Committee, 25 June 1941.

64 This was a recurrent theme in the discussions of the *Girls' Own Paper* and *Boys' Own* by the USCL/RTS Executive Committee.

65 USCL/RTS Minutes of Executive Committee, 18 December 1945.

66 Ibid.

67 Interviews with Marcus Morris and James Hemming.

68 Fenwick (1953).

69 Trease (1948).

70 *Girls' World*, 7 March 1927. The mimetic quality of Victorian girls' fiction is commented on by Bratton (1981) and Rowbotham (1989), p.8.

71 Ang (1985), p.47.

72 Interview with Pat Lamburn.

73 Ibid.

74 Mary Grieve, editor of *Woman*, believed that readers did not know and could not articulate what it was that they wanted in a magazine and that it was up to the editor to intuitively know. Although Grieve was concerned with the production of women's magazines in the 1930s and 1940s, it is likely that similar views prevailed in publishing for girls. See Grieve (1960), p.180.

75 See White (1970), Cadogan and Craig (1986).

76 For an example of the sort of detailed enquiry required see study of contemporary women's magazines by Ferguson (1983) which used in depth interviews.

77 Grieve (1960), chapter 1.

78 On gender inequalities in professions see chapter 2, also Beddoe (1989), Oram

(1987), Lewis (1984), pp.193–200. Interview with Pat Lamburn suggests that women editors were 'cherished' rather than treated as equal.

79 Dyhouse (1987).

80 Interview with Pat Lamburn.

81 See Oram (1987).

82 Lofts (1978).

83 Rosamond Mary Story wrote Sexton Blake stories under the name of 'Desmond Reid' and Westerns under the names of 'Ross Wood' and 'Richard Jeskins'; Cecily Hamilton wrote as 'Max Hamilton'; Gertrude Kent Oliver wrote 'classic' detective stories for the *Boys' Own Paper* under the name 'Kent Carr'. See Adley and Lofts (1970).

84 Cadogan and Craig (1986), p.137 on the editor of *Girls' Favourite*.

85 Gorham (1982), ch.1.

86 Ibid., ch.1.

87 Ibid., p.58; and on the modern girl, ch.3.

88 On the impact of psychological discourses, see Griffin (1993), ch.1; on implications for approaches to girls' leisure in the 1940s see Tinkler (1994a) and (1995a).

89 Cited in Cadogan and Craig (1986), p.242. They also cite the example of gender differentiation evident in the portrayal of Bessie and Billie Bunter for the schoolgirl and schoolboy papers respectively. The contrast between *Girl* and *Eagle* was, according to my interview with Lorrie Purden, similarly based on the assumption of a natural gender difference.

90 Dyhouse (1981), ch. 4. Hudson (1984) argues that for girls today adolescence and femininity are subversive of one another.

91 Dyhouse (1981).

92 Saywell (1922), pp.27–8. See also Dyhouse (1981), ch. 4 on early writers on adolescence.

93 Scharlieb (1924).

94 Lindsey and Evans (1928), p.325.

95 Gorham (1987).

96 Cadogan and Craig (1986), p.316.

97 Griffin (1993), p.144.

98 From Althusser (1970). Thanks to Celia Lury for introducing me to this concept.

99 Mary Grieve (1960), p.90, stressed the necessity of attending to the detail of readers' lives in producing interwar women's magazines: 'Since a woman's magazine strives to reflect the life of the reader, it is of importance that she should see her own life reflected in the pages, not the life of some luckier, richer, cleverer creature. So when we started *Woman* we had to make a deliberate, daily and hourly effort to remember our reader's circumstances.'

100 Interview with Pat Lamburn.

Chapter 4

From School to Work

School followed by paid work increasingly became the norm for girls of all social classes growing up in England between 1920 and 1950. The emergence of magazines for school and working girls in the interwar years testifies to the significance these features of girlhood had attained amongst publishers in this period. This proliferation of papers for different groups of girls is also evidence of the construction of difference as a means of legitimating the differentiation of publishing for a female audience; schoolgirls were distinct from their working sisters who, in turn, had different experiences and interests from wives and mothers. Having said this, the demise of magazines for business girls by the 1930s replaced by the long-running and successful mother-daughter papers, does suggest that the differentiation between adolescent working girls and married women in their twenties was deemed unnecessary or hard to profitably sustain. The publisher's distinction between schoolgirls and working girls was more successful, premised as it was on an important point of transition for girls growing up in this period. On leaving school, as we saw in chapter 2, girls tended to relinquish all things associated with school and being children. Circulation figures suggest that this included schoolgirl papers although they continued to attract some following amongst working girls. How did these different magazines address school and work?

Although leaving school meant a significant break in girlhood experiences, education and employment were intertwined in that schooling was geared around preparing girls of all social classes for the labour market as well as for a domestic and maternal career in marriage. In line with social-class differences in education provision, magazines for middle-class and working-class schoolgirls responded differently to girls' education and work and the transition between these aspects of girlhood. Similarly, magazines for older girls addressed their readers' work in different ways although they shared an avoidance of school matters. Magazines did not merely represent school or work. Indeed, those papers which did address girls' experiences in these areas also assumed an educational role in relation to their readers, one that was spurred in part by the restructuring of the labour market and the effects of the 1920's slump, the Depression of the 1930s, and the mobilisation of women during the Second World War.

School Fiction

The launch of a range of magazines which specifically addressed the schoolgirl suggests that this identity was important for girls growing up in this period. Nevertheless, with the exception of secondary schoolgirl papers, these magazines did not dwell on the detail of schooling, nor indeed on the realities of girls' lives. Instead these magazines offered their readers a diet of fiction which featured girls' boarding schools like Cliff House, which were quite removed from most girls' education experiences. These stories, which were usually written by men, were the female equivalent of the fiction written for the boys' magazines *Gem* and *Magnet*. The deliberate lack of realism is not perhaps surprising. Whilst school experiences were extremely important for shaping the conditions of girlhood in gender and class terms, elementary schooling did not lend itself to a positive schoolgirl identity. Family and home life were similarly problematic. Fictional boarding schools such as Cliff House and fictional representations of schoolgirls were however an ideal vehicle for constructing positive and attractive schoolgirl identities. These facilitated mobility, excitement, action and friendship; they offered freedom from the constraints of femininity and a space untouched by girls' prospects in the labour and marriage markets.

Kathleen Betterton's expectations of boarding school in the 1920s clearly communicates the gap between fiction and reality; they also indicate the possible influence of girls' magazines in shaping perceptions of life outside the reader's own experience. Informed by her reading of Angela Brazil's schoolgirl novels, Betterton recalls how the word 'boarding school' had both glamour and romance for her: 'My imagination had battened on Angela Brazil, lent to me by Flora; the very word conjured up visions of midnight picnics, sweet girl prefects, hockey, house matches, and exploits that saved the honour of the school.' But when Kathleen arrived at Christ's Hospital in Hertford she was bitterly disappointed;

> All my bright illusions about the fun of boarding-school had by now quite vanished. I did not feel at all like Paula on her first day at St Hillary's. Anything indeed less like St Hillary's than the school for which we were bound could be imagined.[1]

As Betterton's account suggests, an important factor in the success of these tales amongst working-class readers was that most of these girls had no direct experience of the type of schooling which these stories depicted. Boarding school education was accessible to only a minority of the girls. In 1921 only 13.5 per cent of girls received their education outside the public elementary system, over half of these (6 per cent of all girls) received a private education at a public school.[2] Within grant-aided schools in the 1930s, only 3 per cent of female pupils were boarders although in non-grant-aided schools over half were boarders.[3] Those readers who did attend boarding schools found that these stories lacked realism. Interviews with ex-boarding schoolgirls educated between 1900 and 1940 suggest that this lack of realism led to girls dismissing these stories at an early age.[4]

This lack of realism was also of concern to the joint principals of a London school who were highly critical of these stories for creating a 'false view' of boarding school life:

> We have looked through several schoolgirls' annuals ... and find they give a false view of school life. The fourth form seem to run the school – the headmistress is generally a dignified but distant figurehead, and the assistant mistresses either young, very girlish and so popular, or middle-aged caricatures. In one, a party of girls were allowed to go for a picnic some miles from school without a mistress. Among them was a 'Ruritanian' princess with a gang of international crooks after her. She had been sent to the school for safety and was naturally kidnapped on the picnic.[5]

This lack of realism stemmed from two key sources. On the one hand, as the joint headmistresses suggest, it derived from the unrealistic freedom allowed to the pupils. On the other, despite many features typical of the girls' boarding school presented by mainstream historians such as houses, dormitories, uniforms, games and an emphasis on 'spirit' and 'honour', these fictional schools did not correspond to the realities of boarding school education for girls.

Drawing upon her experience of a girls' boarding school in the 1950s, Judith Okely argues that unlike boys' boarding schools, those for girls prepared their pupils for economic and political dependency within marriage.[6] Okely goes on to argue that although schools for boys and girls shared similar features they were motivated by different objectives and were experienced differently by their pupils. While Okely's conclusions regarding a boarding school education for girls fit with information about girls' secondary schools, it would be misleading, given the paucity of information on girls' boarding schools for this period,[7] merely to transpose her experiences onto the interwar years. Her comments, supported by her own experience, cannot in themselves be used as the basis for generalisation.

The shape of school stories was based on what was perceived to appeal to readers. This was derived both from the tradition of schoolboys' magazines and the model of schoolgirls' stories made popular by Angela Brazil and other female writers. Magazine authors utilised features which had dramatic potential but they were nevertheless constrained in that they had to avoid challenging feminine ideals and, more importantly, patriarchal interests. Games, for example, facilitated the drama but, more importantly, they allowed girls to escape the restrictions of prevalent notions of femininity which were centrally defined by the roles of wife, mother and home-maker; through games, heroines could be energetically adolescent in ways which were normally the prerogative of boys.[8] Aside from being good at sports, heroines were also portrayed as being clever and studious. In spite of the respect accorded to academic prowess girls were only occasionally portrayed at their studies; lessons were presumably too monotonous and restrictive to serve the narrative usefully. Exams and tests were the exception because they offered an ideal background for schoolgirl rivalries, mischief and accusations.

The letter from the joint principals of a London school quoted earlier, correctly points out that girls' school stories presented a false view of teachers; they were stereotyped as distant, young and popular, or as middle-aged caricatures. In magazines these images were brought to life both in the text and in the accompanying illustrations. The reason for this colourful if exaggerated portrayal again stemmed from the aim of schoolgirl papers to entertain and sell. Miss Bullivant, nicknamed the 'Bull', was the maths and drill mistress at Cliff House. She was a thin and gaunt woman given to 'wearing blouses of dreadful and fearful patterns; a woman with a sharp tongue, more severe than just, seeming to take a delight in punishing girls.'[9] Subsequently Miss Bullivant was an excellent figure of authority who the girls could flout and ridicule. Miss Prim, the headmistress was, in contrast, a distant figure who exercised no direct authority over her girls thereby fostering the illusion of freedom. More importantly, in this distant position, Miss Prim was far removed from schoolgirl pranks and ridicule. This could well have been an object lesson in respect for authority. As Dyhouse notes, by the end of the nineteenth century headmistresses of modern girls' schools had evolved new codes of professional conduct and autonomy and were respected and well paid,[10] although in the interwar years their spinster status came under attack.[11] Dyhouse also cites evidence that many modern heads were indeed distant figures, largely because of the sheer number of pupils their schools catered for.[12] The joint principals may have been reluctant to concede the elements of truth within the admittedly exaggerated portrait of school mistresses typical in the schoolgirl story. In contrast to the distant and aggressive teacher stereotypes, stories also featured young, feminine and kindly teachers like Janey Mathews who was known affectionately to the girls as 'Janey.' Readers were expected to identify with such feminine characters who also served as a focus for struggles between the good and the bad schoolgirls.

Representations of teachers convey a great deal about the limits within which authors were compelled to write. Schoolgirls were not allowed to challenge the authority of respectable figures, only that of ridiculous or unjust teachers. Feminine teachers were always popular and served as role models for readers to emulate. It is interesting that these stories did not feature a Jean Brodie type figure, someone who remained popular with girls despite striving to redefine her femininity to include an active sexuality, independence and autonomy. Within magazine fiction popularity was intimately connected to marriage potential.

The isolation of the fictional boarding school also served dramatic purposes in that it provided an opportunity for fun and tension as schoolgirls sought to contact brothers, cousins and friends at the nearby boys' boarding school. Isolation also served to place girls within a self-contained environment in which they were protected but also allowed freedom from social norms, including prevalent notions of feminine conduct, and the implications of patriarchal relations in the home. The age of schoolgirl heroines served a similar purpose. Schoolgirl stories invariably focused on heroines of 13 and 14 years of age. At this age girls were less circumscribed by patriarchal expectations, particularly within the boarding school environment. This literary strategy is best summed up in the words of Joan in Angela Brazil's novel, 'Joan's Best Chum':

> Under 'twelve' we are apt to have too many privileges, and 'over fifteen' we are generally the victims of preparation for some horrible public examination, and spend all our spare time 'swotting at maths', or committing elusive facts to memory. But those magic years of 'thirteen' and 'fourteen' are a sort of high-water mark, when we have our fling undisturbed by too many restrictions or responsibilities. We have been long enough at school to be entirely in the swim of things, and need not trouble our heads as yet about future careers.[13]

These 'careers' can be interpreted in two ways, in terms of future paid employment and in terms of marriage. Importantly, the fictional school story offered girls a world of women in which the pressures of heterosexuality were largely removed even if, as we shall see in chapter 5, their lives were tightly framed by the heterosexual career.

Adolescence, as we have seen, was widely regarded as the prerogative of boys. Representations of girls as physically active, ambitious and vocal were not generally seen as normal. Instead, girls were expected to display the qualities of self-denial, constraint and self-sacrifice. Such characteristics were deemed inappropriate in the modern fictional schoolgirl. Frith has described the schoolgirl heroines of contemporary boarding school stories as 'ungendered' in that the heroine was suspended between masculinity and femininity.[14] Girls' magazines of the interwar years similarly portrayed heroines in ways which were inconsistent with prevailing feminine norms, but although femininity was not explicit in schoolgirl heroines it was, nevertheless, latent. The buoyant behaviour of schoolgirl heroines was only acceptable at a particular age when the heroine, and also the intended reader, were deemed to be too young to be entering the marriage market. Secondary schools of the nineteenth and early twentieth century often walked a similar tightrope, in this case between encouraging characteristics suitable for academic and career success and at the same time promoting behaviour that did not challenge the expectation that girls would make good wives and mothers.[15]

At Cliff House girls were not organised in any formal way. Minor rules did exist, but these were usually invented and enforced by Miss Bullivant, and it would seem that they were included primarily for the girls to infringe. These rules were invariably trivial; sensible rules, concerned with safety for instance, were rarely broken by the girls. The London joint principals who criticised schoolgirl stories, found this lack of rules and regulations particularly unrealistic. Most private girls' schools were heavily regimented; according to Gathorne-Hardy, the closer a school moved to the public school model the more rules and regulations it introduced.[16] Okely describes how the girls at her boarding school 'were bound in spiders' webs of fine rules and constraints until spontaneity seemed to be a crime.'[17] Free time certainly seems to have been scarce; Roedean actually stated in its prospectus that 'the leisure of the pupils is carefully organised'.[18] The constraints which Okely claims were characteristic of a 1950s girls' boarding school were typical of the organisation of earlier establishments. Okely describes the ban on visits to the nearby town, the termly shopping trip under strict surveillance, the 'crocodile' walk skirting the town, censored mail, separation from parents and boys and the control of reading as some of the ways in which schools maintained their almost full-time and absolute control over the experiences of their pupils. Importantly, these regulations also served to ensure that pupils did not mix with boys and men or members of lower social groups.

Some of these constraints were evident in schoolgirl stories but the gender and class significance of these was not directly articulated and girls were frequently shown breaking the segregation rules particularly where boys were concerned. While corporal punishment was not used in girls' secondary schools, a complex, rigid and often ruthlesss system of emotional and moral restraints, and punishments was implemented.[19] Okely's account of discipline in a fifties boarding school provides insight into the way in which such punishment operated for girls. Fear of exposure was a major device employed by school mistresses at Okely's school; this was particularly effective because the pupils had already internalised modesty and fear of visibility through pre-school and school socialisation. Corporal punishment was not depicted in stories about Cliff

House nor were emotional and moral constraints typical of Okely's experience.[20] Such forms of regulation depended on girls having been socialised into a submissive and subordinate role which would have been incompatible with the liberated, independent and spirited type of schoolgirl heroine which authors believed their readers were attracted to. Moreover, the fear which underpinned these forms of control would have pervaded and corrupted the lively school atmosphere which authors worked hard to create. In order for such constraints to have worked they would have had to be internalised, arising from this any girl who transgressed the rules would have probably suffered agonies of self-recrimination. In place of these types of constraint, Cliff House girls were managed and inspired through appeals to their honour and sportsmanship; school captains utilised these sentiments quite successfully in ensuring that the school ran smoothly. Schoolgirl codes, as Auchmuty points out, drew their strength from the tradition of women as moral guardians, hence the reason why 'schoolgirls should feel at home with honour, loyalty, and discipline'.[21]

School stories created an illusion of freedom. Although this was unrealistic it was crucial to the success of schoolgirl fiction; readers were not expected to want to read about restrictions and deference to authority. Having said this, the appearance during the 1920s of characters such as Betty Barton, a scholarship girl who had responsibility for a younger brother and sister, does suggest that martyr types were attractive although they disappeared by the 1930s with a general move towards more tomboyish and characteristically adolescent characters.[22] The important point about Betty's story was that she finally came into money and could take her place as an equal at Morcove School. While most school stories offered a positive self-image to readers and freedom from constraints, there were clear parameters determining these representations. This fictional liberty was only permissable in particular environments and for a limited period of adolescence and in this way it did not challenge patriarchal expectations of girls as future wives, mothers and sexual servicers of men. These stories were also moral tales which conveyed, through the schoolgirl code and the character of heroines, the values of the social milieu from which the Amalgamated Press writers came. Peggy Preston, for example, represents a typical scholarship girl who won popularity amongst Cliff House schoolfriends in the 1920s for 'her cool clear mindedness, her strong will and determination, her forgiving disposition, and her splendid loyalty.'[23] Drotner argues that Peggy's ability to win popularity and overcome social differences through her good nature and actions formed an important element of the appeal of these early school stories; a fictional recognition and resolution of girls' actual experiences of social and sexual deprecation. The scholarship theme, Drotner points out, emphasised the responsibilities of the individual and obscured the inequalities of education provision.[24] 1930s heroines were wilder than Peggy, these hoydens and 'madcaps' exhibited greater independence and daring in adventures which moved beyond the confines of the school. These heroines, often with names such as Paddy, Sammy and Tony (short for Toinette) represented the coming of age of fictional adolescence for girls, a state clearly equated with boyhood, hence the boyish names and frequent references to girls as tomboys. In spite of this, these characters avoided compromising sexual and moral codes.

School fiction also appeared on occasion in magazines for middle-class schoolgirls although it differed markedly from the school stories which were the staple of working-class magazines. Most noticeably the setting of middle-class school stories was far less fantastic than was common in working-class papers and more directly concerned with communicating a moral message, one which invariably hinged on the work ethic or notions of service. In 'High School' (1941), for example, Hazel Gilmour's mother is widowed and compelled to work at home as a dress maker in order to support herself and her daughter. Mrs Gilmour's one aspiration is that Hazel will be able to follow in her footsteps and attend the local respectable and highly academic High School. Hazel fulfil's her mother's ambition by working extremely hard and eventually winning a scholarship.[25] The use of more realistic settings probably indicates the belief that fiction lost its appeal if it contradicted girls' experience. It is noticeable, however, that this story, like much of the fiction in the *Girls' Own Paper*, engaged with the realities of school experience and also the problems of financial insecurity faced by many middle-class women for one reason or another. Although school stories in the *Girls' Own Paper* were often very different to those which appeared in magazines for working-class readers, what they all had in common was a strong moral tale.

School Talk

Elementary schoolgirl papers generally avoided discussion of the realities of schooling although education was occasionally addressed in editorials and in readers' letters.[26] Secondary schoolgirl papers were, in contrast, far more concerned with these topics. Working girls' papers, with the exception of *Girls' Favourite*, also ignored education issues presumably because readers were assumed to be more interested in work and courtship than their past and unexciting school careers. Three types of discussion about schooling appeared in these secondary schoolgirl papers. Firstly there were recollections by famous women of their schooling. *School-Days*, for instance, regularly featured articles about the education of successful women; these included Rosita Forbes (traveller), Fay Compton (actress), Dame Mary Scharlieb (doctor and surgeon), Ella Bennett (tennis player), Lady Ann Heath (aviator) and Sybil Thorndike (actress). These articles were clearly designed to be instructional about bygone school days, but they also conveyed the author's respect and admiration.

Introducing Dame Mary Scharlieb, the editor commented 'Every person's school life is interesting, and you will enjoy every word of this article in which you will learn a few things about schools of long ago.'[27] Scharlieb proceeded to describe her schooling and then address the question of whether modern schoolgirls were any better off than their Victorian counterparts. Scharlieb's answer was yes, although she added that 'a good schoolgirl will emerge from schooldays, old or new, with an honest and unselfish intention of producing the best of which she is capable'.[28] These sentiments neatly summed up the philosophy of these secondary schoolgirl papers that women should develop their skills and utilise these and their talents in the service of the community. Reinforcing this individualistic perspective, readers were assured that schooling was largely what the schoolgirl made of it.

The second type of education feature involved descriptions, often with photographs, of overseas schools. For example, the *Girls' Own Paper*'s account of schooling in South Africa described the types of school provision, its organisation and content. It also communicated how advanced the British education system was compared to that in other countries although at the same time the *Girls' Own* cautioned readers not to assume that overseas school children were unhappy. This point was reiterated in *School-Days*: 'Schoolgirls abroad enjoy their schools and would be ill at ease in a big British school.'[29] By implication, overseas children did not require the standards of education available in Britain. Given that these overseas schools were largely from present or past colonies, usually outside Europe, it seems likely that these different schooling standards were rationalised in terms of Britain's role as an inter-national leader and as a missionary spreading the Christian message.

The third reference to education appeared in articles which discussed major aspects of school experience such as exams, leaving school and the preparation school provided for future careers. The *Girls' Own Paper* also included one feature on the 1944 Education Act. During the 1920s *School-Days* featured two such series, 'Black Letter Days' and 'Letters of an Old Schoolgirl'. Although presented as factual they were actually penned by fictional characters. The *Girls' Own Paper* also discussed modern schooling, particularly during the 1939–1945 war, but in contrast to *School-Days* it exhibited a more serious approach, one that was typical of this paper but also consistent with its propaganda role during and immediately after the war. Certainly the wartime government regarded the *Girls' Own Paper* highly. Whether volunteered or invited, the appearance of an address from the Right Hon. R.A. Butler, Minister of Education entitled 'The Minister Speaks To You', confirms this impression.[30]

Exams, especially the School Certificate, were the most common topic. In 'Swotting' written by a first year medical student and 'Organise for that Exam' readers were offered tips on how to be successful. Girls were reminded that 'examiners are only human, and are usually only too anxious to pass you, but they get tired of badly-written, untidy papers'.[31] During the Second World War the editor of the *Girl's Own Paper* was clearly anxious that the educational standards and successes of middle-class girls might be under threat. Recognition of the difficulties girls faced in doing exams under war conditions is evident in the article 'Matriculation Under Fire'. Doreen Brown, a 16 year old pupil of St Martins High School for girls, provides a graphic account of the experiences of a group of London schoolgirls who sat the School Certificate exams in June 1944. This article is an extraordinary piece of social history and deserves to be quoted at length. Doreen describes how the girls continued at their exams even though 'the bombing attacks grew steadily worse':

> More and more girls bravely turned up each morning after having their homes damaged the night before. Several girls received phone messages during the lunch break telling them that their houses had been blasted since they had left home in the morning, but they all carried on.[32]

During the morning exam there were usually two or three alerts:

> When the siren sounded nineteen sighs issued from nineteen pairs of lips, but pens continued scratching ... Whenever a bomb came too near, the invigilator would cry, 'Duck!' Simultaneously we would roll off our chairs and try unsuccessfully to sandwich ourselves under the tables. After the crash and blinding flash of light, we would scramble to our feet grinning weakly at each other and, after taking a sip of milk to fortify ourselves, would continue that fateful struggle with our memories.[33]

After an interminable week the exams were over; 16 of the 19 candidates were successful, 10 of them, including Doreen Brown, reached matriculation stand-ard. The message conveyed through this article is clear, education and exams must go on, and with courage and determination schoolgirls could do as well in the bizarre conditions of wartime bombing as in peacetime. We are not told however, whether the girls who had failed their exams had done so because they were the unfortunate pupils whose houses had been blasted!

Issues of schooling were acknowledged as important in secondary schoolgirl papers throughout the interwar and war years, and so too were matters concerning readers' future careers. Indeed, the middle-class *Girls' Own* reveals an approach to girls' careers which was similar to that of many secondary school headmistresses who, whilst not dismissing marriage as a legitimate goal, promoted a liberal education for their pupils followed ideally by a university education or teacher training and a professional career.[34] Magazines for working girls, especially the business girls' papers and the middle-class *Miss Modern*, did not discuss schooling but then their readers would have put 'all things childish behind them'. They were, however, attentive to their readers' work and, in common with the *Girls' Own*, they were concerned about the implications of the economy and especially the labour market for girls' career prospects.

Working Girls

During the period 1920 to 1950 the majority of adolescent girls were potential or actual workers. Magazines responded to this in different ways according to the editorial perspective on, and negotiation of, four main issues. First and foremost, approaches towards women's work were inseparable from attitudes regarding the appropriate roles of women, in particular attitudes towards marriage and its responsibilities for women. Patriarchal interests dictated that women remain primarily located in marriage and the home; these interests were neatly encapsulated within prevalent feminine ideals which naturalised hetero-sexuality and domesticity in women and which presented feminine women as those who anticipated and worked towards marriage and domesticity. The second issue which shaped magazine treatment concerned the implications of women's work for gender relations. The increased demand for women in the paid workforce during this period and particularly during both World Wars, was widely seen as giving girls and women financial independence and a more confident manner – a version of the implications of war which has been widely disseminated in mainstream histories but more recently challenged by historians of women.[35] Reactions to this 'myth' of social change depended on the editor's views regarding the sort of relationship that should, or indeed could, exist between its readers and members of the opposite sex. The third consideration was the editor's construction of the intended reader, her needs but also her interests and fantasies. Lastly, attention to work and careers for girls was determined by the editor's recognition of economic and social changes and the related need of many girls and women to financially support themselves and perhaps their families through short or long-term work. In 1931 single women comprised roughly half of the female workforce aged over 35 years of age, and married women comprised 16 per cent of all working women in 1931 and 43 per cent in 1951.[36] Interlinked with this was attention to the labour market implications of interwar unemployment. The handling of these issues differed according to the publisher's objective, whether entertainment or instruction, and the age and social class of the intended reader.

Elementary schoolgirl papers avoided direct discussion of work in the same way as they avoided issues of schooling. Whilst readers may have been at an age when they gleefully anticipated leaving school, their work prospects were usually drab and often dead-end. Career girls did appear in the fiction of these papers but portraits of heroines as detectives, circus performers and actresses were glamorous and far removed from the realities of the labour market. The fictional representation of acting, for instance, was merely an attempt by editors to pander to their readers' fantasies to ensure that their paper sold. Whilst these stories offered excitement and glamour readers were expected to emulate the heroine's model behaviour, not her career. It is interesting that heroines were rarely depicted as being solely motivated by a desire for stardom. Instead they were usually inspired by the needs of their family, and the fiction documented how the heroine managed to retain her femininity whilst coping with success in a competitive environment.[37] Judging by all the letters subsequently printed regarding stage and screen careers, it would seem that magazines were unsuccessful in achieving a balance between entertaining their readers by appealing to their fantasies whilst also advising girls against seeking careers in acting; the fiction may even have accentuated these ambitions. Middle-class magazines conveyed a very different approach to girls' working lives. Those papers which addressed secondary schoolgirls were firmly committed to careers for their readers. Intelligent girls, they reasoned, should use their intellect to its full. Their attention to careers also arose from the belief that girls needed Christian guidance on how to manage the changing demands of the modern world. In contrast, most of the working girls' magazines treated work in a rather ambivalent manner, if at all; the mother-daughter magazines of the 1930s and 1940s were even less concerned with this matter.

Although working girls' magazines were characterised by the attitude that marriage was the life career and ambition of each girl, they did acknowledge that their readers worked. This is most evident in the use of working heroines, it is also apparent in the appearance of adverts which were premised on the reader's consumer power and which, after 1940, increasingly employed images of working girls and famous career women to promote their products. In spite of this, work was peripheralised. Articles and fiction praised and encouraged girls in their work but at the same time they portrayed it as a means to find a husband or develop skills useful to the potential wife and mother. *Pam's Paper*, for example, described how '[t]he typist is qualified to make a good wife, because she understands men and their business troubles and is not inclined to be jealous if her husband is detained in town or is bad-tempered after a long day at the office.'[38] Attention was focused on the clothes a 'business girl' should wear, how a girl could look smart and professional but also attractive.

This treatment of work suggests that the intended reader was assumed to be uninterested in her job, seeing it merely as a stop-gap before marriage. This reasoning suggests that magazines addressed their readers as 'working girls' merely to establish a common identity. Indeed, as we saw in chapter 2, paid work was, for many girls, characterised by long hours, monotony and poor prospects; contemporary comment and oral history both point to ex-elementary schoolgirls evaluating their jobs in terms of the money and companionship it offered rather than for factors intrinsic to the work.[39] Evidence also suggests that although this may seem a meagre remuneration for work, many women missed both the financial independence and social life if they retired from work on marriage.[40] Those magazines which targeted a middle-class audience proposed more interesting and exciting careers although these were open only to a minority of girls. The fact that romance magazines used the working girl in their fiction does suggest, however, that young workers were excited by heroines in occupations beyond their experience.

Contemporary surveys of the attitudes of ex-elementary schoolgirls do reveal romantic career fantasies. A Mass Observation survey of 200 London girls aged 14 to 20 years of age revealed that only 40 per cent looked forward to nothing more than marriage and children while a third wanted to postpone marriage in order to pursue an interesting job and travel.[41] The Pilgrim Trust survey (1938) of 64 girls who attended a Junior Instruction Centre similarly discovered that while nearly all the girls said that they wanted to marry, most also wanted a 'good time' before settling down to domesticity. A recurrent fantasy running through the answers was a desire for escape from their present situation into some profession already outside their reach: 'One would have liked to be a kindergarten teacher or a dancer, another a trained children's nurse, another a stewardess as a means of seeing the world.'[42] It would seem that while marriage was acknowledged and even desired by many girls, they also entertained fantasies about careers, independence and travel. It is clear that their thoughts on careers were unrealistic, probably unrealisable and transitory; however this interest could explain the use of working heroines in both romance fiction and also, to a lesser extent, schoolgirl magazines.

The Modern Girl

Although fiction utilised the career girl image, representations and discussions of work in other aspects of working girls' magazines remained shallow, suggesting that readers were not assumed to be greatly interested in the realities of paid work. Following the First World War however, these magazines featured a number of articles and stories which suggested that the 'modern girl' may indeed be enjoying her work and as a result delaying or even refusing marriage. This modern phenomenon was clearly attributed to girls' wartime experiences. Magazine responses reveal anxiety about the challenge this could pose to patriarchal relations. It was for this reason that editors felt compelled to address this matter and in the process to redefine women's work in ways which were consistent with traditional expectations of women.

According to working girls' magazines, careers fostered independence and this threatened relations between the sexes, more particularly the heterosexual career and male dominance in heterosexual relations, including marriage. This fear was clearly conveyed in the many appeals to *Miss Modern*:

> the modern girl is very up-to-date indeed; a jolly good sport, and altogether charming. But she's so terribly independent! She doesn't really care whether she gets married or not, so long as she can earn a comfortable income and have a good time ... there is a tendency on the part of the modern girl to over-rate her own good qualities, to consider herself more than the equal of man, and to adopt towards him an objectionable 'we can easily-do-without-you sort of attitude'.[43]

This ambivalence about the modern girl was reproduced throughout these working girls' magazines. The construction and management of the modern girl reveals a number of tensions. On the one hand, editors believed that girls had changed and that they must recognise their readers' new found modernity in order to maintain sales. Editors were also attuned to the contemporary demands of the labour market for young female workers. On the other hand, editors were uneasy about the modern girl, in particular the implications of her work experience for heterosexual relations and the domestification of women in marriage. Her modernity was also inconsistent with prevalent feminine norms. Editors attempted to negotiate a path between these different interests by redefining paid work in ways which re-established female dependence on men and marriage, thereby removing any threat to the patriarchal status quo. In redefining the feared implications of capitalist demands on girls so as to be compatible with contemporary patriarchal interests, magazines also updated notions of femininity to accommodate girls' work experience.

These processes of negotiation and redefinition are apparent in the following extract from *Girls' Favourite* (1927) entitled 'Is the modern girl different?' in which the author describes how girls' work really served very feminine ends: 'I admit we go out to business more. We have to; it's the fashion. And we've found it's also so much nicer than depending on parental generosity for the hundred and one necessities of our existence.'[44] The suggestion is that female work was for pin-money; a trivialisation of the social and economic importance of employment for girls. Ralston continued:

> The modern girl it is true, no longer looks upon marriage as the one and only thing for her. That is all to her good, for she, being content to wait for the right opportunity, isn't nearly so likely to make a wrong choice as grandmamma was. And, on the other hand, if the opportunity never comes she sensibly makes the best of things and determines to be happy with her business chums and her business pleasures. Hence, she doesn't grow into that most unpleasant of persons, a sour old maid.[45]

Work was here described as enabling the modern girl to wait for Mr Right thereby securing a more stable and successful marriage union. It also ensured that the spinster would not become an embarrassing social problem by providing her with useful work and outlets for her 'inevitable' sexual and emotional frustrations.[46]

This articulation was also apparent in the fiction of the 1920s which depicted the heroine rejecting her modernity and also her work as journalist, secretary or stewardess in favour of marriage. Alternatively fictional career girls were portrayed as absorbed in their work but only in the short term and not at the expense of their femininity. In this way editors engaged with their readers' desires for independence and adventure whilst simultaneously reinforcing the message that marriage was a woman's finest destiny.[47] In a similar vein, fiction of the 1930s and 1940s featured career girls who gracefully embraced marriage. Girls who continued to insist that marriage was not for them and who professed to prefer a career were treated harshly in the fiction of these magazines.

In 'Dreams!' (1930) girls were reminded of their dependence on men; in this story the self-sufficient career woman is made to suffer for publicly scorning men and marriage and for encouraging younger girls to emulate her behaviour. Daisy Brentley, the 28-year-old head of a depot at the Argus Shipping Company, was presented as a dedicated and sophisticated career woman who 'scorned the girl who threw up a career to be a household drudge'. In spite of this contempt of marriage, Daisy falls in love; 'for all her talk about liking her independence and never meaning to get married, [Daisy] knew that she had met her fate when Harry Sandford came into her life . . . some day she would renounce all her resolutions, admit she had been wrong, and climb down . . . the high and mighty Daisy Brentley, who had always declared that she was sufficient for herself, was actually going to marry a man who made less than she did.' It turns out, however, that Harry was attracted to Carrie, Daisy's clerk, who was described as motherly, domestic and trusting, her face a 'soft babyish one with its dimples, its rosebud mouth, and its dark blue eyes.' Daisy was distraught when she finally realised this; she

> stared into space. She saw, not the office nor the pile of ledgers. She saw instead a little creeper clad cottage, and chickens clucked in a wee garden; a thrush sang on a bush that was fragrant with roses. And a little toddler stumbled along a crazy path, and nearly fell. Now he was swept up in her arms, and his face covered in kisses. Dreams! Just dreams! Then she turned back to the ledger – and got on with her work.[48]

The tone and message of this story was remarkably similar to that embodied in the Hitchcock thrillers of the forties which were opposed to the independent woman. Rosen argues that these films appeared at a time of unprecedented female economic and social power and that they served in this context to remind women that they were not self-sufficient.[49] Magazine fiction appears to have tackled a similar concern. Although Daisy was not killed as was typical in Hitchcock dramas, she was nevertheless submitted to emotional torture and the knowledge that she would remain a lonely woman.

In contrast to the peripheral or romanticised representation of paid work in most romance magazines, and the depiction of fantastic fictional careers in working-class schoolgirl papers, the secondary schoolgirl magazines such as the *Girls' Own Paper* and the middle-class *Miss Modern*, regularly and seriously addressed girls' employment options. Moreover, whereas working-class magazines discussed short-term semi-skilled or unskilled 'jobs', their middle-class counterparts addressed 'careers', that is occupations which required training and which offered prospects for advancement. Attention to careers must be seen in the context of an increased acceptance of professional employment for middle-class girls.

Belief in the intrinsic value of education and the importance of vocational preparation and careers for middle-class girls was particularly widespread amongst headmistresses; as Mary Pratt argued 'a person is always the richer for the acquisition of new skills and new interests, even if they are not used in gaining a livelihood'.[50] This was a perspective shared by the editor and contributors to the *Girls' Own Paper*. Whereas secondary school mistresses and the *Girls' Own* were strongly committed to education for secondary schoolgirls because of its intrinsic and societal value, the change in parental attitude arose more from the 'growing realisation that a developed intelligence is not incompatible with sexual attractiveness. Thus many parents have come to be less averse to the idea of their daughters entering professions when they find that far from ruining their chances of marriage, it may even extend them.'[51] This suggests that changes affecting girls were often only acceptable if compatible with patriarchal interests; suitable professions were those which did not distract a girl from marriage, nor hinder her chances of finding a husband. It is significant that in their discussions of careers, magazine authors were at pains to stress that femininity was not threatened; some articles, probably copying the example of many girls' secondary schools, went so far as to argue that careers contributed to a girl's marital and mothering competencies. But perhaps the most crucial social change which affected parental attitudes was the recognition of the financial necessity of work: 'Many parents now recognise that a professional qualification is a form of insurance against future economic mishaps even if their daughters do marry.'[52]

The importance of girls being able to earn their own living underpinned coverage of work and careers in middle-class magazines; it was also significant for *Girls' Favourite*'s discussion of careers and the occasional articles in *Girls' World* and *Girls' Friend* during the 1920s. Spinsterhood, whether voluntary or involuntary, was one reason for this but magazines also responded to the possibility of girls being required for financial reasons to return to the labour market after marriage. According to Mary Pratt's estimate, 'the chances are, on a conservative estimate, one in ten that she will some day, by reason of widowhood or hard times of some sort or other, find it convenient, if not necessary, to earn for herself.'[53] This arose from the incapacity or death of a husband, a common occurrence during and after the two World Wars, also the need in some cases to subsidise their husbands' earnings or compensate for their unemployment. Recognition of this can be seen in *Miss Modern* and the *Girls' Own Paper*, both of which considered careers suitable for older women such as window-dressing. Financial hardship faced by the newly engaged or wed who were keen to set up home before starting a family was another common rationalisation of women's paid work.

These concerns and rationalisations of careers prompted middle-class schoolgirl magazines to prioritise work; marriage was treated as peripheral to the reader's interests and ambitions. It would appear that the *Girls' Own Paper* acknowledged the importance of marriage and domesticity for women but felt that its teenage readers should be more concerned with building careers for themselves; marriage could be a future consideration.

Miss Modern's approach was more contradictory. On the one hand it acknowledged the need to advise its readers on work matters. On the other, its readers were perceived to be of an age where heterosexual interests were to the fore and marriage on the horizon; this in fact corresponded with the actual interests of many of its readers encouraged by the poor prospects for women in the labour market.[54] Not only in job descriptions was femininity emphasised, but often the context in which the careers articles were featured undermined the careers advice. For example, *Miss Modern* encouraged girls to think seriously about their careers and yet it printed features like 'On and Off – a moral tale' in which Geranium Jones starts her first job as a junior shorthand typist. Before starting work Geranium's aunt gives her ten shillings 'to buy any little aids to your career – such as a shorthand dictionary and an English grammar.' Contrary to her aunt's advice, Geranium spends the money on a variety of beauty preparations with the aim of winning a proposal of marriage from one of the junior partners in the firm. She soon discovers that both of these were 'yellow and crumpled like the deeds in the files dated 1840'. Instead she catches the eye of Marmaduke Youngman, the unarticled clerk, who we assume she subsequently marries. As this moral tale concluded: 'Our ambitious Geranium had not only got on – she had also got off.'[55] Although *Miss Modern* and the other working girls' papers often contained contradictory messages, *Miss Modern* was more inclined to treat work as a long-term prospect which was genuinely exciting, whereas its working-class counterparts gave the impression that although work was important it was nevertheless a matter of making the best of things. This difference in approach was explicable in terms of the work opportunities available to girls from different social groups.

Impelled by a recognition of the work reality of most girls, the working girls' magazines, also the middle-class schoolgirl papers, felt compelled to offer their readers some advice on work and careers within the current labour market context. Most working girls' magazines restricted advice to the odd article; *Girls' Favourite* and *Miss Modern* took this matter more seriously and along with the secondary schoolgirl papers they offered advice on suitable careers and training.

The provision of work and careers advice in magazines needs to be seen in the context of concern about the lack of vocational guidance available to young people and its significance for economic efficiency and personal fulfilment. Secondary school mistresses were particularly concerned about the information and encouragement available to their female pupils. Surveys discovered that secondary schoolgirls of 12 to 16 years of age were initially excited by the prospect of a career. Lingwood concluded from her survey that 'the majority of the girls took a very serious interest in their future careers'; her research also revealed that most girls were ambitious and quite prepared to enter previously male dominated areas of work.[56] These surveys also showed that these pupils were often compelled to abandon their ambitions. A major problem was that girls had far fewer options than their brothers. As Stott explained:

> The opportunities for the average girl are, in fact, considerably less than for the average boy... For success in the majority of occupations previously the prerogative of boys but now invaded by girls, girls require more ability and unusual determination and enterprise than boys. The girl, in fact, must have the qualities of the pioneer as well as the qualities required for the work itself.[57]

Girls also encountered time and financial constraints. Even where a girl was ideally suited to a particular career, vocational advisers recognised that her choices would be restricted by the fact that most new and exciting careers required long and extensive periods of training which parents often could not afford or were not prepared to invest in.[58] Although parents seem to have been in favour of careers for their daughters they regarded the careers of their sons as more important. According to Stott, 'parents (rather illogically) tend to be more interested in security for the girl and in emotional satisfaction for the boy.'[59] Where girls were concerned, parents seem to have favoured secure jobs with good pay which required only the minimum of training and financial outlay. These jobs also offered few promotion prospects. 'The particular bugbear in this respect – at any rate with us (headmistresses) – is "secretarial work", into which fathers are so apt to push their daughters'.[60] School mistresses tried to counter this trend, but were often unsuccessful in encouraging their students to look beyond office and retail work.

Vocational guidance for middle-class girls was supported as a means of informing them about the range of rewarding professional work open to women. The objective of vocational advice for elementary schoolgirls was concerned to curb what were seen as unrealistic ambitions. Hawkins claimed, on the basis of his research at a mixed urban central (selective) school, that 'boys and girls tended to choose occupations higher in grade than those for which their general intelligence suits them: the girls were more at fault in this respect than the boys.'[61] Arising from this, girls pursued forms of school training which were incompatible with labour market requirements; from a sample of past students (107 girls, 143 boys) only 15 per cent of those who had received instruction in shorthand, 30 per cent of those with typewriting skills, and 25 per cent of those with book-keeping training made any subsequent use of these once they left school. Underpinning this interest was a concern to maximise the efficient use of adolescent labour, an issue of increased significance due to the labour shortage which was anticipated following the raising of the school leaving age.[62] More generally, the observed tendency of young people to seek employment in overcrowded areas of work when other forms of employment were experiencing labour shortages was regarded as highly inefficient.[63] Vocational advisers and other youth workers also suggested that a lack of vocational advice encouraged working-class girls to be dissatisfied with their actual work prospects leading to inefficiency at work and high mobility between jobs. The gulf between expectations and experiences in the labour market was further accentuated by the increasingly automated and routinised character of work which required little or no skill but which depended on the worker having the 'right' attitude.

Work and Careers Advice

In the light of these conditions, a number of magazines took it upon themselves to become careers advisers to their readers. This was a case of magazines meeting the perceived needs of their readers, a need shaped by changing social and economic conditions. Although information was usually conveyed directly, the use of fictional features by some editors reveal attempts to 'sugar the pill'.

The *Girls' Own Paper* featured the longest running careers feature, 'Carol's Career Corner', accompanied by a page of adverts selling training. Careers advocated by the *Girls' Own Paper* were usually highly skilled and required extensive and expensive forms of training. Not all its advice was so elitist: 'These last two months we have discussed medicine as a profession for women, but as there are many girls who find themselves unable to consider the lengthy and expensive training, and yet who still want to do something connected with medicine the *Girls' Own Paper* recommends physiotherapy.'[64] Similarly, kennel work was described as suitable for girls unable to pursue veterinary training.[65] *Miss Modern* on the other hand, provided advice about unskilled work through its series of interviews with young workers, 'Meet These Moderns'; information on professional careers was also conveyed through a series of articles which discussed and described jobs in a variety of fields including horticulture, window-dressing, beauty culture and the film studio. The 11 careers discussed by *School-Days* in its 'As We Grow Older' series were similarly skilled and required long periods of training or apprenticeship; some careers like business management and library work could be learnt on-the-job but promotion prospects were limited by lack of formal qualifications. *Girls' Favourite* suggested to its readers a similarly diverse, if generally less skilled, array of jobs which included tea-room manageress, secretary, reporter, bargain-hunter, hairdresser and cinema pianist. Although articles on careers were rare in working girls' magazines, information was sometimes conveyed through fictional accounts. For example, 'From Kitchen to Cinema Star' was a fictional autobiography which described the pros and cons of the work available to working-class readers.[66] Accounts such as this stressed the necessity of training for girls. However, the mainstay of this fiction advice was that if you want to get on you must help yourself.

In response to labour market conditions, readers of all magazines except the elementary schoolgirl papers, were encouraged to diversify in their work ambitions and thereby avoid overly subscribed occupations. Secondary schoolgirl papers introduced their readers to a range of skilled and professional careers which were either new or recently opened to women. In the thirties the *Girls' Own Paper* promoted dentistry, architecture and veterinary medicine as new careers for girls. *Miss Modern* similarly introduced new areas of employment for its middle-class readers; beauty culture was promoted as an occupation which offered plenty of opportunities to girls who were prepared to undergo some training and window-dressing was presented as 'a career which is now opening up quickly to women. In the past, men held most of the good positions, but within the last year, women display artists, with women assistants working under them, have been appointed in several of the big stores with outstanding success.'[67] Even *School-Days* recognised new career opportunities for girls including work as a barrister, a profession only open to women since 1919. As the author commented, '[w]hether the profession of lady barrister can successfully be carried on I don't think anyone is qualified to say yet';[68] certainly only 20 female barristers were recorded in the 1921 census, although Vera Brittain cited 77 by 1926.[69] In its consideration of teaching, *School-Days* cautioned its readers against pursuing careers in over-subscribed subject areas in which intense competition for posts would limit their options:

> Should she (the would-be-teacher) set out to take honours in English or History she is choosing the most commonly popular subjects but at the same time she is putting herself up against the greatest competition for posts in schools. There are far fewer teachers with honours in Mathematics or Physics, and a girl who has one or another of these will find the final business of securing a post a far easier matter.[70]

Clearly the skewed subject choices of schoolgirls in the interwar years were not much different to the arts and humanities orientation of most of today's female students. Even in unskilled occupations working girls' magazines encouraged diversification with articles on office work alongside more unusual service-sector occupations.

Girls' magazines, particularly those which targeted a mainly middle-class audience, were quite pioneering in the range of careers they suggested to their readers alongside the staples of 'women's work'. They were not, however, blind to discrimination. The *Girls' Own Paper* frequently remarked about the restricted training opportunities available to girls compared to their brothers, especially during the war, but it nevertheless advised its readers to press ahead with their ambitions; 'pronounced capability and enthusiasm sometimes induces employers to relax their prejudices and give their female engineers the special concession of normal works training alongside the men.'[71] 'Reporter Wanted' (1945) tells of the outright prejudice which Patsy encountered in her efforts to become a journalist. The Maxton Mirror where she worked as a proof-reader had a policy which excluded women from the reporting staff; as the boss explained:

> it is part of the paper's policy not to employ women on the reporting staff. There are reasons for this policy. A newspaper reporter has no easy life – he may be called out to an incident at any hour, and very often he encounters unpleasantness in the course of his work which he would rather spare a woman. And if you were a reporter, you know, you would have to interview people who do not want to be interviewed; to be prepared to give up some of your free time to do the work if it should be required of you – and you would have to write a good newspaper story.[72]

After proving her worth by interviewing a famous stage star, Patsy is taken on full-time but it seems likely that her range of assignments would have remained domestic. The story certainly touched on the reality of many women's attempts to enter this profession; when Mary Grieve, editor of *Woman*, started out on her career in journalism in the 1920s she was informed that women could only work on sections of papers which dealt with weddings and charity functions.[73]

In new areas or occupations previously closed to women, magazines employed strategies to render them suitable for their readers. One such tactic was to demarcate a particular sector of an occupation as appropriate for women. However, this segmentation of occupations was, as it is today, problematic in its tendency to construct new areas of 'women's work' with correspondingly low pay, prospects and status. In *School-Days* Phyllis Panting, editor of the children's paper *My Favourite*, described journalism as a suitable career for girls. Her final comment regarding the prospects for girls clearly located women within an area of the profession which could be related to traditional feminine concerns: 'Well the vogue for girls' papers is greatly on the increase, and all the big publishing firms are bringing fresh ones out every year. Therefore, if you decide that you would like to be a journalist, my advice to you, is to make up your mind what type of paper you would like to be on – a girls' paper, a fashion paper, magazine or weekly.'[74] Panting ignored the possibility of women working on either a local or national newspaper.

Another strategy, and one more popular with middle-class magazines, involved the feminisation of new occupations, or aspects of them, in ways which made them compatible with prevalent ideas about feminine skills or qualities. This particular strategy had an established history. Redefining work to use traditionally feminine skills had been used by employers to designate the expanding area of office work as largely 'women's work' enabling them to employ relatively cheap female labour. This feminisation was achieved by redefining the tasks of office work which involved such conceptualisations as comparing the typewriter to a piano, thereby establishing typewriting as a skill suited to female fingers.[75] Ursula Bloom, in her guide to careers for girls, employed this technique in her description of dentistry as a profession for women: women's hands, she argued, 'are smaller, and more delicate' than men's, their manner is more confidence inspiring, and 'they are especially good with young children and nervous patients.'[76] The *Girls' Own Paper* used a similar ploy in its description of veterinary work: 'when it is remembered that nearly every girl is fond of animals and loves to care for them and nurse them, it is obvious that a large number of girls will be attracted to a profession which will give them the necessary knowledge and skill to be a doctor to animals when these are sick or injured.'[77]

Although magazines often feminised careers, some areas of work remained unsuitable for girls. The *Girls' Own Paper*, for example, whilst in favour of women in veterinary work was quite specific about the areas of this profession within which women could suitably work:

> some of the work which falls to the lot of the general veterinary practitioner is very trying, pigs are heavy animals to move when they are ill; they are usually not kept in towns, but on farms in the country, so that distances to be travelled are great; they often fall ill at night, and the veterinary surgeon must be prepared to go out to a case ten or fifteen

miles away in the middle of the night if necessary, and in all weathers. Such work cannot be recommended for girls.[78]

The author did not say that girls should not pursue this type of practice, rather she presented a very unfavourable portrayal of it. In contrast, a town practice dealing with 'dogs and cats and other small animal pets' was perceived as quite suitable for women. Basically the objections to rural work were the strength required and, more importantly, the potential moral danger which girls would be exposed to working late into the night and travelling around on their own. It is interesting that these comments on veterinary work seem to have been taken verbatim from two speeches given by Major F.T.G. Hobday, principal of the Royal Veterinary College, which were reported in both the *Times* and the *Manchester Guardian* in 1927.[79] Certainly the objections which the *Girls' Own Paper* raised are suspect. As Vera Brittain pointed out, women have from time immemorial attended to large animals on isolated farms.[80] Moreover during the war this objection was conveniently forgotten as was the concern about women travelling around at night unaccompanied.

Training came to constitute a significant feature of careers during the interwar period, spurred by increased competition for jobs in the context of unemployment, the Depression, and the rise in professionalism.[81] Both middle-class and working-class magazines emphasised the importance of training; middle-class magazines specifically stressed the acquisition of formal qualifications. As *Miss Modern* advised: 'It never pays in the end to exercise false economy when it comes to training for any career.'[82] In 1927 *Girls' World* featured a special leader entitled 'Learn to Work' in which the editor extolled the necessity of labour market skills:

> In the train I got into conversation with a woman, I should think, somewhere about thirty years of age, and she told me that she had been to London to look for work. She had married young, but owing to money losses her husband was unable to keep up the home, and she wanted to turn to and help him pull round. She had no training and thought of starting to learn shorthand and typewriting, as she could not think of anything else to turn to at her age. I would not discourage her, but with unemployment so rife as it is, it struck me that her task of getting a job was pretty hopeless, and this, added to the difficulties of studying at her age, did not make the prospect hopeful.[83]

The problem of an inadequate training was also taken up in the fiction of working girls' papers. The story of Gwenda featured in *Miss Modern* (1935) is a case in point. Gwenda had been brought up in a rich family, but when her father died she was left penniless and totally unprepared to support herself. 'At first she had thought something would be sure to turn up. At first she refused to believe that anyone willing to work and really on their uppers could not find something, somewhere, somehow. Now she was not so sure.' Gwenda drifted into an assortment of unskilled poorly paid jobs; she chaperoned an aunt, she 'worked in an office through hot summer months, with every window sealed, and with the most ghastly smell of stale smoke and bad paste blending together.' She reflected on her early life and how unsuitable her education had been:

> People wanting servants, offices wanting secretaries with knowledge of queer languages, and all manner of certificates. Gwenda had no certificates. There wasn't anything she could do. Just look beautiful, just speak beautifully, just be exquisite. Hard-hearted business people wanted more. Oh yes, they wanted a great deal more.[84]

Eventually Gwenda secured a job as an ice-skating instructor and, rather typically of the fiction in these magazines, she was reunited with her past lover whom she subsequently married. Whilst in fiction there could often be a happy ending, the letters received by Labour MP Ellen Wilkinson were testimony to the fact that most young women continued for many years to bear the burden of inadequate training.[85]

Concern about high unemployment also prompted working girls' magazines to address the issue of mobility between jobs, a characteristic of unskilled and semi-skilled employment. Magazines stressed that high mobility was not only dangerous but also immoral.[86] Although motivated by concern for the reader, magazines appear to have had another agenda, namely the interests of employers. As we have seen, employment prospects for most ex-elementary schoolgirls were quite restricted and as contemporary studies stressed, this was not likely to change; indeed conditions of work were likely to become even more monotonous. Young workers would have to dismiss their fanciful career ambitions and learn to extract enjoyment and fulfilment from their rather mundane job prospects. Within this context magazines took it upon themselves to persuade girls to adopt a different and more positive attitude to their jobs, one that was consistent with the need of employers for contented, hard-working, loyal and reliable staff. Magazine editors would have been familiar with the problems of management. After all, they were responsible for the women who worked on their papers and would themselves have had a vested interest in girls acquiring this approach to their work.

A clear example of this encouragement to readers to change their attitude to work is presented in this extract from 'Is Office Work Dull?'. On one side, Miss A represented the views of 99 per cent of office staff that office work was indeed quite dull, also monotonous and physically restrictive. Counterpoised to this was Miss B, 'the one-in-a-hundred':

> I say that office life isn't dull, with an accent on the n't. In my opinion
> no work can be dull if a proper interest is taken in it. If you take an
> enthusiastic interest in your duties you will find that these duties are
> congenial and pleasant. Office girls who complain of their work being
> dull have only themselves to blame . . . Nothing is interesting unless you
> invest it with interest.[87]

Miss B went on to describe how there was 'romance' even in typing routine
letters –

> Letters are the bricks that go to the building up of gigantic business
> concerns. They are also the connecting links of business houses all over
> the world, and those who type them are helping in the forging of these
> bricks.[88]

Even ambitious girls will not find the work dull, she claimed, because she will
be 'keenly alive to the importance of her work, and it naturally follows that work
which is important cannot possibly be uninspiring . . . letter typing and ordinary
office routine, which to some girls may seem humdrum and monotonous, are
stepping stones to a more responsible nature.' *Miss Modern* similarly extolled
the wonders of work to its readers, 'no real work is without its own personal
romance; try and find it in your job. Trace the history of the work before it comes
to you and follow its course to a final transaction, you'll get a new angle!'[89] The
conceptualisation of work in terms of romance was a particularly interesting
feature of these attempts to reorientate readers' attitudes, one which was
consistent with strategies to make extended education provision attractive to
girls in the 1940s and 1950s by linking it to girls' 'personal' interests.[90]

Working-class magazines discouraged their readers from being choosy
about their work and rarely addressed the poor conditions which many girls
worked in except when they wished to make a moral point. Trade Unions were
not discussed although they occasionally featured in the fiction. In 'Mill Lass
O'Mine' Ray Elderwood worked at one of Mr Burton's mills and was an active
member of the union. When Mr Burton the mill owner enclosed what the mill
workers regarded as common land, Ray led the workers in a revolt leading to the
burning of the fence which surrounded the land. The next morning Ray was
called to Mr Burton's office; she had quite expected to be fired, even to be black-
listed. Burton, however, realised that being a free spirit, the threat of
imprisonment would be intolerable to Ray. He subsequently used this to
persuade Ray to marry his rather unworthy nephew and to prepare him for taking
over the running of the mill sometime in the future. Unbeknown to Burton or
indeed Ray, the nephew was already pledged to another woman. After an unusual
start the drama returned to the traditional formula of romance and intrigue.[91]

The sexual vulnerability of many female workers was acknowledged in letter replies but like the fictional treatment of this topic the root cause, namely the behaviour of men and unequal gender relations, was never tackled; magazines treated it as an individual and isolated occurrence. Magazines were not unaware of the inequalities of power between the sexes which was at the root of harassing behaviour even if, at this time, the concept of 'harassment' had not yet been established. Magazine fiction deliberately utilised scenes of working-class girls being harassed precisely because of the vulnerability it imposed on the heroine, a vulnerability that was gender and class specific.

The overwhelming concerns of magazines seem to have been for the girls' chastity and the position of men in the servant-keeping or employer class. Magazines avoided detailed discussions of the incidents which were reported to them through readers' letters and shied away from acknowledging the extent of sexual harassment. In response to one girl's letter, the correspondence editor advised the reader to hand in her notice promptly. Although she was assured that she had done nothing wrong, the responsibility for handling this situation was firmly attributed to the maid; a classic example of the sexual double standard: 'Your mistake was in not nipping this thing in the bud. Had you taken a firm line about it at first, you would not now be facing this difficult situation.'[92] No advice was offered on how to 'nip' such problems 'in the bud' and help was not forthcoming on how to find a new job. It is ironic that while girls were brought up to be sexually innocent they were, at the same time, expected to possess a 'worldly' approach to men and sex. As we shall see in chapter 6, this innocence was key to feminine sexuality and throughout the interwar years magazines avoided the public provision of information concerning the female body and sexuality. Magazines similarly avoided the subject of how to handle amorous advances and the fiction heroines were invariably naïve like the readers were supposed to be. Where were girls expected to acquire this knowledge? This laissez-faire attitude which characterised magazine responses cannot be solely explained in terms of the expectation that the readers' working life would be temporary. As we have seen, magazines increasingly acknowledged that many girls would not marry. A more likely explanation is that editors felt unable to do anything constructive; underpinning this was their own vested interest in the continuation of domestic service and their inability to challenge the behaviour of men from their own social class.

The sexual vulnerability of working-class girls in domestic service may not have been broached, but magazines were more forthcoming when girls were sexually threatened or abused by working-class or foreign men. In an article entitled 'Perilous Paths' (1919) girls were warned in dramatic tones against applying for overseas posts as governesses or nurse maids: 'You will remain without hope of rescue until body and soul are lost. When your beauty is gone, and your health shattered, you will die in a garret or cellar, neglected and alone.'[93] *Polly's Paper* went on to describe how girls who applied to work in a ballet troupe ended up working in 'a fifth rate beer garden', the 'sort of place where actresses are expected to go amongst the audience.'[94] A similar tone appears in this advice to readers of *Girls' Weekly* prompted by a letter from Maudie:

> Just now lodgings are very scarce, and before leaving home girls should realise that every large station is used by people of bad character, who are ready to decoy simple country girls, who, in their ignorance take the apparent sympathy and wishfulness to help them as a sign of goodwill and friendship. Quite recently a young country girl answered an advertisement which offered a good situation in London ... The place that seemed so desirable proved to be one of the most notorious and evil dens of vice in the city.[95]

On the one hand this advice fits into a long tradition of concern to protect the morals of young girls travelling and working away from home; the Girls' Friendly Society was established in 1874 with this purpose.[96] On the other hand such advice reveals the class and race dimensions of magazine treatment of sexual harassment. The fact that magazines suspected foreign men of being involved in the white slave trade was not inconsistent with concerns to protect the chastity of white British girls; it also reveals the prevalent stereotype of lascivious foreigners discussed further in chapter 6. Similarly, while the dangers confronted by many working-class girls in middle- and upper-class households were minimised, magazines were much quicker to warn girls against the dangers of being drawn into prostitution, probably servicing men of their own class.

And so to war

Concerns about the conditions of girls' work were pushed aside in wartime when the magazines most vocal on careers and training addressed 'the nation's need' for young female war workers. Both *Miss Modern* and the *Girls' Own Paper* assumed an active role in encouraging girls to join the women's Services. The *Girls' Own* was actually enlisted by the government to disseminate information and facilitate the recruitment of young women into war work and pre-Service training:[97] this it did through careers advice, propaganda fiction, and by featuring colour photographs of smiling uniformed girls on its covers. These features of magazine propaganda stressed the fun aspects of war work and appealed to the reader's patriotism; they also conveyed the personal value of war work. In recognition of the propaganda potential of fiction, the Ministry of War also commissioned W.E. Johns, of Biggles fame, to write recruitment fiction for the

Girls' Own Paper.[98] The 'Worrals of the WAAFs' which ran from 1940 through to 1946 was principally a detective series which conveyed the excitement and adventure of being in the Services although little detail about Service work was actually presented. Most romance magazines responded very differently; the war only intruded into their pages as a backcloth for the staple fiction dramas although letter pages and articles acknowledged readers' war work and issues relating to the wartime separation of lovers, spouses and families. Before they folded, the editorials of working-class schoolgirl papers similarly presented only passing acknowledgement of the war with references to domestic economies, the blackout, girls living in unfamiliar places and, on occasions, older brothers going away; the fiction remained unchanged except for the occasional war setting. It seems likely, as Drotner argues, that '[w]ithin the recognizable universe of serial girls' fiction, the war, apparently, could not become a regular theme without impairing either the entertainment value of the stories or the protagonist's credibility as basically unspoiled English girls.'[99]

Miss Modern and the *Girls' Own Paper* were however compromised by their promotion of war work. The propaganda imperative encouraged the *Girls' Own Paper* to present a misleading impression of Service life, although this was consistent with publicity produced elsewhere. For example, the arduous work often from 8am to 11pm and deplorable working and living conditions (which for one NAAFI manageress included rats in the skirting boards), were not exposed.[100] The features which were stressed included the uniform and drill, that is those aspects of the Service life which had proved attractive to women in the First World War.[101] The portrayal of uniformed girls stressed not only efficiency and smartness but also how attractive a girl could look. These descriptions convey the dual responsibilities of women at war, they were citizens contributing to the war effort and they were women who had to please men and desire marriage and motherhood. It is difficult to determine whether this duality was unconsciously presented or whether it was a deliberate effort to appease public criticism of women in uniforms who were often regarded as masculine or alternatively as sexually promiscuous.[102] This image does seem to have been used quite deliberately to recruit girls by emphasising how attractive and marriageable they would be in uniform. This certainly was the underlying message of wartime advertisements aimed at young single women.

Fiction was similarly harnessed to the war effort and often focused on the patriotic ambitions of girls to do some form of war work in spite of opposition from elderly relatives.[103] Similar to the tactic employed in school stories, parents were not portrayed as the obstacle to girls' ambitions and they were never the subject of direct criticism. The fact that so many war stories referred to adults restricting girls does suggest that this was a common experience, although it is likely that in reality it was parents who were most likely to prevent girls from 'doing their bit'. It seems that magazines were trying to identify with the problems of their readers and influence the parents of these girls without posing a direct challenge to parental authority or suggesting disrespect of them. Acknowledgment of tensions between adults and teenage girls was also broached although neatly contained by using distant family members as the focus of tension.

A more ambivalent attitude to the war lurked behind this propaganda; both the *Girls' Own Paper* and *Miss Modern* had to negotiate a path between recruiting girls to the Services whilst at the same time encouraging them to pursue professional and long-term careers in a wide range of occupations. On one hand the demands of war opened up new areas of work and training to girls, in the field of radio for instance. On the other hand, the war diverted many girls into attractive but short-term jobs. Victoria Stevenson confronted this problem in *Miss Modern* (1940);

> It's a strong temptation to take a job with a good salary and no prospects rather than toil on with training you had arranged to undertake at the beginning of the war. 'What's the point of bothering?' is an easy slogan now, but what are you going to do when the war is over?[104]

As Stevenson pointed out, 'when the war is over, the trained girl will have the pick of the labour market, and her untrained sister, who would not look ahead, will probably find that she's struck a very bare patch.'[105] Although occupations with more secure prospects and training were available, these tended to be in traditional areas of women's work such as catering, child care, nursing and domestic work. It is questionnable whether the *Girls' Own* was pleased about the effect of the war in diverting girls away from a broader range of often pioneering careers.

More worrying for these papers was the increased tendency for girls to leave school before acquiring a School Certificate. It is somewhat ironic that the *Girls' Own Paper* had to persuade readers to stay on at school because their propaganda encouraging girls to 'join up' and 'do their bit' was so effective and because war conditions had led them to question the relevance of their studies. The editor was clearly anxious about the letters she received from girls of 14 and 15 who were determined to leave school to take up what they described as 'more important work'. As one reader explained: 'it [school] all seems such a waste of time. Heaven knows why we have to keep on doing Latin when it can't be of any use to us, and I've cost my father enough money already.'[106] The editor replied that the best possible way that she could repay her parents' self-sacrifice in sending her to a good school, and the first way in which she could serve her country, was by putting the idea of leaving school out of her head. Instead girls were advised to join pre-Service training corps like the St John's Ambulance or the Girls' Brigade. As the editor explained, 'where would all the young doctors, lawyers, journalists, scientists, architects, teachers and artists be found in the future?' She went on to describe how 'it is the boys and girls who are at school to-day who can become the clear-headed, God-inspired men and women needed to build up the better world we believe we are fighting for.'[107] This reply clearly conveyed the preoccupation of the *Girls' Own Paper* with the maintenance of Christian ideals through an educated, professional middle class. It also embodied wartime propaganda that the British were fighting for what was right, and that God was on their side.

War also raised problems of another sort for girls' magazines concerning the compatability of femininity with fighting and killing. This matter was addressed by W.E. Johns in the *Girls' Own Paper*:

> If a person is properly trained, I can't see that it makes much difference who sits at the controls, a man or a woman. The aircraft will respond equally well for either sex. But has a woman sufficient nerve, sufficient of what in the Army is called 'the fighting spirit' to undertake these duties, duties which, don't forget, mean the dealing of death, even though the result may not be seen – as in the case of bomb dropping. This is a question I would prefer not to answer, although there is not the slightest doubt that many girls would volunteer for such work, given the opportunity.[108]

Evidently Johns did not want to suggest that women were less patriotic than men, but he clearly thought, or rather hoped, that women would be averse to the idea of killing. Johns went on to admit that he was personally against women fighting, though he acknowledged that this could be viewed differently depending on the circumstances. While male fighting could be both premeditated and offensive, in contrast aggression in women was only acceptable in defence of her home and her young.

Even in the fiction the heroines were not portrayed as intent on killing although these stories recognised the contradictions which arose for girls between the messages of war propaganda and prescriptions of femininity. For example, in 'Invasion' (1942) two sisters found what they believed to be an enemy parachutist drowning near the beach. Although they considered leaving him to die, they eventually decided that 'the only sporting thing to do' was to save him. This proved a fortunate change of heart as the parachutist turned out to be a young RAF boy.[109] There is an obvious contradiction here, in that whilst it was unacceptable for girls to kill an enemy or knowingly allow one to die, girls were nevertheless expected to join the Services which enabled men to fight and kill.

Throughout the hostilities, the *Girls' Own Paper* featured much praise of girls' work in the Services and in the immediate post-war years it shared the optimism of many feminists that the war heralded a change in the position and status of women in society. As Gertrude Williams sums up:

> For thousands of girls whose lives have been lived within very narrow boundaries this has meant an extraordinary widening of mental horizons, and for the first time a large proportion have learned something of leadership and its responsibilities . . . The girl with a stripe on her sleeve or a pip on her shoulder has discovered that she can take command as well as a man . . . and that both the men and the women . . . are ready to recognise her rightful exercise of authority.[110]

However, in 1945 the *Girls' Own Paper* printed an essay apparently written by an officer who had ATS under his command during the war, which undermined the contribution of Service girls and criticised the way in which they had responded to Service life and duties. This man clearly did not recognise women's rightful authority as Gertrude Williams had anticipated. The 'Open Letter to a Service Girl' began with a somewhat begrudging praise of the Service girl,

> I think you've done, on the whole, a really good job of work – especially on the gun sites. . . . We realise that we caught so many 'jerry' planes and 'doodle-bugs' very largely owing to your efficiency on the radio-location equipment.[111]

But the reader was warned not to 'preen' herself; Service girls, the Army commander argued, were not as thorough as men and although they were generally quicker they lacked intuition in emergencies. He further criticised Service girls for grousing and for wearing heavy make-up, he also claimed that 'you girls don't stand up to discipline anything as well as men.'[112] Perhaps the most interesting criticism which he levelled against Service girls was that they had a tendency to throw their weight around and parade their uniform as if they were the only ones to have done any real war work. In the light of post-war criticism of working women the tone of this article suggests that the commander sought to undermine the war contribution of women in order to justify the pressures on them to retire from men's work and return to pre-war standards of femininity. This was, however, an isolated voice in the *Girl's Own Paper* but one that illustrates the ways in which patriarchal interests were restated even within a quite progressive middle-class girls' magazine.

Work and Marriage

As we have seen, the issue of girls' work was characterised during this period by considerable tensions between the demands of the labour market, the needs and the fantasies of readers, prevalent feminine ideals and also patriarchal pressures to maintain the domestication of women and the sexual division of labour within the paid workplace. Arising from the location of married girls and women in the family which was, and still is, an institutionalised form of patriarchal relations, the issue of married women's work represented a prime area of tension between patriarchy and capitalism. This tension, as Summerfield shows, characterised the state's management of the mobilisation of married women during the Second World War. In this context, assumptions about women's role in the home remained resilient to the demands of war and worked to constrain provisions for the mobilisation of married women.[113] How did girls' magazines address this issue?

During the period 1920 to 1950 married women increasingly undertook paid work outside the home in the formal economy. Whereas the proportion of married women registered as employed in 1921 was 8.7 per cent this had risen to 10.04 per cent in 1931 and 21.7 per cent in 1951; this represented roughly 16 per cent of the total female labour force in 1931 and 43 per cent in 1951.[114] During the twenties the issue of married women's work was rarely aired; working girls' magazines assumed that once a girl got married she was centrally located in the home and family. Opinions shifted somewhat by the 1930s. Although romance magazines maintained a strong commitment to the domestic ideal they also confronted the issue of married women's work openly and even positively in their correspondence columns. This approach was facilitated by an increased acceptance of young wives working especially in areas of demand for their labour;[115] it was also a response to the financial pressures which magazines acknowledged as curtailing their readers' ability to live out patriarchal expectations and the feminine ideal. In reply to Ruth, *Oracle*'s letter editor (1933) wrote, 'Many girls are breadwinners now, and in many cases I have seen it makes for happiness and not for discontent.'[116]

Arguments for and against married women working were drawn out in a letter competition in *Miss Modern* in 1935. Those against working wives referred to the conflict which must inevitably result for a married woman between meeting the needs of her husband and also those of her (male) boss. Repeatedly these letters also stressed the argument that by undertaking paid work outside the home a woman deprived a man of a job. In contrast, those in favour of office wives pointed to the delays to marriage and starting a family which could result from depending solely on a man's income. A further point stressed the skills and experience of young married women; 'Why should her talent henceforth be "hidden under a bushel"?' A number of these letters recognised the importance of financial independence and also the difficulties of adjusting to housewifery and were in favour of a gradual apprenticeship to home life so that 'when the domestic call proves the stronger, she can forsake the typewriter for the cradle.' The editor agreed with the pro-'office wife' lobby, and after commenting that most of the letters she had received had been against office wives, she concluded 'I do think that many of you overlooked the fact that the alternative to the "office wife" in many cases is an exceptionally long engagement with no prospect of marriage for years and years.'[117]

The above article from *Miss Modern* suggests that some married women, especially those employed in professional careers sought work for its intrinsic satisfaction. Magazines which targeted working-class readers did not usually mention this motivation for paid work, but then the majority of their readers were in jobs characterised by routinisation and poor prospects. This motivation was however strong in the *Girls' Own Paper*, which featured biographies of successful married women and articles which favoured the combination of marriage and a career. Marjorie Tiltman (1945) explained this position:

> I would like to see almost every girl married. Even more fervently I would like to see her equipped for a career. Both offer different ways of enriching and fulfilling her individuality. Marriage and motherhood can, of course, be a whole-time-job, and the most selfless career in the world. But motherhood should be regarded as a temporary one, for the sake of the children as well as the parents.[118]

In one sense magazines can be seen as responding to the increased participation of married girls and women in the labour market, but their acknowledgment of working wives varied according to whether they could be accommodated within their different philosophies. Romance magazines, for example, argued that it was necessary to accept working wives because marriages would otherwise be delayed interminably due to insufficient savings; they also argued that the working partnership in marriage promoted greater mutual respect and fostered a more stable and happy marriage. The *Girls' Own Paper* was able to accommodate the careers of married women because this was compatible with its concern to promote a liberal version of equality, and maintain the dominance of the professional middle classes; middle-class women had a duty to themselves, to God and the community to combine marriage and a career.

Conclusion

Magazines directly addressed their readers as either schoolgirls or working girls. These identities were conveyed through the titles of these papers and their cover images. Attention to the detail of schooling or paid employment for girls, however, differed according to the social class of the intended readership. Reflecting the importance attached to the education of secondary schoolgirls, magazines for these readers did address educational matters. In contrast, elementary schoolgirl papers avoided their readers' experiences of schooling which had little to commend them as the basis of an attractive identity and instead offered readers a fictional identity within a fictional school far removed from their experience and the constraints which characterised it. Future careers were similarly not mentioned in elementary schoolgirl papers which is not surprising given the conditions of employment available to girls who left school at 14 years of age. Magazines for secondary schoolgirls were far more attentive to careers and seem to have shared the objectives of secondary school mistresses on this matter. Ironically, this promotion of professional careers was far removed from the actual work prospects of most middle-class girls who, as we've seen, entered clerical and retail work on leaving school. Work-related issues were also addressed by magazines for working girls. Paid work was the reality for the majority of their readers and this could not be ignored. This arose, on the one hand, from the magazines' commitment to offer their readers some guidance on survival in a labour market characterised by considerable insecurity. It also stemmed from the utility of this identity as a means of signifying the readers' modernity and establishing the specificity of their readers relative to older married women and also younger schoolgirls. On the other hand, acknowledgment of readers' paid work can also be attributed to the disruption of gender relations which was perceived to arise from women's employment outside the home. Given that their readers were at an age where heterosexual coupling in preparation for marriage was expected, romance magazines felt compelled to address this issue.

Treatment of schooling and paid work varied along the axis of social class and age although the prevailing conditions of the economy and labour market had significant cross-class implications which were acknowledged by most magazines for older readers. Nevertheless, magazines for most working girls of all social groups recognised and indeed promoted an alternative career structure, the heterosexual career. There was also another type of work which was more central to femininity namely the servicing of others, in particular men and children. Paid work was, in these magazines, most usually employed as a backdrop for the real business of girlhood which revolved around relationships. In this way magazines were in tune with a quite widespread view, one which was articulated in this contribution to the *Times Educational Supplement* on the subject of technical education for girls: 'The majority of our pupils find their fulfilment in life, not in careers, nor in institutions, but in relationships.'[119]

Notes

1 Betterton (1982), p.207.
2 Board of Education (1933).

3 Ibid., p.233, note.
4 Interviews with two ex-pupils of boarding schools.
5 Cited in Trease (1948), p.125.
6 Okely (1978).
7 Oral history and autobiographies offer glimpses of boarding school life especially the regimentation and sports preoccupation. See Avery (1991), ch.8; Bowen (1984), Arnot Robertson (1984).
8 Ibid., on the centrality of games.
9 *Schoolgirl*, 3 August 1929, p.30.
10 Dyhouse (1981), pp.57–8.
11 Oram (1987).
12 Dyhouse (1981), pp.70–1.
13 Freeman (1976), p.72.
14 Frith (1985).
15 Delamont (1978), also Dyhouse (1981), ch.2.
16 Gathorne-Hardy (1977).
17 Okely (1978), p.126.
18 Gathorne-Hardy (1977), p.262.
19 Summerfield (1987a) and (1987c), pp.24–5.
20 Wells (1993) discovered that, in response to a reader's enquiry, the editor of *School Friend* stated that corporal punishment was used at Cliff House. This answer, which was not consistent with the fictional depiction of this school, was probably spurred by the editor's desire to foster the reader's identification.
21 Auchmuty (1992), p.81.
22 *Schoolgirls' Own*, 5 February 1921.
23 *School Friend*, 6 May 1922, p.14.
24 Drotner (1988), pp.204–5.
25 *Girls' Own Paper*, April 1941.
26 Wells (1993) notes in her research into elementary schoolgirl papers that letters sometimes referred to school matters including scholarships.
27 *School-Days*, 17 November 1928, p.16.
28 Ibid.
29 *School-Days*, 3 November 1928.
30 *Girls' Own Paper*, October 1944, pp.6–7.
31 *Girls' Own Paper*, October 1942, p.9.
32 *Girls' Own Paper*, February 1945, p.10.
33 Ibid., p.11.
34 Summerfield (1987a).
35 Marwick (1991), p.151. This interpretation criticised by Braybon (1981) and Summerfield (1984).
36 Lewis (1984).
37 An example of this type of story is 'When the Limelight Shone on Celia', *Schoolgirl*, 16 November 1929. Readers' letters seeking advice on stage or screen careers, generally received this type of reply: 'I don't want to discourage you, girls, but unless you have strong influence to get you started I think you would be happier as you are'. *Girls' Weekly*, 27 November 1920, p.420.
38 *Pam's Paper*, 7 May 1927, p.5.
39 Jephcott (1948), p.121. On present-day parallel see Pollert (1981).

40 Roberts (1984), p.62.
41 Mass Observation (1949) *File Report 3150*, p.12.
42 Pilgrim Trust (1938), p.254.
43 *Girls' Weekly*, 24 January 1920.
44 *Girls' Favourite*, 12 March 1927, p.122.
45 Ibid.
46 Jeffreys (1985).
47 'Little Miss Mirror', *Girls' Friend*, 25 September 1920.
48 *Girls' Friend*, 15 March 1930.
49 Rosen (1973).
50 Pratt (1934).
51 Ibid.
52 Ibid.
53 Pratt (1934), p.285.
54 Contemporary research points to this correlation. See Sherratt (1983).
55 *Miss Modern*, November 1930, pp.30–1.
56 Lingwood (1941), p.191. See also Pratt (1934); Mercer (1940), pp.19–20; Stott (1939).
57 Stott (1939), p.122.
58 Lingwood (1941), p.191. See also Williams (1945).
59 Stott (1939), p.128.
60 Pratt (1934), p.288.
61 Hawkins (1943), p.105.
62 Ibid.
63 Ministry of Education (1947), p.63; see also Ministry of Labour and National Service (1945), p.22.
64 *Girls' Own Paper*, August 1943, p.40.
65 *Girls' Own Paper*, October 1944, p.40.
66 *Girls' Weekly*, 7 August 1920, p.99.
67 *Miss Modern*, June 1935, p.32.
68 *School-Days*, 21 September 1929, p.25.
69 Brittain (1928), p.75.
70 *School-Days*, 5 January 1929, p.25.
71 'Engineering as a career for girls', *Girls' Own Paper*, October 1941.
72 *Girls' Own Paper*, January 1945, pp.6–8.
73 Grieve (1960), p.15.
74 *School-Days*, 26 January 1929, p.13.
75 Davy (1986), p.216.
76 Bloom (1944), p.53.
77 *Girls' Own Annual*, 1939, p.369.
78 Ibid, p.319.
79 Brittain (1928), pp.104–5.
80 Ibid.
81 Dore (1976), pp.22–6.
82 *Miss Modern*, April 1935.
83 *Girls' World*, 14 March 1927, p.2.
84 *Miss Modern*, November 1935, p.24.
85 *Woman*, 12 June 1937, p.10.

86 See for example, *Girls' Favourite*, 2 December 1922, p.420.
87 *Girls' Favourite*, 11 November 1922, p.346.
88 Ibid.
89 *Miss Modern*, February 1935, p.49.
90 Tinkler (1994b).
91 *Girls' Friend*, 12 June 1920.
92 *Silver Star*, 16 October 1930.
93 *Polly's Paper*, No.1,1919.
94 Ibid.
95 *Girls' Weekly*, 26 June 1920, p.520.
96 Dyhouse (1984), pp.104–14.
97 Cadogan and Craig (1986), p.273.
98 Ibid., p.273.
99 Drotner (1988), p.216.
100 National Panel Member (1984), pp.136–42.
101 Crosthwait (1986), p.172.
102 Ibid., on First World War. On the Second World War see Summerfield and Crockett (1992), pp.437–8.
103 For example, *Girls' Own Paper*, July 1944, pp.28, 30, 32; also March 1941, pp.23–6.
104 *Miss Modern*, April 1940, p.14.
105 Ibid., p.14.
106 *Girls' Own Paper*, April 1942, p.3.
107 Ibid.
108 *Girls' Own Paper*, February 1942, p.31.
109 *Girls' Own Paper*, January 1942, pp.16–17.
110 Williams (1945), p.97.
111 *Girls' Own Paper*, August 1945, p.17.
112 Ibid., p.44.
113 Summerfield (1984).
114 Halsey (1972), table 4.7.
115 Lewis (1984), p.151.
116 *Oracle*, 9 December 1933.
117 *Miss Modern*, January 1935.
118 *Girls' Own Paper*, November 1945, p.6–7.
119 *Times Educational Supplement*, 15 May 1943 cited in Thom (1987), p.129.

Chapter 5

Relationships

According to popular psychology, girls were naturally disposed to take a great interest in relationships, especially those with men and children.[1] It is perhaps not surprising then that kith and kin were such a central feature of girls' magazines. What is interesting, however, is the sorts of relationships acknowledged and depicted in different types of magazines. Most notably, papers for schoolgirls focused almost exclusively on friendships and also rivalries between girls while those for older readers were preoccupied with romantic encounters between the sexes, courtship and marriage. In this respect, magazines mapped out the heterosexual career and worked to monitor the boundaries of girls' relationships. This was an ongoing process and one influenced by wider socio-economic and cultural changes, in particular the perceived implications of the two world wars for relations between the sexes, the interwar suspicion of close associations between girls and between women, hostility towards the spinster, the demographic imbalance and also concerns about the falling birth rate. Magazines depicted girls' relationships both within and outside the family as changing and they offered their readers ways of understanding and managing these perceived shifts in attitudes and practices. Although magazines acknowledged the modernity of their readers and their desire for 'modern' relationships, representations of girls within the family, friendships, courtship and marriage were clearly underpinned by patriarchal interests. Most magazines were, however, dedicated to the provision of entertainment and for this reason some identities were more attractive, versatile, and subsequently visible, than others.

Daughters and Sisters

Girls were generally more closely involved in family and home life than boys even though a number of middle-class girls were sent away to boarding and finishing schools. However, girls' magazines devoted relatively little space to discussions of readers as daughters and sisters and fiction generally allotted the family a background role, albeit with notable exceptions. Romance papers frequently portrayed girls as working away from home; even when they did live with their parents, the focus on romance meant that the girl as daughter or sister was barely visible. Schoolgirl papers, particularly those aimed at working-class readers, also favoured dramas set outside the family and home in girls' boarding schools or, alternatively, girl-guide camps, foreign lands and circuses. Whereas the freedom of the working-class heroine from filial responsibilities was dependent on her removal from the home, middle-class heroines were often portrayed in domestic settings as unsupervised by parents and unfettered by the constraints of the daughter's role. This was a representation of family life typified by Arthur Ransome and Enid Blyton in which parents smiled benignly on their children from a distance, providing no hindrance to girls' expeditions and antics.[2] Alternatively, middle-class heroines were left in the care of a governess, either a dragon whom girls rebelled against or, more frequently, an accomplice in their adventures. The 'substitute mother' scenario, popular in working-class schoolgirl papers of the 1920s, was an obvious exception and provided heart-rending portraits of girls battling to support their dependants in emotional as well as economic and domestic terms. This scenario was more complex in romance magazines and involved a triangle of conflicting needs which featured the heroine, her dependent family, and her lover or, more commonly, a blackmailer who sought sexual and emotional possession of the heroine; this dimension to the 'substitute mother' plot was indicative of the preoccupation of these papers with sexual relations.

The 'substitute mother' theme was successful for a while because it played to feelings of martrydom and suggested that girls would be eventually acknowledged for their sacrifice and commitment to family. This story-line clearly offered rather limited options for the heroine who appeared like the Victorian 'Angel in the house'.[3] Such representations were not consistent with a 'modern' interwar schoolgirl identity and entertaining fiction. Domestic and familial settings raised two particular problems. Firstly, as we saw in our overview of the conditions of girlhood, the exacting nature of domestic responsibilities combined with poor quality and often overcrowded homes, did not offer the basis of a positive fictional representation of girlhood. As Dyhouse argues of working-class girls growing up in late Victorian and Edwardian England, the demands on working-class girls were often inconsistent with the characteristics attributed to adolescence, indeed many girls did not seem to experience a childhood removed from adult responsibilities.[4] This insight into the nature of girlhood also applies to girls growing up in the interwar period. A further reason for the marginalisation of the daughter in fiction stemmed from patriarchal relations in the home, namely the father's authority, which girls could not be seen to challenge. Independence and adventure were unlikely to be consistent with parental expectations of daughters. As with the management of the headmistress in school fiction, possible disrespect and disobedience towards parents was avoided by placing them at a distance or removing girls completely from the familial setting.

Glimpses of parents in working-class magazines reveal that they were heavily stereotyped. Home and family were visibly central to the identity of the working-class mother who was typically portrayed wearing an apron and ministering to the needs of her family. Middle-class mothers were also depicted in the home, usually as home-makers rather than as domestic workers. On occasions, especially during the Second World War, mothers were also portrayed doing some form of voluntary or home work. Middle-class fathers existed on the margins of the fiction, their place being in the public sphere. Working-class fathers were peripheral but utilised more within the fiction as foci of servicing in some 'substitute mother' stories and as sources of tension in romantic fiction. He was typically portrayed sitting comfortably in an armchair smoking while mother, or her substitute, stood in waiting. Both middle-class and working-class fathers were represented in the fiction as the final arbiters of power within the family; they established the rules and regulations of the home which were administered by their wives.

Innate gender differences were the explicit and implicit rationalisation of the sexual division of labour in the family both within the fiction and non-fiction, an assumption which accorded with the expectations which most girls lived with during this period. Discussing the tomboy, *Girls' Favourite* advised that 'girls have got to remember always that they ARE girls, and therefore cannot let their zest for "fun" spoil their girlish charm.'[5] This 'girlish charm' consisted of a disposition towards domestic and caring pursuits which was consistent with popular and psychological discourses on female adolescence. Helen Thorndike, for example, in her evidence to the Board of Education in 1923 referred to 'the strength of the fighting instinct in the male and the nursing instinct in the female'.[6] In 'A Real Tonic' (1940), the editor of an elementary schoolgirl paper wrote that 'a good many schoolgirls are what we might call born nurses, gentle, patient and soothing – a comfort to have around when there is sickness in the house.'[7] The assumption that these skills were innate was clearly elucidated in this doctor's reply to an expectant mother who wrote to the romance magazine *Lucky Star* (1945) enquiring about what to tell her 12-year-old daughter about her pregnancy:

certainly tell your daughter, also let her cooperate in the preparation for the new baby. Enlist her help, sympathy and love. If you let her help you with the baby for instance, and tell her that she will have to be a 'little mother' to the others when you are in bed, you will awaken that

121

maternal spirit which exists in every girl child, and you will find too, that she becomes more sweet and gentle.[8]

Efforts by magazines to cajole readers into fulfilling their domestic and care obligations suggests a fundamental inconsistency. If girls were naturally disposed to such tasks why did they need persuasion to undertake them? Arguments which normalised domesticity were, it seems, employed to rationalise and justify the contemporary status quo. Board of Education deliberations on the education of girls reveal a similar process of rationalisation in order to perpetuate and strengthen the sexual division of labour which traditionally located girls and women in the home.[9] Within magazines, as within education discourses, assumptions about feminine nature had different implications depending on a girl's social class.

Glimpses of the working-class daughter in working girls' magazines reveal that her responsibilities were closely aligned to those of her mother; indeed, girls and their mothers were often interchangeable. Articles in romance magazines constantly encouraged readers to assist their mothers in the care of family and home. In 'Labours of Love' Joan grumbled about her domestic chores, but 'Peg's Man Pal' reminded Joan of her mother's untiring and uncomplaining work and advised her to help out.[10] Similarly in 'Always Out' Margery was depicted as so preoccupied with life outside the home that she failed to keep her mother company and assist her in domestic tasks;

> Mother turned disconsolately to her task of mending the smaller children's socks. Why was it, she wondered, that Margery was always so anxious to be outside the home rather than inside? It was the rarest occurence for her to spend an evening in the house, and there were many little things she could do to help mother, apart from attending to little needs of her own.[11]

While the feature asked girls to consider their mother's need for companionship, it also conveyed the isolated nature of domestic and child-care work in this period.

Eldest daughters, as we saw in chapter 2, often had a crucial role to play in the working-class home. This was recognised in the 'substitute mother' fiction in working-class magazines which clearly articulated their obligations. In an article entitled 'The Hard Case of the Eldest Sister' (1922) the fictional author, apparently speaking from her own experience, realistically described the domestic and child-care tasks which often fell to the eldest girl in a working-class home:

Looking back down the years, I can always see myself in the position of little 'mother'. It was my duty to look after my sisters when they were tiny tots, and I was frequently kept away from school to look after the children when mother, through illness or some other cause, was unable to do so herself.[12]

The eldest sister was described as mother's adjutant, her second in command,

and during the absence of the C.O., it naturally falls to the lot of the next in command to take charge of affairs ... To the eldest daughter often falls the lion's share in contributing towards the expenses of the home, and in helping to keep the house in order. She is often an outdoor worker and an indoor worker as well. Next to her parents, she is also responsible for the conduct of her younger sisters.[13]

The phrase 'little mother' was extremely apt as an expression of the daughter's role in usurping the duties and responsibilities of her mother. Editors recognised the hardship and sacrifice this role entailed, particularly if girls stayed at home after leaving school. In these cases girls were exposed to isolation, lack of personal time and income:

I rarely have any new clothes, and having no pocket-money of my own I am absolutely dependent upon my parents for what money I require, and people more or less rightly argue that, being at home most of the time, I do not need to be so well dressed as my sisters ... The future is none too promising. By-and-by my brothers and sisters will be leaving home. They will be having their own homes, leaving me alone and with no prospects of ever marrying and having a home of my own. I have seen this sort of thing happen in other cases. It is the inevitable fate that befalls the daughter who stays at home.[14]

Whilst the restrictions imposed on the 'stay-at-home' girl were acknowledged, these articles were nevertheless resigned to the fact that this was the 'lot' of the eldest daughter.

The 'substitute mother' embodied the ideal of both the daughter and the sister; somewhat disconcertingly these identities easily conflated with that of the mother. This is clearly the case in the following story (1922) in which two orphaned sisters, Alice and Mabel, are looked after by a selfish and aggressive woman who eventually deserts them. Alice was only 14 but she appeared older than her years because of the substitute-mother role she assumed in relation to 11-year-old Mabel. This role was communicated through the language and the tone used to describe the sisters' relationship. Alice had 'mother pity in her heart', she 'had "mothered" Mabel since she was little more than a baby herself; and she loved her with the self-sacrificing affection that the true mother always has for her little ones.'[15] A similar elision of roles occurred in 'Her Ne'er Do Well' (1930) in which, after her mother's death, Jane assumes the maintenance of the home for her father and brothers. The inset picture depicts Jane dressed in an apron listening to her father speak whilst he is seated in an armchair smoking a pipe. Fittingly, her father comments that 'since your mother went, Jane, you've been like a mother to me and the two boys.'[16] In this story, our heroine was both daughter and mother to her father!

Whilst the responsibilities of daughters often dovetailed with those of the mother, the specific relationship between girls and their brothers seemed to prepare girls and boys for their future heterosexual relationships. Sisters were expected to be 'chums', moral guardians and emotional servicers of their brothers:

> no matter whether he is younger or older, a brother appreciates a little bit of 'mothering' from his sisters and rarely forgets any little kindnesses he receives from them. And another thing, don't 'squash' your brothers. Encourage them, take an interest in their doings – always keep their confidences.[17]

Importantly, girls were attributed responsibility for how boys grew up to perceive and treat women. As *Girls' Favourite* explained, 'brothers will largely form their opinions of other girls by comparing them with you ... a sister, after all, is the person to help a fellow to understand girls, and to give him a high ideal of womanhood.'[18]

Overarching the representation of the roles and responsibilities of daughters and sisters was a concern for the family. This was manifest in two ways: concern for the maintenance of the girl's family and concern to ensure girls behaved in ways which safeguarded their moral and sexual purity for the sake of future families. Interlinked with this was a determination to protect and uphold patriarchal relations, in this instance the authority and status of the father and the servicing role of girls and women in relation to the males in their family. In order to protect these interests, girls had to comply with the dictates of their parents and chiefly their father.

Girls were constantly reminded that they owed their parents obedience: 'No matter what your ideas or feelings may be in this matter, you should not openly defy your parents ... One is never old enough to be disrespectful to one's parents.'[19] Although this advice referred to 'parents' it is obvious that it was fathers whom girls must principally obey as they laid down the law within the family. Even a 22-year-old girl was scolded by 'Peg's Man Pal': 'In minor things you are old enough to act for yourself, but while you are under your father's roof and he is responsible for you, you ought to study his wishes when they are reasonable.'[20] Girls were told that these rules were there for their own well-being. 'Advice For Every Girl' delivered in *Every Girl's Paper* (1924) suggested that brothers were motivated by a similar concern in their dealings with their sisters:

> I wish all you girls had a dear, protecting father and brother on which to lean. Their dictates are often hard, but many a girl has been saved by them from moral sin, who have been grateful for their harshness in the years that followed.[21]

Although patriarchal relations of power were crucial it was still regarded as essential that girls obey their mothers. This seems to stem from the specific responsibility which mothers had for the moral and sexual purity of their daughters. It also arose from the vested interest these magazines had in promoting the status of motherhood which was central to the definition of contemporary woman, crucial to family stability and, for most girls, a necessary part of their adult role. Whereas fathers had power, mothers had influence which, magazines suggest, was not always effective. In fact the mother's authority depended heavily on her daughter's cooperation, an impression reinforced by magazine attempts to cajole girls into obedience.

Magazines extolled the trust and confidence which could exist between a mother and her daughter: 'Take mother into your confidence, Alice. You paid me a great compliment, but mother's opinion must rank first. She is hardly likely to turn on you as you suggest. A mother's love is deeper than you think.'[22] During this period magazines often suggested that the mother-daughter relationship was becoming more sisterly and companionate. Macalister Brew's discussion of this topic in the *Girls' Own Paper* (1946) acknowledged tension between mothers and their daughters but also advised girls to devote time and attention to their mothers, 'tell your mother things or ask her advice on matters that somehow seem too shy-making at home ... Don't lose your mother, take some trouble over your friendship with her – even if she infuriates you sometimes.'[23] This companionate relationship portrayed between mothers and daughters can be interpreted in a number of ways. In view of the role of mother as moral guardian it was essential that mothers had an authority more extensive than mere physical restrictions and this depended on her influence. During the interwar period the opportunities which parents had to physically restrict and monitor their daughters were considerably less than prior to the First World War. Because of this, a closer mother-daughter relationship based on shared confidence, trust and respect was essential to the regulation of daughters. It is also likely that this sort of relationship was promoted in recognition of the frictions which could arise during adolescence between a girl and her mother; a close and supportive relationship could overcome some of the worst effects of the confrontation between adolescent daughter and menopausal mother. It is also probable that editors recognised and responded to the feelings of estrangement which mothers confronted as their daughters grew up and away from them. Perhaps this distancing between a daughter and her mother would not have been so significant in communities where extended family systems persisted. However, during the interwar period many working-class families were relocated in suburban housing estates. In this context, it is likely that the locational bond which traditionally characterised mother-daughter relationships was replaced by a greater reliance on emotional forms of connectedness.[24]

The concern for family and patriarchal relations clearly determined the ways in which magazines treated and responded to instances of parent-daughter conflict and tension. Surveys of the 1950s reveal that this form of tension was common during adolescence. It was certainly an experience of girls who wrote to *Girl* between 1953 and 1955. Twenty-one point seven per cent of the problem letters received by the editor concerned family relationships and roles; 'not infrequently, the tension and sensitivity find an outlet in the mother-daughter relationship.'[25] Although similar information is not available for the period prior to 1950 it is likely, as other sources suggest, that such conflict was common.[26]

There was, however, little in the way of explicit acknowledgement of this in schoolgirl magazines with the exception of the occasional feature in the *Girls' Own Paper*. Similarly it was unusual for parent-daughter tension to emerge in schoolgirl fiction. A notable example was 'Just A Modern Schoolgirl' (1931) which focused on the misunderstandings between a father and his daughter. Initially it appears as if the tension between father and daughter arose from an accentuated generation gap; 'Mr Gaynor was a stern man. He was, most people said, a little old-fashioned, so that his ideas seemed unusually strict.'[27] The story opens with an interesting scene of conflict which developed when Celia, who was reading about films and film stars, failed to promptly respond to her mother's request for assistance. Angered by this, her father launched into a tirade against modern girls; 'the girls of today seem to imagine . . . that they are queens of the earth, to be waited on hand and foot. That is an idea you had better get out of your head!'[28] He then proceeded to tear up Celia's magazine. This interaction is interesting in focusing on a key cause of parent-daughter conflict, as Celia lamented, 'Why didn't Daddy move with the times? Why didn't he realise how things had changed since he was a boy?'[29] Shifting the focus of the drama it is then revealed that Celia had once been accused of theft, as a consequence of which Mr Gaynor did not trust his daughter and felt compelled to rear her strictly in order to prevent further such occurences. The end of the story sees Celia vindicated and her father revealed as a caring, more liberal man. This story is particularly interesting for its reference to the generation gap and adult contempt of the modernity of contemporary girls, a theme which also emerged in magazine representations of older working girls.

In romance magazines, the dramatic role of these tensions was to present conflict between the duties of girlfriend and daughter. Letters in working girls' magazines reveal that girls in fact experienced tensions in a wider range of areas. In contrast to the fictional representation of tension in which the father was highlighted, letters suggest that the mother was also a major source of conflict thereby contradicting the fictional representation of mother as passive and quietly supportive. Contemporary and recent sources offer discrepant accounts of the mother-daughter relationship. On the one hand a Mass Observation survey of girls in 1948 revealed that mothers were much more popular than fathers, a conclusion supported by Jephcott.[30] This popularity arose from the support and sympathy which mothers offered their daughters and the girls' respect for their mothers' self-sacrificing work. On the other hand, recent autobiographies and oral history reveal a different perception with daughters recalling extremely ambivalent, if not hostile, feelings towards their mothers; Maggie Fuller, for example, vividly describes her feelings of hate towards her mother.[31] These autobiographical perspectives may be a product of the re-evaluation of relationships and increased courage to examine feelings and actually criticise the hitherto sacrosanct mother.

Advice on how to handle disagreement with parents was tempered by the editor's commitment to parental authority. Editors clearly negotiated a path between the wishes of their readers and those of their parents whom they were loathe to criticise. As girls got older, however, editors recognised their need and desire for independence and, in many cases, marriage. This is illustrated in this reply to 'Broken Hearted Baby' (1930);

> If you are very young, as I gather from your letter, it would be wisest to do as your parents wish, and wait, hoping they will like him better in time if there is really nothing against the boy. But if you are old enough to know your own mind, and know he is really what you say, then be frank with them and tell them you care for him and want to go out with him more. It would be better to do so with their approval.[32]

Another common form of tension arose for girls in their late teens who were contributing to the family exchequer but who were denied control over their earnings. In contrast to articles which usually stressed the positive aspects of mother-daughter relationships, these letters suggest that girls' relationships with their mothers were often characterised by tension. The editor dealt with these problems sympathetically; a 22-year-old girl who gave her mother £2 10s wages each week to receive only five shillings pocket-money was told, 'I see your mother very plainly from what you write. She is a good, kind mother who can't realise her girl has grown up. The kind of person who wants to rule others for their own good can be a very tiresome burden.'[33] The correspondent was advised to stand up to her mother tactfully. Magazines were also sympathetic to girls who were tied too closely to their mothers, particularly once they reached courting age. In response to one reader, whose age was not clear, the editor cautiously replied, 'if you are not too young, there is no earthly reason why you should be tied to your mother's apron-strings in this way, and she is exceedingly selfish to expect you to put up with it. Mothers so often forget that they were once girls themselves and although I am not advising you to defy your mother or to be rude to her, I think you should point out that you have your own life to live and tell her you're not content to be treated as a child.'[34] Defiance of parents was not usually tolerated but rules could be bent once girls reached courting age; 'Obedience to parents is all very well, but sometimes it amounts to a form of bullying when mothers are so exacting, and you are quite right to rebel against it.'[35] In spite of this advice, it is not clear what the girl should do if her mother would not listen; 'mothers and fathers do make rules that perhaps are hard to obey. But if girls can't talk it over with their mothers, and get them to amend their rules a little in certain cases, they should obey.'[36] Magazines were harder on mothers than fathers because they perhaps recognised the closer involvement of mothers with their children and the problems of relinquishing control over the detail of their lives as they grew older.

Relationships between daughters, mothers and fathers appear to have been constructed around patriarchal relations which were manifest in the maintenance of the power of the father in the home, and in a concern to protect the sexual purity of girls in the interests of their future husband and family. Representations of the roles of daughters and sisters shows how extensive the domestic and maternal responsibilities were; indeed the role of daughter or sister and mother were often indistinguishable and also interchangeable. From an early age girls were prepared for the responsibilities of adulthood within the family, not just in terms of domesticity and motherhood but also in terms of servicing boys and men in ways which maintained heterosexual relations.

Friends

Friendships between girls were, during the nineteenth and early twentieth century, also justified in terms of their role in preparing girls for a sound adjustment to the demands of heterosexual relations.[37] Within girls' magazines during the interwar and war years, however, this particular emphasis was not apparent. Moreover friendships between girls were marginalised in all but the schoolgirl papers, where they were most commonly addressed within fiction.

The best chum was a central character in schoolgirl fiction; she was a companion, emotional support, confidante and the person with whom the heroine discussed school matters. Friendships between girls were characterised by loyalty and self-sacrifice which was reflected in fiction titles, for example, 'Peggy Preston's Loyalty'. Friends were affectionate and loved each other but contact and emotions were restrained; when Betty had problems, Polly 'was the loving friend, standing close to Betty with a hand resting sympathetically on the girl's shoulder'.[38] The way in which schoolgirls were portrayed fitted closely with the 'stiff upper lip' tradition of the boys' public school. It also reflected the increased suspicion of expressions of love between girls and women and the twentieth-century trend to curtail this.

Autobiographies and studies confirm the importance of schoolgirls' friendships. Angela Rodaway developed a close school friendship with Sonia and when their study periods did not coincide so that they could talk together they would skip off lessons, in particular gym.[39] The importance of friendships between girls and also the problems they gave rise to were a major concern of schoolgirls according to Hemming. Of the letters he received, 13.2 per cent concerned girl friends and, as he explained, 'Many correspondents seem to be engaged in a passionate struggle to establish or maintain a friendship'.[40] The fiction in schoolgirl magazines acknowledged the importance of female friendships for their readers and the isolation which could ensue when girls did not have female friends. These aspects of girls' friendships were presented in a rare article on girlfriends which appeared in *School-Days*. Jean described how when she started at Ethelreds she 'didn't want to get sloppy over girls, but I did want to make some real and lasting friendships'. Jean was disappointed, 'I imagined they would flock around me, but, on the contrary, they left me severely alone.' Eventually the headmistress took her aside and explained 'we only get out of friendships what we put into them. Try and be friendly yourself, and you will find that others must respond to you. Don't be afraid of being snubbed.'[41] Jean tried hard and eventually discovered another girl who was equally lonely.

The importance of being able to make friends was accentuated during the Second World War when many girls were evacuated into unfamiliar surroundings. *Schoolgirl* responded to this in one of its rare acknowledgments of the war by offering tips on how to make new friends: 'Perhaps one of the biggest difficulties you have encountered has been the making of new friends, for this isn't easy, is it?' The editor advised girls: 'If you feel you'd like to be friends all round, then what you must do is set out to be friendly yourself.' The editor suggested a friendly smile and a little conversation; 'at first it's a good idea to go rather slowly, not to pour out your whole heart to her. Instead, encourage her to talk to you . . . . Then once the friendship is firmly established – you'll find yourself very much happier and your little worries and problems much smaller by comparison.'[42]

In her study of the appeal of schoolgirl stories for readers in the 1980s, Frith argues that their popularity stemmed from their depiction of a world where 'to be assertive, physically active, daring, ambitious, is not a source of tension':

> The significant point here is that the school story presents a picture of what it is possible for a girl to be and to do which stands in absolute contradistinction to the configuration of 'femininity' which is to be found in other forms of popular fiction addressed specifically to women and girls.[43]

Auchmuty in her reflection on the continued appeal of boarding-school stories similarly points to the power accorded girls and also the opportunity these stories provided for girls to identify with strong female heroines.[44] The possibilities of independence within a world of girls no doubt appealed to schoolgirls in the period 1920 to 1950. Older readers were also attracted by the prospect of power and autonomy but romance magazines foreclosed an all-female environment as a site for this. In these magazines, as we shall see in chapter 6, autonomy could only be achieved vis-à-vis men and in her pursuit of this independence the woman was revealed as unprincipled and evil. For girls growing up between 1920 and 1950 it is also likely, as with readers of today, that the positive depiction of female friendships in schoolgirl magazines would have been welcomed given the centrality of these to girls' experiences. Readers of romance magazines were denied this affirmation of female bonding. However, whilst schoolgirl fiction enthusiastically promoted friendships between girls it was nevertheless quite clear that these were temporary. The flip side of the concentration on girls was the marginalisation of boys and the virtual exclusion of sexual interest between the sexes. Whilst not wishing to denigrate this important female space in popular literature, it is nevertheless important to acknowledge the organising principle of schoolgirl magazines. The marginalisation of boys and their representation as brotherly in these magazines stemmed less from a celebration of female friendships than editors' determination to manage compulsory heterosexuality;[45] schoolgirls were not of an age to frolic with boys.

Studies of the experiences of older working girls reveal the central place of female friendships; 'Without a friend a girl is often completely lost in an office, an evening class or a youth group.'[46] Pearl Jephcott described the character and prevalence of these friendships amongst the girls in her studies: 'If the girl does not actually work at the same place as "my friend", she probably lives two or three doors away from her and will go round each evening as soon as she is home from work and has had her tea.'[47] These friendships, Jephcott revealed, were not necessarily constant or long-term and often when a girl left school she changed her set of friends, but they were vitally important, indeed leisure was largely dependent on the co-operation of a female companion:

She will go to the Palladian on Sunday if 'my friend' also wants to do this. If she planned to go dancing on Saturday it will almost certainly be on the understanding that 'my friend' goes with her. 'I go because my friend goes' is an accepted reason for almost any activity.[48]

An important bond within many adolescent friendships was a shared interest in boys. Once girls left school the primacy of boys increased and the importance of a girlfriend with whom to share confidences and compare experiences was heightened. Moreover, for girls seeking to meet boys it was generally accepted that she needed a friend to go out with. Whilst the boy-centred interest of the reader was assumed and catered for in working girls' magazines the importance of the girlfriend was marginalised even in the role of courting aid. In contrast to schoolgirl papers, both the fiction and articles in working girls' magazines denied female friendships. The possibility of romance between working girls, expressed either verbally or physically was also not entertained by magazines, just as it was overlooked in surveys such as that by Jephcott. In many respects, working girls' magazines seem to have assumed the role of the reader's best friend in these matters: they encouraged the reader to confide in them; they invited her to share her romantic fantasies; and through their articles, fiction and letter pages they disseminated information about other girls' experiences and established etiquette and guidelines concerning the management of relationships. These magazines also sought to guide girls in making sense of changing gender relations and their implications.

Rules which prohibited associations between schoolgirls and boys were a common feature of fictional school life although they were occasionally evaded. Representation of the segregation of the sexes was consistent with contemporary boarding school practice although in the context of magazine fiction these regulations served principally as a device for generating mischief and intrigue. Where a platonic 'chum' relationship between girls and boys was featured, especially after 1930, it tended to involve older schoolgirls and often embodied a humorous competition between the sexes with at least one boy emerging as the superior character. In 'Warned by the phantom' (1936) this boy was Dave; he was portrayed as cool and intelligent, 'the level headed, clever lad with all his instinctive chivalry . . . It was he who spoke next, without any self important airs although he must have realised that supreme decisions were being left to him. One must be guided by Dave, he always understood.'[49] Co-education settings introduced into the *Girls' Crystal* in the 1940s also provided opportunities for chum relationships: the 'Worst Boy At The Co-Ed School' featured Vincent who had a very bad reputation and his female friend Paddy who, with sisterly devotion, fought to clear his name and foster his best features.[50] As if to contain any resonances of heterosexual romance in descriptions of boys and girls together the heroine was frequently given a tomboy name.[51]

The working girls' magazine, *Girls' Favourite*, also addressed platonic relations between the sexes. Girls were advised by this paper to treat boys in much the same way as they did their brothers. They were also expected to educate boys in the correct way to interact with girls; in effect they were made responsible for teaching boys how to perpetuate a gendered society and reinforce feminine norms. Independent girls were admonished for promoting undesirable male attitudes which threatened the viability of standards of feminine behaviour; 'Nowadays girls like to assert their independence but this can certainly be carried too far'.[52] One aspect of a girl's responsibility towards boys was to encourage them to be courteous; 'See to it, dear readers, that you help boys to be courteous to the feminine sex, by appreciating the little things they do for you.'[53]

Whilst it is often difficult to distinguish clearly between platonic and romantic relationships between the sexes, it is noticeable that during the late 1930s and 1940s schoolgirl magazines more frequently featured platonic friendships between boys and girls. Whilst these relationships were similar in tone to that between a girl and her brother, they were nevertheless the first stage of the heterosexual career providing girls with the necessary experience of the opposite sex to make future decisions about men and marriage.

The Heterosexual Career

Throughout the period girls' magazines defined their intended readership in terms of their occupation, whether at school or at work, and in terms of their location in heterosexual relations. Magazines for a female readership marked the stages of the heterosexual career in their representations of relationships between the sexes and through the ways in which they constructed their intended readership and the type of content deemed appropriate for this audience. But whereas relationships between the sexes appeared to have been essential to the identity of the working reader, they were marginal to that of schoolgirls, at least until 1940. Heterosexuality nevertheless worked as a 'structuring absence' in schoolgirl papers in that the idea that readers were too young to be engaged in relationships with boys permeated all aspects of the magazine.

The lack of romantic interest in schoolgirl papers was seemingly inconsistent with the experience and interests of school-aged girls, particularly those of working-class girls many of whom expected to marry before their 23rd birthday. Contemporary studies reveal that many of these girls were very interested in boys: 'The school child of fourteen, when confronted with the possibility of joining a social group, will ask quite frankly, "will there be boys there?"'[54] Boyfriends were also a major interest and anxiety of the magazine readers who corresponded with *Girl* magazine in the early 1950s.[55] Contrary to the popular notion that elementary schoolgirls had the opportunity to develop an interest in boys at an earlier age than their secondary school sisters, segregation was a common practice in elementary as well as secondary schools; inter-mingling of the sexes was not even guaranteed in a mixed-sex school.[56] Despite this segregation, elementary schoolgirls often had boyfriends. Similarly, some secondary schoolgirls also developed an interest in boys which resulted in clandestine meetings; 'Of course we used to meet these grammar school boys, you know, and we got to know them waiting for trams, and we used to chat them up and so forth, you know, but we had to be very careful we weren't seen, or else we were in hot water.'[57] It was because of these interests that elementary schoolgirls in particular turned to romance magazines to supplement their reading of school fiction.

While schoolgirl novels by Elsie Oxenham and Elinor Brent-Dyer positively celebrated a 'world of girls' for schoolgirls and married women, schoolgirl magazines were usually produced by men and were specifically concerned with these relationships during only a brief spell in adolescence. Whilst the all-female environment was portrayed positively this was more to do with the heterosexual career than female bonding. Magazines denied relationships between older girls. Similarly the denial of readers' romantic interest in boys stemmed from ideas about the appropriate age for such preoccupations. As we have seen, where boys were featured in schoolgirl fiction the different roles and status of the sexes was clearly conveyed. There were inconsistencies, however, as schoolgirl magazines occasionally portrayed older fiction characters such as form mistresses having 'amorous encounters with handsome coaches or substitute masters'[58] and from about 1929 these papers recognised and catered to their readers' interest in contemporary films, many of which had a romance theme, and film stars. According to *Schoolgirl*, 'Every schoolgirl dreams of a fairy prince – every schoolboy of a princess, and sometimes in filmland these wonderful dreams come true'.[59] The parallel boys' papers give no indication at all of boys being interested in princesses and, as this quote reveals, girls were not expected to be engaged in romantic encounters, although to fantasise about future selves in such relationships was legitimate given their assumed destiny of marriage. Whereas schoolgirls were prohibited romantic relations with boys, older girls were expected by editors to be motivated by an interest in the opposite sex and this greatly shaped the form and content of these magazines. The flip side of this, as we shall see in chapter 6, was that girls were denied an identity as single women or as lesbians.

With the onset of the Second World War the middle-class *Girls' Own Paper* did change its depiction of the middle-class schoolgirl, thereby symbolising a shift in this paper's perception of its intended reader, most significantly she was portrayed as having a boyfriend. Although not leading to engagement and marriage, the introduction of boyfriends to the *Girls' Own Paper* marked an important and exploratory stage of the heterosexual career, a career which was increasingly important to the construction of its intended readership. Macalister Brew, a prominent youth leader, provided this account of boyfriends for the *Girls' Own Paper* in 1946:

> Friendship with a boy is quite a different thing from friendship with a girl. As a woman oneself one understands fairly well how other women think about things, how they talk, how they react to certain situations .... Boys think about things rather differently and therefore unless you take a fair amount of trouble to understand them you may find they have entirely misunderstood you.[60]

Interest in boys, holding hands and kissing were, she stressed, quite natural at this stage when girls were exploring boys and their own sexuality. These exploratory relationships did not involve the selection of a life-long marriage partner although they were defined as a necessary aspect of heterosexual development; 'It is the experience of friendship with boys which helps one to judge and decide carefully before taking the solemn step of marriage.'[61] Such a shift in the perception of girls seems to have been linked to the interwar sexualisation of the adolescent and the moral panic of the Second World War, in particular the spectre of young girls engaging in pre-marital sexual relations with soldiers, apparently proved by increased rates of VD and illegitimacy amongst young women.[62] This atmosphere of concern about the girls' sexual practice probably spurred the *Girls' Own Paper* to a quite explicit management of their reader's assumed heterosexuality.

While there was some change in terms of how the intended reader was constructed within magazines, representations of relations between the sexes also reveal change. Firstly, as was apparent in the shifting character of the *Girls' Own*'s intended reader, papers for middle-class schoolgirls started to acknowledge relationships between the sexes. Secondly, romance magazines featured shifting attitudes towards heterosexual relationships, courtship and marriage.

The 1920s Bachelor Girl

The prospect of marriage was the keystone of articles and fiction in working girls' magazines throughout the period 1920 to 1950. Marriage, and later motherhood, were presented as the ambition and fulfilment of every 'normal' girl. Magazines subsequently had much to say about 'affairs of the heart', courtship etiquette and marriage. Such interests were deemed to be appropriate to girls in their mid to late teens in line with prevalent discourses on heterosexual development and current conventions which they served to justify. In contrast to Edwardian magazines, interwar girls' papers did not expect their readers to be totally engrossed by the prospect of marriage. As we saw in chapter 4, magazines for working-class workers acknowledged, albeit with ambivalence, the work prospects of their readers although they attacked girls who prioritised careers over marriage.

In the midst of what editors perceived as an anti-marriage fashion, magazines continued to present marriage as woman's first and finest ambition during the immediate postwar period and, indeed, throughout the 1930s and 1940s. Editors' insistence that their readers desired marriage thus acquired a defensive note. Even the 'modern' girl who professed to be a 'bachelor girl' was presented as concerned with marriage in the long term:

> But is there a single modern girl for all her modernity and, perhaps, her occasional scoffs at romance who doesn't deep down in her, look forward to a time when she will make a little home for herself and the boy she loves? Even though she may affect to despise and detest housework, and threatens to expire at the mention of darning a manly sock, doesn't she in her inmost thoughts rather love the idea of doing these same despised things for the one who can endow them with magic charm?[63]

Fiction reinforced this image of the modern girl. For example, in 'Secrets of the Heart' (1927) Cassie explained to her father that she did not want to marry, 'I'll just be a jolly care-free bachelor girl'.[64] The mere fact that she described herself as a bachelor *girl* quite clearly conveys that Cassie will eventually marry; there were no popular bachelor *women* or spinsters in these magazines. In spite of this, as we saw earlier, magazines conveyed unease that their readers were being side-tracked by fashion and a desire for independence. In response to these fears editors attempted to persuade girls that they still wanted marriage, domesticity and motherhood. On occasions they abandoned persuasion in favour of outright attacks on the bachelor girl;

> The modern girl is very up-to-date indeed, a jolly good sport and altogether charming. But she's so terribly independent! She doesn't really care whether she gets married or not, so long as she can earn a comfortable income and have a good time ... there is a tendency on the part of the modern girl to over-rate her own good qualities to consider herself more than the equal of man, and to adopt towards him an objectionable 'we-can-easily-do-without-you' sort of attitude ... What-ever you do, girls, don't lose your femininity, it's your greatest charm.[65]

Femininity as defined by these magazines centred on a girl's desire for marriage. It is possible that the magazines focused on marriage as a preferable condition to the limited alternatives for girls in contemporary society. The editor Nell Kennedy certainly saw it as the only viable option for her working-class readers. The historical reality was that a large minority of women were compelled or chose to stay single, to earn their own living and support themselves and sometimes dependants through their careers; 'as things are, some girls must perforce remain unmarried, and all honour to them, when they look around and find their own work and demand a place in the respect and honour of their fellows'.[66] The sympathetic approach to the unmarried girl crucially depended on whether she had desired marriage; if this was the case her spinsterhood was not interpreted as a rejection of the institution of marriage and she was not presented as a threat to patriarchal relations. In spite of the lip-service paid to the unmarried career woman, the needs of spinsters were not addressed. Heterosexual relations and marriage dominated the working-class romance magazines. Perhaps this focus can be interpreted as optimism; at this age magazines assumed that no girl was destined to be a spinster within the heterosexual scheme of things.

While magazines for working girls tried to come to terms with the careers of modern girls, their possible independence and spinsterhood, the middle-class *Girls' Own Paper* had no such problems and was extremely positive about the post-war 'bachelor girl' who pursued a career. The *Girls' Own* was perhaps most concerned that girls should have an objective in life as all service ranked the same with God. Although marriage was an appropriate objective, as we saw in chapter 4, professional spinsterhood also had much to offer:

> Girls very naturally look forward to marrying; it is girlhood's right and reasonable climax. But if this does not come to pass, some girls seem to lose heart, and to feel that life has little else to offer. Yet there are a hundred other interests which can be most absorbing. And the un-married woman is often freer to enjoy outside pursuits than the wife and mother within the home.[67]

Whilst the *Girls' Own* acknowledged marriage as a feminine goal, unlike other magazines it avoided romantic fiction and advised its readers to steer clear of such literature. Referring to novels on 'sex matters' the *Girls' Own* warned, 'it is a law of Nature that all such spurious emotionalism has a damaging effect both on the bodily and on the spiritual faculties of those who allow it to develop unchecked.'[68]

Courting Practice

Romance magazines suggest that girls were tired of the Victorian convention whereby girls remained passive in relations with men. At the same time, they tempered signs of female independence:

> There are a few ultra modern spirits who profess to see no reason why woman should not openly show her inclinations and do her best to win the man to whom her heart has gone out. These urge that it is mere folly for a woman to permit her chance of happiness to pass her by without an effort to retain it, just as it is unworthy of her new-found spirit of independence to meekly pick up the handkerchief when the gentleman deigns to throw it. All of which is very amusing nonsense![69]

Girls were told that it was not their place to initiate contact with the opposite sex be it for platonic or romantic purposes; 'it would be forward of you to take the first step. You must not dream of doing such a thing.'[70] Once in a relationship girls had to continue to play the waiting game and anxious correspondents who feared their boy was on the retreat were told not to pursue; 'listen, no man was ever brought back by running after him. The more you pursue, the further he will fly.'[71] Similarly it was not the girl's place to propose. The implication of this was that girls could only indicate their interest in subtle ways, and that their role was limited to one of response. It is ironic that although girls had to secure a husband they were not expected or encouraged to take any positive steps to initiate or maintain a relationship.

Courting custom traditionally bestowed the right to propose on males. Since it was part of the masculine model, a girl emasculated her boy if she took the lead in this matter. The rationalisation of this practice was that,

> No man is too shy to speak when he loves a girl – sooner or later. If you were to speak first, you'd give him a terrible shock. He will never think quite the same of you again – and you'll damage his own self confidence for ever. He will never forget that you thought him such a coward that you could not trust him to do what has always been a man's job. And later on, if you married, when the first rapture had worn off, as sure as I am here, the day would come when the horrible doubt would steel into your mind as to whether he ever intended to propose at all.[72]

This practice emphasised male power, hence a girl's rejection of these norms was perceived as a direct assault on male dominance. 'My Pal Peter' described the acceptable limits of female independence such that he accommodated the manners and mores of modern girls without disturbing patriarchal social relations;

independence is all very well at the right and proper time, but sweetheart this is not the right time. A boy likes to feel himself his girl's protector. A man prides himself on his superior muscular strength, and has no greater delight than when using that strength to save the girl he loves . . . If Dolly learns to leave to the next sweetheart . . . the things she now insists on doing for herself she will advance a good step to the top rung of the ladder that leads to a wedding ring.[73]

In a similar vein *Girls' Favourite* (1927) advised girls '[n]ot to assume a great air of ownership over your fiance. He likes to think that he owns you. It flatters his manly conceit.'[74] Male confidence appears to have been incredibly fragile. The fact that girls wanted to and actually did propose, that they desired to initiate and lead in relationships, was antipathetic to the notion of man as hunter and woman as passive hunted. Girls had to be cajoled into passivity and they were encouraged to accept these standards in order to secure a husband.

To simply characterise relationships between men and women as one of power versus powerlessness and activity versus passivity is to miss the complexity of magazine representations. Males were presented as the initiators of relationships but representations also suggest that girls had an active role in manipulating a man through, for example, 'playing hard to get'. Courtship advice revealed that securing a future husband was a very calculated business; 'She must get on pleasant, although not familiar terms with him; make him feel that here is a girl who shares most of his views; let him see that she thinks for herself sometimes; takes an interest in what concerns him, and what goes on in the world.'[75] In spite of the representation of men as the initiators of relationships, girls were told that they in fact controlled the level of intimacy. This reasoning excused men from responsibility for their actions and was the prime rationalisation of the sexual double standard; girls and women were made the guardians of public morality and patriarchal standards. Males, in contrast, were not expected to judge the implications of their attentions, they were not able to gauge how far they could go. As *Girls' Friend* explained (1920), 'a man is sometimes a little puzzled to know how far he can pay attention of a purely friendly character to girls without leading the recipient to suppose he means more by them than is actually the case.'[76] Central to this representation, as we shall see in chapter 6, was the notion that there was a fundamental difference between male and female sexuality. The influence accorded to girls in relationships was double-edged and left them responsible for the conduct or misconduct of heterosexual relations. Men, on the other hand, were effectively freed from responsibility and also criticism.

It is difficult to evaluate how far courting etiquette and models of behaviour served the interests of girls and women. Boys and men were expected to finance courtship; girls who insisted on paying their own way could be seen as rude.

Boys were also expected to show certain courtesies to the female sex; girls who questioned or rejected these practices were castigated. While the courtesies bestowed on girls as part of this etiquette were presented as some of the privileges of being female, they actually imposed constraints on girls. The superficial character of feminine 'privilege' was on occasions clearly revealed; take for example this comment from *Every Girl's Paper* (1924):

> Ladies are only considered first by courtesy. Perhaps the man didn't behave in quite a gentlemanly manner, but it was no business of yours to call him to account. He must have thought less of you than you did of him. If you really mean to be a lady you will have to bear many things in silence, that you grumble so much about now.[77]

The 'privileges' of the female sex were actually an illusion conferred or retracted at the whim of a man. The ideal of the 'lady', for instance, was a device whereby females were constrained into patterns of behaviour which served patriarchal relations and which denied girls the right and the power to counter male abuse of the social standards which enmeshed such ideals. These courtesies were, in fact, more important to the maintenance of masculine identity; through enacting these courtesies men demonstrated and reaffirmed their economic and social power in heterosexual relations.

In return for the compliment a boy bestowed on a girl by asking her out, girls were expected to entertain and please their partner. While males were expected financially to invest in the outing, girls were told to invest themselves in entertaining their male companion. The 'girls boys like best' according to an article in *Girls' Favourite* (1922), are those 'who will be at all times eager to hear of his prowess at sports or in other directions. There are some girls who find great difficulty in getting away from that fascinating subject of "I", and they are by no means favourites among the male members of the community.'[78] *Miss Modern* was similarly concerned with the ornamental and servicing role of girls in relation to boys and advised its readers to 'take trouble with those who think you worth knowing. Flatter, listen, chatter, glisten, put on your act to the height of your powers because that's why you're there.'[79] Once again female behaviour was referred to as an act necessary to ensnare a future husband.

Courting etiquette of the twenties differed from pre-war days in that it was increasingly acceptable for the modern girl to have a number of male friends before finally marrying. Once she accepted an offer of marriage she was expected to devote all her attentions to her prospective husband (1924):

> It certainly is a little hard on a girl that she should reserve her company for some boy who has not yet given her any definite cause to consider that he is seriously in love with her ... Of course, if she becomes

engaged to him that is a different matter. Then he would expect her exclusive attention.[80]

Initially this tolerance of pre-engagement relationships was a response to the demographic imbalance of the 1920s, when girls outnumbered men. In this context, girls could not risk waiting for a boy. This practice, which was well established by the 1930s, also served male interests in allowing them to take the opportunity to court a number of women before finally settling down. This new type of relationship posed problems for girls because it was unclear how they should be managed and interpreted. As Pam explained (1924):

> Gone are the days when girls had to be virtually engaged before they could enjoy a man's companionship. That is all to the good, but the pity is that sometimes girls begin to hope that the nice boy in question is a lover before the idea has entered his own head, or heart. It doesn't do to assume that because he thinks you pretty or has kissed you once or twice that he is making up his mind to devote his life to you. Therefore be kind and friendly, but take his compliments lightly, make no demands on him, leave him free as the wind, and whatever you do don't ask him when he is coming round to call for you again.[81]

Given the prevailing double standard, this new practice meant that girls were increasingly vulnerable to male attentions and abuse.

Flirtation was a recurring topic in working girls' magazines during the early twenties when there was, according to magazines, a 'fashion' for it. This was one of the ways in which modern girls could influence relations with men whilst avoiding directive behaviour, which was a male prerogative. Flirts were usually portrayed as somewhat misguided young women who eventually grew out of this stage. Magazines were broadly tolerant of these girls in so far as they were understood to have been borne along by contemporary trends. Girls were warned, however, that flirting was not in their long-term interests; 'a reputation for flirting very often keeps men with honest intentions away from you' and 'the flirt very often ends up by becoming a lonely old maid'.[82] The flirt was sometimes harshly criticised for attempting to exercise power over men; a flirtatious girl was described as cold-hearted and calculating, she led men on 'merely for the sake of displaying her power over them.'[83] Flirts were also criticised because 'through contact with such girls some of our best and truest men have been spoiled'.[84] Girls were advised, 'Have as many friends as you like, but have them on a fair understanding. A flirt can do incalculable harm, not only to men, but to her own sex. She embitters a man, and he is never the same in his treatment of women.'[85] Girls were once again responsible for the ways in which men perceived and treated women. Fiction reinforced this message and conveyed the seriousness of heterosexual relationships; flirts were not good material for a stable and harmonious marriage.

Concern regarding the exercise of female power through flirtation was ironic. Girls were presented as possessing considerable influence over men through their roles as sisters, wives, and mothers, and this was frequently used as a justification for the necessity of female purity in both physical and moral terms. Demonstrations of power were, however, seen as unfeminine because of the threat they posed to male superiority. If women were to exert any influence they had somehow to do so invisibly. Once they overstepped the mark, the fears they provoked could dissuade men from marriage. In the context of the 1920s demographic imbalance such behaviour was portrayed as particularly foolish in that it could seriously exacerbate the already precarious nature of woman's future livelihood. The importance of marriage was also at the heart of the critical stance adopted towards male flirts. Whilst not wishing to inhibit male privilege it was not acceptable for men to ruin a girl's chances of marriage. Preservation of the institution of marriage was of paramount concern in that it secured male interests but also, according to magazines, the future interests of their readers. Within this context magazines were intolerant of men, and also women, who disabled others in the marriage market.

Once engaged, flirtation was forbidden and girls were supposed to be totally loyal. In answer to a reader's enquiry as to whether an engaged girl should flirt, *Polly's Paper* replied: 'If she does it is to be hoped that her fiance will discover what she is doing and will jilt her straight away. A girl who cannot keep true to her lover before marriage will make an unfaithful wife afterwards.'[86] In this instance, the magazine's response was also shaped by patriotism. During both the First and Second World Wars girls were separated from fiancés for long periods and unlike in peace-time conditions they had the opportunity to mix with other men. In spite of this and the obvious loneliness of many girls, magazines had no sympathy for engaged girls who flirted. Florence, for example, was clearly rebuked in *Polly's Paper* for such behaviour; 'I have no patience with girls like you, who become engaged and then, when your boy has to go away from you for a time, find someone else to fill his place and wish to break the engagement.'[87] No mention was made of male infidelity in wartime.

Magazines received numerous letters concerning the right age to get engaged and married. Girls were usually advised to wait until they were at least 20 before getting married:

The heart is never too young to love, but the mind of seventeen is too young to be sure of itself. Real love, like wine, is all the better for keeping, and no girl ever loses a lover worth the having because she is bound to ask him to wait awhile until their love is tested and found genuine.[88]

While 20 was considered a good age for a girl to marry, it was not considered sensible for a boy to consider such a commitment until he was in his mid twenties; before this he was neither emotionally mature or financially stable. Although it was acceptable for a woman to marry a man up to five years her junior, magazines preferred a man to be older than his bride as 'Peg's Man Pal' explained: 'I believe myself it is far better for the man to be older than the woman, for I also believe in him being the head of the house, not in a bossy, domineering sort of way, but in a steadfast, dependable manner, and this answers best when he is some years older.'[89] As this quote illustrates, the age differential was highly significant for gender relations within the home, in particular the husband's authority. Religious differences only emerged as an issue in the *Girls' Own Paper* because of its strong Christian ethos and girls were advised against inter-faith marriages.[90] Class differences were, however, a more commonly depicted obstacle between lovers but one which was confined to the fiction; it is notable though that successful romances either involved a woman with a man from a slightly higher social class or a couple who shared the same social standing.

'Affairs of the Heart'

Love was presented in romance magazines as the most powerful force in a woman's life and readers were repeatedly warned against turning their back on it. While it would be wrong to argue that material conditions and patriarchal social relations were no longer able to uphold the institution of marriage, it is clear that ideological sanctions were crucial to the stability of heterosexual, and more specifically marital, relationships. Love was, moreover, the rationalisation of women's acceptance of marriage and her subordination within it.

Romance fiction relied upon three key scenarios. Firstly there were stories in which the heroine initially fell in love with a villain later to discover her error and transfer her affections to the hero who has been waiting in the wings of the drama. The second scenario focused on the unravelling of misunderstandings which had prevented the hero and heroine from realising their love for each other. The final story-line, which was a transformation narrative, involved a flirtatious and/or tomboyish young woman casting off her modernity in favour of traditional romance culminating in marriage.

A contextual examination of this transformation fiction in romance magazines reveals that editors juggled with what they believed to be a fashion amongst modern girls and what they thought girls should aspire and conform to. An important attraction of the initial independence for the heroine, and from articles we can also assume for the intended reader, was the modernity and freedom it promised from the constraints of patriarchal marriage and motherhood. Audrey

Challoner, for example, 'believed it was old-fashioned to fall in love and have orange-blossoms and bridesmaids at a wedding, and, to show how up-to-date she was, she left a comfortable home and lived in a tiny flat'.[91] Independent or tomboyish behaviour which represented a rejection of patriarchal norms regarding girls' conduct and ambitions, was clearly presented as a desire for the power embodied in masculinity and a rejection of the passive role and inferiority accorded to traditional femininity. Whilst this was acceptable for pre-courting girls depicted in schoolgirl papers, working girls' magaziners could not easily accommodate such heroines. In order to persuade the heroine to accept a monogamous heterosexual identity magazine fiction had to show the heroine discovering the error of her ways and voluntarily choosing marriage and motherhood. This usually occurred after some horrendous sexual encounter or rejection. For Audrey Challoner it was the latter:

> Eric Mathers has taken you out and given you a good time, and he has only asked for a few kisses in return. Now he has got tired, or perhaps he met somebody else he liked better. So he just means to fade away. He doesn't think he has done anything wrong. This is the modern idea.[92]

Reinforcing the message of non-fiction features, these stories clearly caution readers about the possible dangers of modern ways. The transformation of the heroine was completed, however, only when she fell in love with the hero; indeed, heterosexual love was presented as the primary rationalisation of a girl's acceptance of the constraints of femininity and marriage.

By the close of each story when the heroine had usually found a man whom she loved or would learn to love, she had also undergone a transition. In contrast to her initial depiction as independent, the heroine is finally revealed as child-like and as dependent on the hero for love, protection and tenderness. As Dick explained to Audrey:

> My darling, of course it is true that people love each other now just the same as they always will. I love you and I'm going to make you love me. We're going to be engaged, you and I, for just a bit. Then we'll be married ... Then, according to fairy stories which are a lot truer than some of the rot talked nowadays, we're going to live happily ever afterwards. Do you understand?[93]

In this capacity the hero appears like a father in relation to his child, that is the benevolent patriarch; the hero's masculinity is authoritarian and also protective and in this way it reinforced prevailing notions of relations between the sexes.

Radway argues that women who read romance novels often extract positive reinforcement and pleasure from seemingly restrictive story lines.[94] Magazine fiction contained a range of different features and explicit titles and illustrations which, intentionally or otherwise, framed the fiction in quite specific ways. Whatever pleasures girls extracted from these stories two key skills would probably have been acquired from a regular diet of romance serials. One of the lessons conveyed in fiction, which was reinforced elsewhere in these magazines, concerned the identification of a good man worthy of being a girl's future husband. Heroes tended to be serious and quiet men who worked hard, and although strong they were also restrained. The hero's competitor was, in contrast, frivolous and fun-loving and loved conspicuous consumption as much as he hated work. Bourgeois morality, the work ethic in particular, was at the core of this distinction between the hero and his unworthy competitor; for all the romance in these magazines the message conveyed to girls was that they had to secure a husband who would financially support them. As *Girls' Friend* reminded its readers:

> The only love that a woman is justified in putting any faith in is the love that expresses itself in action, ... when a man really loves a woman he rolls up his sleeves, squares his jaw, and works as he has never worked before ... The truth is that marriage on nothing a year leads only to happiness in novels. In real life, where people have to eat, and be clothed and have doctors, it is about the shortest known cut to certain misery.[95]

In this way the hero bore a resemblance to the boy-next-door whom readers were encouraged to marry. The main difference between the boy the intended reader was expected to marry and the man portrayed in the fiction was that the latter was forced to display in actions and words the depths of his love for the heroine. In reality, the reader's boyfriend was rarely given the opportunity to demonstrate his feelings so graphically. Magazines suggest, however, that given the same circumstances the reader's 'man' would probably behave in the same way.

The second skill which girls were encouraged to learn and use involved interpreting male behaviour in particular ways. Whether this accorded with girls' actual experiences of men is another matter. As Radway argues of modern romances, readers were encouraged to understand male behaviour in certain ways through being privy to the meaning, attributed by the author, to the actions of the hero. These meanings readers were encouraged to transpose on to their own relations with men. In fiction for example, when the hero appeared to punish the heroine, the reader was informed that his behaviour was motivated by pain at the heroine's perceived infidelity or failings; this device subsequently rationalised acts of sexual violence towards women as passion. The hero's violence was also explained as a symptom of his ambivalence towards the heroine as he struggled not to fall in love. It was precisely this reason which, readers were informed, underpinned the actions of Peter when he violently 'kissed' Sally: 'Down came his hard, contemptuous mouth upon her soft lips. It hurt her. The bruising pressure of their brutal demand was mingled with savage joy.'[96] As Radway suggests in her analysis of this 'double perspective' in romance novels, 'What she [the reader] is encouraged to do is to latch on to whatever expressions of thoughtfulness he might display, no matter how few, and to consider these rather than his obvious and frequent disinterest, as evidence of his true character.'[97]

Interwar magazines, like the modern day romances examined by Radway, utilised a double perspective to shore up patriarchal relations. That is, they offered readers an interpretation of male behaviour which was not usually obvious from the actions depicted. Indeed, the importance of love as a device with which to rationalise girls' acceptance of patriarchal relations could only work if they perceived male behaviour in such a way as to read love from it. It was through using this device that magazines rationalised double standards as regards the character of male and female love. The love of a girl or woman was described as deep and permanent. Male love, in contrast, was often shallow, more easily controlled and redirected. This notion of male love, as we shall see in chapter 6, stemmed from the belief that men were dominated by their sexual urges rather than any 'finer' feelings. Even when a man found his ideal partner, his love was nevertheless different from that of a woman. In reply to Margaret, Peg wrote 'There is a little quotation which every girl ought to learn by heart; "Love in man's life plays but a part, 'tis woman's whole existence".'[98] Peg went on to describe how men continued to need the variety and stimulation of their careers and sports once they were married. This interpretation of male and female love served patriarchal interests in that it rationalised women's total commitment and sacrifice within marriage, and at the same time it justified men's involvement in both the public and private spheres and excused them of any heavy emotional investment in their family and home.

It is not surprising that magazines devoted so much attention to love and the interpretation of male behaviour in positive ways given the magazine's depiction of the demands of contemporary marriage and motherhood.

Marriage

In modern marriages, according to the middle-class *Miss Modern*, young wives often continued to work and couples were more companionable. Having said this, *Miss Modern* and particularly the working-class romance magazines, presented marriage as characterised by a strict division of labour which heightened once the couple had children. The roles of young wives and mothers required energy and skill to negotiate to the satisfaction of both husband and children since they were often contradictory or in tension; a fine line existed between success and failure as a wife and mother. Women's contribution to the family involved various forms of servicing – physical, domestic, emotional, sexual – which were highly labour intensive and they were subsequently torn between meeting the needs of different family members. Moreover the types of servicing which fell to the wife and mother were often difficult to combine, the most obvious example of this being the combination of sexual and domestic servicing which, even today, remains a problem for many women.[99] Husbands, in contrast, were not portrayed as experiencing these tensions as their responsibilities as father and husband were entirely consistent, depending as they did on their ability to support their family financially.

Given the multiple responsibilities of the wife and mother it is not perhaps surprising that magazines warned girls not to get obsessed by domestic management; 'I admire the way you run your home, but I do not admire the way you have slumped down into it as if it were the only place on the earth.'[100] Advice regarding motherhood broached a similar difficulty, how to care for baby without neglecting one's spouse. Those readers who neglected their husband's needs in caring for their children were admonished; 'You're making the mistake so many young mothers make – you're putting the baby first. Put your husband first and arrange your day so that you are free for him when he is free.'[101] This advice was premised on the certainty that if a husband and wife were happy together then their children would grow up content but it is also clear that if a woman neglected her husband she woud lose him and the security which he provided for both herself and her children.

Fiction also addressed the often fraught role of the young wife and mother and the specific problems which she might encounter. The 'Night She Said "No"' (1940) featured Jim and Molly Fenmore and baby Michael. From the beginning it is clear that with the arrival of Michael, Molly and Jim had been drifting apart;

> It wasn't that Jim begrudged the attention Molly lavished on the precious little spark of life that was jointly theirs. He just couldn't help feeling that now she had Michael, Molly had hardly any time for him. Hardly any interest, either, when she was turning down all the plans he had made for their anniversary.[102]

Jim also noticed how Molly had lost interest in herself and he could not help making an unfavourable comparison with a close female friend of theirs called Norma. One evening Norma called round with tickets for a show but Molly felt unable to leave baby Michael so Jim subsequently went along with Norma. In their absence Molly became anxious, 'She had sacrificed everything in order to give her time to her baby, and in doing so it looked as though she had lost her husband's love.'[103] It is eventually revealed that Jim had actually fixed up the evening with Norma in order to bring Molly 'to her senses'. The story ended with Molly and Jim reaffirming their love for one another and promising never to let the baby push them apart again.

The wife's servicing of her husband was complex and demanding; she had responsibility for her husband's physical, emotional and psychological needs. Importantly, it was she who determined whether he made a good husband. This responsibility for male behaviour and attitudes represented a common theme in magazine constructions of girls and women. A wife's role in relation to her husband was often comparable to that of a mother to her children. Again this elision of roles was a recurring feature of representations of girls in relation to boys and men whether as daughters, sisters, friends, lovers, wives or mothers. Women's servicing of their husbands in the home was presented as an essential corrective to the physical and psychological buffeting which men received in the world of paid work. Women, it seems, had no such antidote either to their position of powerlessness in the relations of capital or those of patriarchy except perhaps the precarious illusions of power which magazine fiction and occasionally articles offered their readers in their bid to entertain and to ease them into a graceful acceptance of 'woman's kingdom'.

Conclusion

Girls' magazines talked about women's new found modernity but this did not extend into the home nor, indeed, into girls' relationships. The portrayal of schoolgirl friendships were the exception. Even though romance magazines referred to changing relations between the sexes, especially in courtship, these were presented as double-edged. Representations of girls in relationships reveal the tensions inherent in the roles and responsibilities which girls and women were expected and encouraged to assume as daughters, sisters, lovers or wives. Advice to girls was also contradictory in that while they were presented as responsible for relations between the sexes and the stability of marriage and family, they were denied any direct control or authority. Given the complexity and demands of these different relationships it is not surprising that they so often seemed to dominate the lives of girls and also women. This complexity and constraint also accounts for the marginalisation of certain identities, for example that of the daughter in schoolgirl papers. Magazines for courting girls had, as usual, less leeway and were indeed commited to informing readers of the detail of their obligations towards men, especially prospective husbands. Central to magazine rationalisations of these feminine roles and also the sexual double standard was the notion of innate gender difference which, as we shall see in chapter 6, was writ large both on the outside and on the inside of the female body.

Notes

1 For example, Wall (1948), p.102. See also note 6.
2 Townsend (1983), ch.14.
3 Gorham (1987), pp.41–6.
4 Dyhouse (1981), ch.4.
5 *Girls' Favourite*, 29 April 1922.
6 Board of Education (1923), pp.89, 91.
7 *Schoolgirl*, 10 February 1940, p.13.
8 *Lucky Star*, 12 February 1945, p.4.
9 Dyhouse (1978); Hunt (1991).
10 *Peg's Paper*, 22 April 1930, p.12.
11 *Girls' Favourite*, 18 February 1922, p.66.
12 *Girls' Favourite*, 18 November 1922, p.379.
13 Ibid.
14 Ibid.
15 *Schoolgirls' Weekly*, 21 October 1922, pp.3–5. See also *Schoolgirls' Own*, 5 February 1921.
16 *Red Letter*, 8 February 1930, pp.175–7.
17 *Girls' Favourite*, 15 April 1922, p.247. See also *Girls' Own Annual*, Vol. 6, 1927, p.34; *Miss Modern*, June 1935, pp.7, 57.
18 *Girls' Favourite*, 15 April 1922, p.247.
19 *Peg's Paper*, 19 August 1930, p.20.
20 *Peg's Paper*, 15 April 1930, p.20.
21 *Every Girls' Paper*, 6 October 1920.
22 *Every Girls' Paper*, 20 October 1924, p.42.
23 *Girls' Own Paper*, September 1946, pp.13, 46.
24 Young and Wilmott (1990), ch.5, 9, indicate that family members saw each other significantly less once they moved away from each other.
25 Hemming (1960), p.89 and pp.26, 88.
26 See Forrester (1981) and Jamieson (1986), pp.61–5; also Wall (1948) and Ministry of Education (1947), p.99. On tension between Victorian middle-class mothers and daughters see Dyhouse (1989), pp.22–33.
27 *Schoolgirl*, 22 August 1931.
28 Ibid.
29 Ibid.
30 Mass Observation, *File Report 3150*, p.5; Jephcott (1948), p.44.
31 Rowbotham and McCrindle (1977), p.116.
32 *Peg's Paper*, 8 April 1930, p.37.
33 *Fortune*, 31 October 1936, p.31.
34 *Oracle*, 4 March 1933, p.14.
35 Ibid.

36 *Girls' Favourite*, 27 May 1922, p.395.
37 Vicinus (1985), pp.35, 189–90. See also Blanchard (1929), pp.136–7; Wile (1929).
38 *Schoolgirls' Own*, 5 February 1921.
39 Rodaway (1985), p.87.
40 Hemming (1960), p.34 and ch.5.
41 *School-Days*, 8 December 1928, p.10.
42 *Schoolgirl*, 18 May 1940, p.13.
43 Frith (1985).
44 Auchmuty (1992), ch.1.
45 Rich (1980), p.647 coined the phrase 'compulsory heterosexuality' to describe the material and ideological enforcement of a heterosexual orientation on women.
46 Jordan and Fisher (1955), p.73.
47 Jephcott (1942), p.129.
48 Ibid.
49 *Schoolgirl*, 4 January 1936.
50 *Girls' Crystal*, 8 April 1950. See also *Girls' Crystal* 1950, 'Merryman's Island College'.
51 Thanks to Alison Oram for this point.
52 *Girls' Favourite*, 24 June 1922, p.490.
53 *Girls' Favourite*, 13 May 1922, p.343.
54 Jephcott (1942), p.132.
55 Hemming (1960), pp.34, 81.
56 Summerfield (1987c), pp.25–6.
57 Ibid., p.25.
58 Drotner (1988), p.210.
59 *Schoolgirl*, 22 August 1931.
60 *Girls' Own Paper*, July 1946, pp.13, 46.
61 Ibid. See also *Girls' Own Paper*, September 1946, p.41.
62 Board of Education (1943). See also Tinkler (1994a) and (1995a).
63 *Girls' Favourite*, 12 March 1927.
64 *Girls' World*, 7 March 1927.
65 *Girls' Weekly*, 24 January 1920.
66 *Girls' Weekly*, 21 January 1922, p.67. See also *Girls' Own Annual*, No. 9, 1927, p.528.
67 *Girls' Own Annual*, Vol. 7, p.433. On sublimation see Oram (1992).
68 *Girls' Own Annual*, Vol. 9, p.557.
69 *Girls' Friend*, 31 January 1920.
70 *Polly's Paper*, 15 December 1919, p.14.
71 *Peg's Paper*, 29 April 1920, p.28.
72 *Peg's Paper*, 15 January 1920.
73 *Peg's Paper*, 12 April 1924.
74 *Girls' Favourite*, 12 March 1927, p.127.
75 *Girls' Friend*, 11 September 1920, p.387.
76 *Girls' Friend*, 17 April 1920, p.135.
77 *Every Girls' Paper*, 20 October 1924, p.42.
78 *Girls' Favourite*, 4 February 1922.
79 *Miss Modern*, May 1940.
80 *Poppy's Paper*, 2 February 1924.

81 *Pam's Paper*, 1 March 1924.
82 *Girls' Friend*, 19 June 1920, p.243.
83 Ibid.
84 *Girls' Friend*, 24 April 1920, p.152.
85 *Girls' Friend*, 19 June 1920, p.243.
86 *Polly's Paper*, No. 2, 1919.
87 *Polly's Paper*, No. 4, 1919.
88 *Girls' Weekly*, 18 February 1922, p.154.
89 *Peg's Paper*, 29 July 1930, p.22.
90 *Girls' Own Paper*, October 1945, p.32.
91 *Peg's Paper*, 11 February 1930, pp.310–11.
92 Ibid.
93 Ibid.
94 Radway (1987).
95 *Girls' Friend*, 18 September 1920, p.405. See Fowler (1991), p.65.
96 *Peg's Paper*, 27 April 1940, pp.8–10.
97 Radway (1987), p.148.
98 *Peg's Paper*, 6 May 1920, p.30.
99 Delphy and Leonard (1992), ch.9 on the variety of work done by wives.
100 *Peg's Paper*, 25 March 1930, p.15.
101 *Peg's Paper*, 29 June 1920, p.22. See fiction in *My Weekly*, 1 January 1930, pp.40–2.
102 *Peg's Paper*, 22 February 1940, pp.42, 44–5, 46.
103 Ibid.

Chapter 6

The Embodiment of Femininity

Adolescent girls were, throughout the period 1920 to 1950, a focus of attempts by the government, schools, employers and youth organisations to construct and regulate their bodies in relation to their potential maternity, their assumed heterosexuality and their wage labour.[1] While interest in girls' health as future mothers was principally concerned with their insides, concerns about girls' sexual conduct and the bodies of female workers were increasingly preoccupied with the body's external dimensions. With regard to wage labour, this attention was related in part to the increased employment of girls in service work where appearance was central to the servicing of male colleagues, clients and customers. More generally, the focus on appearance was linked to the growing physical culture movement at this time, which encouraged an interest in the external as opposed to the internal 'uterine' aspects of the body and fostered the equation of health and fitness with appearance: comparisons of youth in Britain and on the continent during the 1920s and 1930s, which had industrial and military connotations, contributed a further dimension to this concern with the visible aspects of the body.[2] Girls' magazines of the period 1920–1950 were also involved in the construction and regulation of the body, processes which, as Scott and Morgan point out, are often intertwined; 'To construct some bodily feature or process, to describe it in a certain way or to lay emphasis on some aspect of the body is, in some measure, to exercise control or constraint.'[3] An important aspect of this construction was the cross-cutting of the internal/external dimensions of the body by a public/private division. While magazines were clearly interested in certain external features of their readers' bodies such as their face, hair, hands, limbs and anything clothed, other elements, namely the torso and especially the breasts and genitalia were defined as private. Similarly, while the heart and mind were presented as public, the internal workings of the body and the changes associated with puberty and pregnancy, were only obliquely referred to.[4] Magazine silence on sexuality and on aspects of the body's insides and outsides was central to the tension these papers encountered between meeting their readers' need for information and at the same time constructing the female body in ways which supported the sexual division of labour and heterosexual relations.

Magazine treatment of the female body and sexuality reveals the complex, and often insidious, workings of magazine representations of femininity. Editorial constructions of the body represented a negotiation of different interests. On the one hand, editors were keen to present attractive and appealing images of girls which conveyed the modernity of magazines and contemporary young women. They also sought to respond to their readers' desires for fun, freedom and mobility and to address their interest in the female body and its changes. On the other hand, editors were clearly keen to adhere to traditional representations of femininity which were more in line with prevailing patriarchal interests in passive, heterosexual young women who desired men and marriage for their fulfilment. They were also, in tune with the interests of capital, concerned to promote motherhood. The result of this negotiation was that the female body and its functions remained cloaked in obscurity beneath a lively modern demeanour on which magazines spoke volumes. The effects of magazine representations of the body were cyclical. Magazines reinforced the particular constructions of the female body which they labelled as feminine; they stressed the normality of these constructions and offered girls detailed guidelines on their realisation. Most notably magazine representations worked to naturalise heterosexuality and dependence on men; heterosexuality was inscribed both on the outside and on the inside of the female body. Through these constructions and ways of understanding female experience of the body and sexuality, magazines worked to shape the way in which girls perceived themselves. In effect, they contributed to the realisation of their ideals of girlhood.

The influence of magazines was secured in particular through their utilisation of various forms of blackmail. Girls were encouraged by magazines to regard the winning of a husband as essential to their future happiness and security. This was a message which was reinforced through other mediums of formal and informal education. In stressing the centrality of their prescriptions of femininity for success in the heterosexual career, magazines fuelled and at the same time addressed girls' vulnerability which would have been particularly acute arising from the often unexplained physical changes of adolescence. Girls' magazines subsequently had considerable leverage in encouraging readers to follow their advice and set themselves up as authorities on femininity and also courtship, love and marriage. They were perhaps successful in this because they were one of the few mediums to address the feminine body from the perspective of girls. Although what they said was not necessarily novel, they offered their audience a privileged 'insider's' view and detailed step-by-step advice on becoming visibly feminine. Evidence that these magazines did influence their readers can be found in the correspondence columns where girls of 12 years and upwards sought advice on how to follow prescriptions of femininity. For all the letters which were printed, there were many more which were received; some of these were dealt with personally, others were ignored.

Keeping Up Appearances

Of all the messages delivered in romance magazines, perhaps the most powerful was the emphasis laid on appearance. Articles and adverts constantly stressed the importance of this: 'in my estimation, and I'm sure you will all agree with me, details in dress and manners are the things that matter most of all.'[5] Beauty articles described how to make up one's face, neck, arms and hands; how to groom and wear one's hair; how to position one's hat; what clothes and shoes to wear; how to sit and walk like a film star; how to look composed whilst dancing. As this list suggests, the emphasis was on the creation of a particular look. General health in terms of sleep, food, exercise and fresh air were necessary preliminaries but they were not in themselves enough.

Why was a feminine appearance given such a pivotal place in romance magazines? Matthews has suggested in her examinaton of the rise of beauty culture in England that attention to health and beauty became ends in themselves for women during the interwar period. Moreover, she argues, women who wanted to be modern, to experience adventure, power, and liberation, could do so through the transformation of the body. Magazines for schoolgirls but especially magazines for working girls did embrace and present the female body as a site of girls' modernity; this was most clearly represented, especially in cover images, through the girl's appearance – her clothes, hair, skin and bodily shape – which together conveyed youth, liberation, mobility, and fun. Girls looked very different from their Victorian and Edwardian forebears, but then they were *modern girls*. Matthews argues that the staple justification for female physical culture in the twentieth century was to be 'fit and beautiful for herself and in order to catch and keep a husband, as well as or instead of to raise healthy children'.[6] Magazine constructions of the female body were, however, only skin deep. Modern she may look, but as magazines were at pains to stress, the interwar girl had not really changed in any significant ways from her pre-war counterparts. Reinforcing this, fictional images of girls powerfully contradicted any idea that they were independent modern young people.

The centrality of appearance in romance magazines was linked to the fact that the majority of magazine readers were considered to be at the age when they would be preparing for, or already in, the marriage market. At this stage, according to magazines, femininity was vitally important; but girls did not just have to be feminine, they had in a very real sense, to be *seen*, and to see themselves, as feminine. The key to magazine presentations of femininity and concentration on appearance was female heterosexuality which, it was supposed, would find expression in marriage and motherhood. Marriage and its obligations were central to the way in which women were defined in society; the prospect of marriage also defined magazine prescriptions of femininity. However the prescriptions concerning a feminine appearance related to the intended reader's place in the heterosexual career; this was bound up with the age and social class of the reader. Magazines aimed at married women emphasised the importance of looking good in order to maintain the love and fidelity of their husbands; papers for adolescent working girls who expected to be engaged by the time they were 20, communicated that feminine beauty was vital to success in securing a husband.

Even schoolgirl papers described to their readers how to keep fit and attractive: the *Schoolgirl*'s readers (1940) were advised about good looks problems – 'It's no longer the thing to have a shiny, well-scrubbed look, and that horrid starched feeling your face gets if it is washed too vigorously' and 'rough red hands are admired by no-one'.[7] Although schoolgirl papers presented beauty as an important asset for girls, it did not receive the attention nor the importance attributed to it by romance magazines. This was because readers of the older girls' magazines were considered to be at a key stage in their heterosexual career, that of finding and securing a future husband. Elementary schoolgirl papers were positioned differently in this career and the maintenance of a feminine appearance was subsequently less significant. The fact that schoolgirl magazines did divert some attention to questions of appearance and beauty does suggest that girls were expected to think of themselves as different from boys; reliance on looks was fostered from a very early age. The *Girls' Own Paper*, a secondary schoolgirl paper which targeted a mainly middle-class audience, also avoided a heavy emphasis on appearance throughout the interwar and war years despite the fact that its intended readers were aged between 12 and 18. This was because many of its readers were considered to be too young to be interested in such advice. The *Girls' Own Paper* also appears to have been protecting the innocence of its older readers who were not expected to marry until their mid- to late twenties; a policy which was consistent with strategies employed by some interwar secondary schoolmistresses in their attempts to minimise distractions to their pupils' pursuit of professional careers.[8] Rather than advice on appearance, the *Girls' Own Paper* offered its middle-class readers information on careers; this changed during the late 1940s when the paper merged into the *Heiress* and increasingly targeted working and courting girls. While attention to 'good looks' was a somewhat marginal topic relative to its coverage in romance magazines, schoolgirl papers, especially those aimed at secondary schoolgirls, were keen to stress the importance of general health and fitness. The *Girls' Own Paper*, for example was an avid supporter of physical culture for its readers. Physically active, and often sporty, heroines were also a feature of schoolgirl fiction as we saw in chapter 4.

Related to the heterosexual significance of a feminine appearance was its centrality as a means of differentiating the sexes and thereby rationalising patriarchal social relations and the subordinate place of girls in relation to boys and men. Representations of femininity in girls' magazines artificially differentiated the sexes, particularly with regard to appearance and sexuality. As Susan Brownmiller has observed in her analysis of contemporary feminine norms, a 'major purpose of femininity is to mystify or minimise the functional aspects of a woman's mind and body that are indistinguishable from a man's.'[9] Such representations of femininity in magazines were only possible because of those dominant patriarchal relations which structured society in such a way that girls already believed that the sexes were different and that they should fulfil different roles.

The emphasis in magazines on a girl maintaining a feminine appearance was particularly strong in periods when gender relations were disrupted. In the 1920s, as we saw in chapters 4 and 5, magazines voiced popular anxieties about the independence of modern girls in the labour market and in relationships which were implicitly attributed to the emancipatory tendencies of the First World War. The main concern was that these changes threatened the traditional relations between the sexes and the dependence of girls on men and marriage. One response to this was the 'back-to-the-home' movement evident in domestic pressures on readers of women's magazines; this represented a particularly important aspect of the post-war patriarchal backlash against the perceived independence of women.[10] Girls' magazines did not usher their readers out of the labour market, on the contrary, their readers needed to work and there was a demand for young female workers. Magazines nevertheless assisted the patriarchal cause through their production of sexual difference and, more specifically, their encouragement to girls to maintain a feminine appearance. As Coward argues of 1980s constructions of women: 'Women's bodies, and the messages which clothes can add, are the repository of the social definition of sexuality.'[11] During the Second World War magazines similarly placed considerable importance on a feminine demeanour, this was in spite of shortages of raw materials. Adverts, in particular, described beauty as a girl's chief contribution to the war effort – 'Beauty goes hand in hand with the service of King and country'.[12] Feminine beauty was not likely to win a war but it was crucial to patriarchal relations which depended on the maintenance of an artificial difference between the sexes. This was of particular import given that patriarchal roles and expectations of girls were under attack due to the demand, arising from wartime production and the call-up of men, for girls and women in the labour market. In fact, many of the pre-war restrictions which had operated to differentiate the sexes were eroded (if only temporarily). Magazines such as *Miss*

Modern and the women's service magazines such as *Woman* and *Woman's Own* responded to this situation by focusing more heavily on features which did not suggest that the war contribution of women should be restricted, but which nevertheless served the purpose of differentiating the sexes. Other romance magazines whilst not vocal on this subject nevertheless continued to reinforce the femininity of their readers despite the demands of their war work.

Girls' magazines responded to perceived disruptions of gender relations in both the 1920s and 1940s by concentrating on appearance, in particular facial beauty and mannerisms. They may even have attempted to counter fears that women were becoming lesbians as their secondary sex characteristics were modified by fashion and life styles and many women were thought to be acting like men. According to Faderman, critics of women during the two world wars complained that with 'the increasing female freedom which encouraged women to develop not only athletic skill, executive ability, and professional success but even develop boyish figures, the secondary sex characteristics were becoming so modified that lesbianism was inevitable.'[13] A feminine appearance diffused the fear that girls' wartime independence would threaten male dominance. There is certainly an element of truth in this statement from *Woman* magazine that women served King and country through their femininity: 'Try to look like a woman, a pretty and charming one too, that's a better contribution to the general happiness than looking as if you'd just called round to do the handyman's job.'[14] Amidst social and economic change and the disruption of gender relations the female body was constructed in such a way as to embody the heterosexual imperative which was at the core of patriarchal relations.

The constant stress on a feminine appearance was closely tied to the developing cosmetics and fashion industries which both benefited from this emphasis and also fuelled it. During the thirties advertisements for clothes and beauty products increased in magazines for working girls and mothers. Even during the Second World War, when raw materials were in short supply, adverts continued to remind women and girls of their products. Tensions did arise, however, between the interests of the cosmetics industry and girls' magazines; the clash over the use of lipstick in the 1920s is one such example. During the 1920s magazines began to receive increasing amounts of financial support from the cosmetics industry. However, adverts encouraging girls to wear make-up contradicted magazine advice which encouraged girls to foster a natural and innocent feminine look. The growing cosmetics industry represented the interests of capital but girls wearing heavy lipstick clashed with prevalent norms of femininity. Indeed, the wearing of lipstick was associated with an autonomous and active sexuality which, as we shall discuss below, was inconsistent with conceptions of girls and women as sexually passive and dependent on men and as requiring monogamous marriage, motherhood and domesticity for their fulfilment. This issue revealed tensions within the relations of capital between attention to girls as consumers and as potential mothers. Commercial exploitation of girls also clashed with patriarchal interests in a domesticated and male-controlled female sexuality. Girls' magazines finally achieved a compromise with this rather contradictory advice: 'The colour of a lipstick should be the colour of the lips. Then its use will not be seen.'[15]

In order to appreciate the vital role of a feminine appearance in maintaining the status quo it is necessary to examine what this ideal entailed. Fictional representations of feminine beauty did change over time but they maintained a remarkable consistency in their implications. Little Lil was a typical fictional heroine of the 1920s, described as 'golden-haired, young, pink and white and dimpled, with the wonderful freshness that England gives, with red, passionate lips.'[16] Later in the 1940s a typical heroine was described in the following way: 'She was so little and slender and breath-takingly lovely! She had dark, almost blue-black hair, and skin white as a camelia. Dark blue eyes and a sweet red mouth that seemed to invite him enticingly, even though, at the same time, she possessed a look of untouched freshness.'[17] Although separated by 20 years both girls were portrayed as dolls, very child-like, but at the same time extremely sensual although not actually possessing an independent and active sexuality. These descriptions also suggest the heroines' virginity and their potential for sexual responsiveness (if they met and married the right man). The emphasis of these descriptions was on fragility and passivity, the personalities of these characters was not discussed in any detail and it was not expressed through the facial descriptions. The significance of this portrayal is apparent when compared to the fictional representation of men. Male heroes had faces with character. For instance, Paul Grey's face conveyed to the heroine, and presumably the reader, that he had 'carved his own way in the world, and won what he sought; it was the face of a fighter, of a man who only falls to rise again, stronger, more resolute, and undaunted than ever.'[18] Paul's appearance indicated action, independence and individuality, whereas the heroine's appearance suggested that she was passive, weak and immature. It was in these ways that magazines artificially differentiated the sexes. On the basis of this, magazines allotted male and female characters different roles.

Magazine representations of femininity, in terms of appearance, were full of contradictions and tensions. On the one hand, a feminine appearance was described by these papers as natural; girls were innately feminine. On the other hand, romance magazines in particular, devoted considerable space to information on what constituted a feminine appearance and how to create it. In fact, appearing feminine was generally portrayed as an art form to be acquired by girls, rather than as a natural endowment. Adverts were often the most open about the artificiality of beauty: 'You're his dream girl. Don't disappoint him, give yourself a new look.'[19] Looking feminine was, however, more than just an art, constructing difference was quite literally body work; ironically, this constituted a substantial element of girls' leisure.

This contradiction between the rhetoric of naturally endowed feminine beauty and advice on the construction of the feminine look posed a major problem for magazines; somehow they had to ensure that girls would adopt their models of femininity. Magazines seem to have invited their readers to collude in the creation of an illusion of femininity. But these girls were, in a sense, being blackmailed by a fear of failure as women. The main device used in these magazines to encourage girls to co-operate in the construction of feminine beauty was the argument that their heterosexual identity depended on it as did their future marriage and happiness.

Magazines presented a number of positive images of girls in their late teens. What they all had in common was heterosexuality and potential or actual marriage and motherhood. Single and childless older women were never presented as models for girls to emulate; their sexuality was increasingly questioned and they were frequently depicted in magazines as physically unattractive. This conveyed a clear correlation between femininity, feminine beauty and heterosexuality. Readers were subsequently encouraged to construct their own adult self-images around marriage, motherhood and domesticity. To achieve this state a girl had to attract and marry a man. But to secure and maintain a marriage and a positive self-image of themselves as an older woman, girls and young wives had to look both pretty and young. The link between femininity and youth explicitly denied readers' experiences of growing up and growing old and seems to have been the cause of much anxiety. Indeed magazines, especially adverts, exploited readers' subsequent vulnerability (which is apparent in magazine correspondence) to persuade them to comply with their advice and prescriptions of femininity. For instance, James Drawbell, the editor of *Woman's Own*, recognized women's vulnerability about ageing but he actively worked to perpetuate the beliefs that created and sustained it. In his autobiography Drawbell described females as 'objects of curiosity and pity' because of their dependency on men:

> This dependency, calling for affection and companionship makes a woman painfully vulnerable. She is always in need of reassurance, always aware that every day she is growing older and that her face and her figure (the mainstay of her personal security) will soon be challenged by the hordes of fresh young girls to whom men are always attracted.[20]

Although this example refers specifically to a woman's magazine, it does indicate that at least some editors deliberately utilised this strategy to promote their prescriptions.

A girl's fate depended on her face; a feminine appearance was a commodity to be bartered in exchange for love, food and shelter. Consistent with this, girls were told to be feminine *for* men or to conform to *male* standards of feminine beauty; such a policy rested on the assumption that the majority of girls would want to, or feel they should, get married. *Girls' Favourite* in 1922 advised its readers that 'there are certain things a boy notices a great deal in connection with a girl. The way she dresses for instance ... They love to see a girl turned out in neat and pretty, and yet smart clothes.'[21] Advice regarding what constituted a feminine look was often delivered by a male figure such as 'Peg's Man Pal' and girls were frequently encouraged to seek a man's advice and approval on matters of appearance:

> Your father knows what men like about women. Therefore take his advice. If he says you are making yourself cheap, or you look terrible with your hair like that or in that dress, remember he has a masculine point of view and take his advice.[22]

The emotional and economic argument that if a girl wanted to get and keep a man, wanted a home and family, she must always appear feminine, was used throughout adverts, articles, fiction and letter pages in romance magazines. During the twenties magazines flattered girls' intelligence and spirit, and female heroines were portrayed as adventurous, mischievous and plucky. In spite of this, fiction and articles continued to focus on appearance; heroines were introduced face first and girls were constantly reminded not to be apathetic about their looks. Love was presented by romance magazines as the crucial factor in marriage and yet young wives were warned that their husband's affections depended on them retaining a feminine appearance.[23] Magazines were well aware of the rigours of child care and domestic work but in encouraging readers to maintain the illusion of a feminine appearance they also fostered the idea that domestic work was light and easy; implicit in this was the assumption that man's work in the public sphere was more arduous and also superior to women's domestic work. As women grew older the focus on feminine beauty lessened and they were judged increasingly on their domestic competence. Magazine covers reflect this shift in emphasis. Covers on girls' magazines and papers for young wives and mothers featured models who shared youthful faces; the only differences between a teenage girl and a young married woman in her thirties were their hair-styles, clothes and posture. In contrast, magazines for middle-aged readers featured distinctly older women portrayed with children or engaged in domestic or craft activities.

Magazine messages regarding the importance of a feminine appearance seriously and overtly undermined the reader's confidence. Some magazines even denigrated a girl's employment capabilities in stressing the importance of appearance. Guest contributor, F.E. Bailey, writing for the monthly magazine *Miss Modern* in 1930 addressed the 18-year-old office worker and advised her to 'use your sex-weapons with discretion in the battle of a career':

> In my opinion you would be foolish not to use your good looks
> discreetly in order to help your career, . . . Besides, if you want to carve
> a career, some day you must graduate from secretarial work to
> something more important, and then you may have to compete with
> men, and men have better brains than women. Consequently you must
> use your looks to supplement your brain.[24]

Readers were told that not only was a career likely to depend on good looks, but
also their efficiency and self-respect. Many girls who wrote to the magazines
were greatly influenced by these messages which the correspondence editor was
frequently forced to contradict. Writing to *Girls' Friend* in 1930, Tillie told how
she 'has always been the pretty one of our family, and great things are expected
of me, as far as marriage is concerned'. In reply, Tillie was told that 'it isn't
always the pretty girl who wins the rich husband you know. That's a fallacy.'[25]
The reply is ironic as within these magazines the pretty girl nearly always won
the rich and handsome husband. The contradiction within a magazine between
fiction and articles could hardly have been reassuring for the reader.

Not only did marriage depend on looking feminine but, according to these
magazines, so did one's popularity. Girls were clearly told that their posture,
voice, clothes and body were reliable indicators of personality and through
numerous articles they were schooled in how to read facial beauty, dress, posture
and voice as clues to the character of a woman, be she real or fictional. A
feminine appearance indicated a feminine personality. If a girl did not look
feminine then she was not feminine and was therefore a disagreeable person.
Throughout the period romance magazines featured numerous articles judging
personality from all types of physical characteristics; there was never any
indication that personality may have been socially determined. Fiction reinforced this association between looks and personality. In schoolgirl papers the
popular girl always had curly hair and a round face, in contrast the bad girl had
lank hair and a sharp face;[26] similarly in romance magazines the difference
between the older heroine and the evil woman was manifest in their appearance.
Imagery was very important in conveying this difference. Doris Langley was
described in child-like terms as a 'pretty, fair-headed girl'; in contrast the evil
Belle Hammond's beauty was described in terms of a deadly sweet poison, she
had a 'sharp alluring beauty' and Sadie, who bore the mark of Satan, was
described as 'lovely with a dark passionate loveliness'.[27] The contrasting of fair
and dark which was typical of comparisons between heroines and female
villains, was, as we shall see, clearly linked to prevailing racist stereotypes.
Animal images and colour were also commonly used to convey personality in
magazine fiction. For example, Carmen Beresford, the haughty, selfish and

heartless actress was presented 'curled up on a big black couch, with he
pillowed against a huge purple cushion'.[28] When Carmen was angry sl
'hiss of an angry cat'. This imagery is interesting in that it conveys the sense
and the cruelty of Carmen, but most importantly it suggests her impotency; the
hiss of an angry cat seems trivial when pitted against the aroused wrath of the
male hero.

Although a feminine face was vital as a sign of acceptability, magazines also
placed considerable emphasis on dress; the impression was that clothes and hair-
style acted as a reinforcement to feminine behaviour. During the 1920s, for
instance, the fact that girls wore short skirts was widely interpreted as a sign of
their modernity, especially in sexual matters. This was a misleading interpretation of dress which some historians of the First World War have
replicated.[29] The link between clothes and gender identity was quite hotly
debated in the magazines of the forties when girls were wearing trousers for
heavy industrial and agricultural work. According to some this was entirely
inconsistent with femininity. Derek Bond, a film star of the era, was asked to
comment for *Red Star Weekly* (1950) on whether girls should wear trousers. His
reply clearly reveals that the issue of gender identity was at stake:

> You don't really want to be equal to men, do you? Wouldn't you rather
> remain a woman with all the respect and privileges of your sex? ...
> Look like a girl and men will consciously regard you as such. That's the
> way it should be in the natural order of things ... she provides a
> complement to my own sex.[30]

Dress, according to this statement, was vitally important for the way girls were
regarded and treated, in fact their 'privileges' depended on it. But as we saw in
the discussion of the 'lady', these privileges were often double-edged. In this
case, 'privilege' merely allocated females a restricted sphere of activity which
was labelled inferior to the public sphere occupied by males.

Body Matters: Puberty and Pregnancy

Presentations of femininity and feminine beauty in magazines were quite
separate from discussions of the functions of the developing female body. While
appearance was an appropriate topic of concern and discussion in girls'
magazines, the physiological development and maturity of the girl's body was
not; it was either ignored, diminished or treated as abnormal. In its place
magazines presented a particular form of socially constructed body as the norm.
What magazines demonstrate here is the changing and also age-specific division
between public and private knowledge, a matter which had significant implications for girls' control over their own bodies.

Presenting certain body images as the norm for girls was a powerful argument to persuade readers to conform. For example, hair-free limbs were defined by magazines as feminine, heroines never had hairy legs or armpits. Throughout the period many adverts appeared in magazines selling depilatory creams, which referred to female body hair as 'superfluous', 'unnatural' and 'masculine'. This advert from *Poppy's Paper* in 1930 was typical:

> There is nothing more repellant to a man than a masculine growth of hair on the limbs and arms – it robs a woman of every vestige of daintiness and charm. Remove this disfigurement which breaks romance and spoils your happiness and joy.[31]

This advert clearly shows how a natural female characteristic was re-defined as unfeminine, even as an exclusively masculine feature. It also points to the artificial separation of the sexes which was frequently used to justify the different and inferior status of women in society.

Magazines presented a very unreal picture of adolescent girlhood. Characters in magazine fiction did not manifest any physical changes during adolescence and articles did not deal with these matters. This insistence on an asexual adolescent model was most extreme in the Amalgamated Press schoolgirl papers whose artists were told to 'play down' girls' breasts, and in swimming scenes to keep the girls submerged up to their armpits.[32] Letters concerning pubescence only occasionally featured in the mother-daughter magazines in the forties though it was not the case that magazines did not receive such letters. Evidence of the concern generated by puberty can be found in the study of letters addressed to *Girl* between April 1953 and March 1955. Although this study is outside the period being discussed its results and observations are nevertheless very relevant. James Hemming, education consultant for *Girl* and *Eagle* examined 3259 problem letters from girls. He noted that 16.1 per cent of problems were associated with anxieties about physical characteristics and deportment. A major worry for girls was the size and shape of their breasts. Hemming also discovered a 'continuing obscurantism' concerning the physical aspects of sexuality which resulted in many anxious letters about menstruation, sexuality and the 'facts of life'.[33] However, *Girl*, like earlier schoolgirl papers, did not feature any discussion of the subject and fiction heroines always conformed to the asexual ideal of the female adolescent.

It would seem that magazines experienced tension as the needs of their readers could not always be publicly recognized and catered to. Athough schoolgirl papers were keen to avoid a public discussion of puberty they were aware of their readers' anxieties and prepared to answer queries personally:

I am sure there are lots of readers of the *Schoolgirls' Weekly* who are sometimes at a loss to know what is the right and wrong thing to do in matters of etiquette. Well, if there are such readers, I shall be delighted to answer such queries through the columns of the paper. Or, if there are other matters, and you desire a personal reply, just write to 'The Editor' ... and enclose a self-addressed envelope.[34]

In this way, the physical changes associated with puberty remained a private and highly individual matter.

In spite of the fact that the magazine readers were pubescent girls and newly matured women, menstruation was considered a taboo subject by girls' magazines and it was not until the thirties that letter replies concerned with menstruation occasionally appeared in romance magazines. Magazine silence about menstruation was typical of society's reticence in discussing this matter. The effects of this division between public and private information probably accentuated the stresses experienced by many girls at adolescence as few received any sex education. Griffith noted in the 1940s that while many boys received sex education at school, 'I am doubtful if the same can be said for girls. Far too many girls' schools ignore the subject altogether or deal with it in a wishy washy way.'[35] In recognition of this, the Board of Education issued advice to teachers and youth leaders on providing sex education for young people, especially young women. In spite of this, magazines continued to avoid the issue. Despite their 'personal' relationship with their readers, girls' magazines were too much a public medium to address such matters overtly.

Denied explicit information from home, school or the media, many girls were quite frightened at the onset of menstruation. Angela Rodaway suffered agonies from ignorance: 'I was almost certain that I should die. Everyone else in my form at school, next day, was almost certain too.'[36] Girls may have turned to magazines but with the exception of occasional letters on the Doctor or Nurse page and adverts for 'Dr William's Pink Pills' and sanitary towels, which appeared in the mother-daughter magazines in the forties, periods were not mentioned. Nevertheless, adverts were important. They were the only sign that Fiona McFarlane had when she was growing up that periods happened to other women besides herself:

> they never did mention it in those days, this would be 1946 to 1947, it just wasn't mentioned – I gradually worked out that these periods must happen regularly, because look at all the advertisements for sanitary towels there were, and if it only happened once in a lifetime you wouldn't need this massive advertising campaign.[37]

The advertising that concerned periods came in two forms with adverts for sanitary towels and iron tablets. In both, periods were treated as an ailment and handicap, rather than as a healthy sign of female reproductive maturity. Many sanitary towel adverts revealed an ambivalence between recognising girls as capable individuals in the social and employment spheres and feeling that they were inferior because 'handicapped' by a periodic loss of blood. For example, a 'Lilia' advert (1932) described how

> Modern women cannot afford to be handicapped by Nature's disabilities. In the very full and active lives we lead there is no place for woman's weakness, no room for off days ... The freedom of full health for every day in the calendar is a stark necessity for every woman who works.[38]

It is strange that sanitary towels were advertised as if they were some sort of medication which would cure women of their natural disabilities. Adverts for 'Dr William's Pink Pills' which appeared throughout the interwar years similarly treated periods as a problem when they referred to the onset of menstruation as those 'perilous years'. As this advert (1940) explains,

> In her teens many a girl outgrows her strength. She is entering womanhood and can't meet the demands made on her system. She becomes thin, pale and irritable: her head droops, she is languid, has headaches and backaches and the least exertion leaves her breathless – she is anaemic.[39]

Whilst it is difficult to be precise as to the extent of anaemia amongst adolescent girls, it is likely to have been quite prevalent arising from poor nutrition; the Women's Health Enquiry noted that 588 out of the 1250 women in its sample suffered from anaemia in the thirties.[40] What is significant about the advert for 'Pink Pills' is that anaemia was treated as a problem of adolescent female physiology rather than as an outcome of poverty and poor nutrition.

Pregnancy was also a taboo subject in girls' magazines in the twenties, in spite of the fact that motherhood was constantly presented as a woman's fulfilment. Magazines appeared to be reflecting the attitude that pregnancy was 'low', an attitude endorsed by Miss Helena Powell in an essay entitled 'The problem of the adolescent girl' (1924) in which she claimed that the 'beauty and the essence of motherhood lie not mainly in the bearing of children, but in the devotion, the patience, the understanding which makes the real mother.'[41] The realities of pregnancy were never discussed in the fiction or in the articles of girls' magazines although, in line with government maternal welfare schemes, advice on mother and child nutrition was featured.[42]

During the 1930s mother-daughter magazines began to discuss more openly the moral and economic implications of pregnancy. These magazines featured a number of letters from readers who had been abandoned after having conceived out of wedlock. For some this had occurred in the First World War, while for others it was more recent. The dilemma which most of these readers raised was whether they should admit they had an illegitimate child to a current suitor and thereby risk jeopardising their chances of marriage. Correspondence editors were sensitive to their readers' problem (1935): 'Many girls like you have paid the penalty of trusting and being deceived. There is little shame if you do your duty by your child, and pick up the threads of your life afresh.'[43] As this reply suggests, a girl was not harshly treated if she devoted herself to the care of her illegitimate child. In the context of the Second World War when mother-daughter magazines received numerous letters from girls and women who were pregnant out of marriage, these magazines remained supportive of their readers. This was partly in recognition of the prevalence of pre-marital sex amongst young people intending to marry. It was also linked to a concern for the health of the unborn child. In a letter to *Lucky Star*'s 'Ask the family doctor' in 1940, a girl wrote that her friend was having a baby outside marriage, the father having been killed before he could return to marry her. The doctor was quite sympathetic, but his major concern was for the child; he reminded readers to help girls who were pregnant outside wedlock because a harassed mother harmed the child she carried. Referring to the suffering of unmarried mothers the doctor revealed how strong opposition to pregnancy outside marriage remained in the forties:

> It is very terrifying for a girl who has always lived a straight life to find that she is going to be an unmarried mother. She knows she will lose her job, she realises that she will be blamed and probably scorned, and having a baby is quite a big and perilous enough adventure in itself.[44]

While the treatment of pregnancy in mother-daughter magazines corresponded to a more open approach arising from recognition of the importance of a mother's health during pregnancy, numerous taboos still remained around this subject.[45]

The biological and social reproduction of children was a major rationale behind the increased discussion of women's bodies and health in the late 1930s and 1940s. The demands of heterosexual development as a prelude to marriage and motherhood, were similarly frameworks in which information about the adolescent girl's body and sexuality could be addressed. For example, the discussion of menstruation and sex education in mother-daughter magazines during the thirties followed on the heels of debates which drew attention to the inadequacy of sex education and the need for sex instruction through schools. These debates were couched in terms of managing heterosexual development, promoting the family and the reproduction of the race.[46] Such concerns also defined the advice of magazine correspondence editors. Robin Kent suggests that by the 1940s there was an opening up of sex discussion in women's magazines, what she calls the 'breakthrough into the bedroom'.[47] My survey suggests that although mother-daughter magazines increasingly tackled matters concerning marital sex, birth control and pregnancy in their correspondence features, especially their medical columns, very little detail was actually presented to the reader. Moreover, magazines for working girls continued to be reticent in discussion of the female body, sexuality and sexual practice. Letters dealing with such matters were often given only brief and cryptic replies – in reply to 'Curly Tops', in 1940, *Peg's Paper* replied 'Yes; pregnancy can follow then just as easily as any other.'[48] Frequently readers with sex-related problems were invited to send in a self-addressed envelope so that their queries could be answered personally. In reply to a troubled wife, Nurse Janet (1940) wrote:

> I cannot discuss your question here, but I should like to help you if you will write to me privately... I feel you are not being fair to your husband and you too must change your views if your married life is to be really happy. Why not read a thoroughly practical book dealing with the problems of married life? I shall be very pleased to recommend one. It has helped a great many people to start their married life with mutual understanding. You are wrong in thinking there is anything ugly or gross. It is simply that you do not understand these matters properly.[49]

While this can be seen as modesty on the part of correspondence editors as open discussion of sex was not generally acceptable, it also conveys an acknowledgement of the importance of marital sex. Nevertheless, these magazines were most interested in the promotion of healthy babies and families. Consistent with these concerns and with government pronatalist policies, editors were against providing information concerning birth control, particularly to young couples: 'My advice to all healthy young people is to have babies early in marriage.'[50]

Sexuality

Female sexuality was a central theme of the fiction in romance magazines and although an assumption of heterosexuality permeated every corner of these papers they rarely addressed this topic directly. Schoolgirl magazines avoided sexuality almost completely although glimmers of sexual attraction can be seen in some of the fiction, especially that featuring heroines in their late teens.[51]

Romance fiction invariably portrayed female sexuality as latent, clearly signalling the heroine's virginity, and the drama unfolded around its arousal. A favourite phrase of magazine fiction was an initial description of the heroine as a 'sweet untaught girl'. Female sexuality, except in the case of the overtly sexual and bad female character, was described as passive and it was often characterised as a fruit, nearly ripe and waiting to be picked and eaten. Men, in contrast, were sexually pro-active and it was they who aroused the heroine's sexuality. Because an active, independent female sexuality was labelled as unfeminine, fiction heroines became pregnant either through innocence, being misled, or through the unconscious workings of their maternal instinct; girls rarely took the initiative in lovemaking.

It is significant that a heroine in love was nearly always reduced to a child-like stature and behaviour; she was described with 'a glow of almost childish pleasure on the softly contoured face', she had the 'face of an innocent candid child', and after marriage she was frequently referred to as a 'girl-wife'.[52] This was a very impotent, passive and innocent image of mature adult females and it would seem that her powerlessness was one of her chief attractions. For this reason the heroine was frequently portrayed in the presence of an over-bearing or bullying person because this enhanced her desirability in the eyes of the hero. It was not only her sexuality which was portrayed as child-like, but also her body, which was devoid of body hair and denied physical maturity.[53] The presentation of the adult female as emotionally, physically and sexually child-like was a clear denial of female independence. The message of femininity portrayed in the magazines served to reduce the adult female from mature adulthood, thereby creating a wide separation between adult male and artificially child-like female; implicit in this was an assumption of male superiority. This distinction between male and female sexuality was carried over into the non-fiction elements of romance magazines. However, even the schoolgirl magazine, the *Girls' Own Paper*, made this distinction in a rare article on boyfriends (1946) in which girls were informed about the different 'make-up' of the sexes and the misunderstandings that could often arise:

> boys do not always realise how very little holding hands in the 'flicks'
> or a goodnight kiss often mean to a girl, because although men always
> tell us how sensitive and emotional *we* are, the fact is that most of us
> do *not* get excited about bodily contacts.[54]

Although women were apparently emotionally altered by sex experience they were otherwise somewhat unmoved by sexual foreplay. Boys, girls were warned, could get terribly excited: 'Little things that mean nothing to you may cause him to lose his self-control altogether.'[55] Girls were clearly responsible for ensuring that 'things' did not go too far.

Female sexuality was alternatively described in maternal terms and a heroine was frequently depicted drawing her lover's head down onto her bosom offering motherly reassurance and security. A clear example of this can be seen in this story from *Woman* in 1937. Jim and Celie had been married two years,

Celie was concerned for Jim's health – 'suddenly she felt rising in her that emotion that usually came when her babies were in her arms.'[56] This comment suggests that Celie felt a maternal protectiveness towards Jim. Often a girl's romantic adventures or her pregnancy were presented as a search for emotional satisfaction that had otherwise been denied her; in this context, it invariably meant the satisfaction of the maternal instinct. This was reiterated in the articles and letters of mother-daughter magazines of the forties once discussion was more open in these papers. Nurse Elizabeth's advice to a 31-year-old reader of *Silver Star* in 1950 who enquired about sex outside marriage clearly conveys this link between sex and motherhood:

> A girl suffers psychologically, although I cannot go into that fully here. Sex experience is much more profound than most of us realise, and with a girl it is intermingled with her desire for a home and children, and so a sense of disappointment, of something missing, is bound to follow. She is conscious of a feeling of frustration, of a certain amount of strain.[57]

Linking female sexuality to the maternal 'instinct' was common during this period. Judge Lindsey excused the sex delinquency of adolescent girls by arguing that a girl's interest in boys may 'be regarded as maternal, just as the liking of a little girl for dolls may be interpreted as maternal'.[58] He went on to claim that female sex offenders did not have sex for its own sake – 'They are not fresh bodies offered for the pleasure of men but bodies offered to the agony and bloody sweat of motherhood. That is what it really means with most of them whether they and we are conscious of it or not.'[59] Similarly during the Second World War, Russell attempted to explain female promiscuity in terms of the maternal instinct:

> A woman (whether married or not) who has begun her active sex life is meant to become a mother, you cannot first rouse, and then frustrate, basic human instincts and expect to get off scott free. The very impulse which drives her towards motherhood may (unless she marries) turn her into a woman that mothers despise.[60]

There are a number of possible reasons why the idea of a maternal sexuality gained popularity in this period. Motherhood was central to femininity. By defining female sexuality as controlled by the maternal instinct, psychologists and social commentators could continue to maintain that all females were driven by a desire for motherhood; contrary evidence regarding female sexuality could be encompassed and redefined within this model. The case of unmarried mothers did, however, reveal tensions between patriarchal and capitalist interests embodied in this notion of femininity. On the one hand, unmarried mothers produced children and thereby fulfilled one of the demands of the state for an increase in the birth rate. On the other hand, in being pregnant outside of wedlock, an unmarried mother was not under direct male control through marriage. Single, childless women were, in contrast, quite clearly a threat to the interests of both patriarchy and capital in that they did not bear children and they remained independent of male control. Perhaps this explains Judge Lindsey's more lenient treatment of the young unmarried mother than the single school teacher in this description; 'she went to one of her teachers, an old maid, who would have been a far better and wiser and more charitable person if during her own childhood she had been guilty of the same misstep this child had made.'[61] The recognition of female sexuality, albeit in a limited form, was also related to the changing place of sexuality within marriage. Jeffreys argues that the role of the wife changed during the twentieth century and that in effect she replaced the prostitute in satisfying her husband's sexual needs.[62] This required that the married woman should enjoy sexual intercourse, and that she regard her sexuality as good not immoral; this could be achieved, in part, by linking sexuality to her maternal impulse. It is also possible that attempts to define unmarried mothers in a more positive light were linked to government policies to promote motherhood arising from official concerns about the declining birth rate which, it was feared, would lead to a population crisis. The philosophy that women had a sexuality but that it was really motivated by the maternal instinct made a restricted form of female sexuality respectable, but once again it denied women a sexuality in their own right and reduced female sexuality to a controllable form.

Motherhood appears to have been a crucial consideration in the ethics of romance magazines. By protecting the status of motherhood, magazines achieved more long-term protection of patriarchal interests as well as meeting capital's need for a new generation of workers. It is also likely that magazines avoided estranging many readers who had illegitimate children or who were close to a woman in this position, as was particularly likely during the Second World War with the increase in illegitimate births among young women. During the 1930s magazine fiction introduced the young distressed unmarried mother figure. Magazines appear to have been quite daring in their pursuit of new story lines and they probably recognised the semi-tragic appeal of the virtuous unmarried mother. They were, however, anxious not to challenge patriarchal interests which promoted the image of woman as sexually naïve and passive. Magazines achieved a compromise. Although pre-marital sex was discouraged, unmarried mothers were not harshly depicted in the fiction as long as their case fulfilled three main qualifications. Firstly, that the girl had not sought sex for itself, she had either been misled by a man, or consciously or unconsciously sought the fulfilment of her maternal instinct. In this way she remained ignorant about sex and her sexuality. Secondly, the heroine's pregnancy was never mentioned or revealed in the illustrations. Thirdly, once the girl had given birth to the child she had to be a devoted and proficient mother. Given these exacting conditions it is not surprising that some unmarried mothers were treated somewhat harshly in the fiction. In 'The Sin In The Preacher's House' (1935), Lily Mar was married to a preacher who was ignorant of the fact that she had 'abandoned' her illegitimate baby when she was 16 years of age. After 17 years Lily meets Rachel, her illegitimate daughter, who does not know her mother. Rachel is presented as an unruly adolescent, full of anger at her unknown mother's desertion. Indeed she tells Lily how much she hates and despises her mother and when she becomes pregnant outside wedlock she blames her mother for her predicament. The crisis peaks when Rachel reveals that the father of her illegitimate child is Dick, a respected member of the community and Lily's best friend and confidant.[63]

It is interesting that although we are told that Lily became pregnant as a result of being misled by a man who promptly deserted her, Lily was nevertheless punished in the story; her disgrace in the eyes of the author is apparent in the choice of her name Lily *Marr*. It would appear that Lily was harshly treated not because she became pregnant outside of wedlock but because she abandoned her child, inevitably causing her much damage. Throughout this period the mother was believed to be essential to the full and healthy development of a child. Abandoning a child was a terrible crime and any problems in the child's subsequent development could be blamed on the mother. This emphasis on the mother-child relationship received a boost in the forties and fifties with the arguments of Bowlby.[64]

Female sexuality in magazine fiction was acceptable if separated from a desire for sex, and if it was either child-like in its passivity or maternal. However there were some anomalies in magazine fiction. Leila Brandon is an unusual fiction character. She was a likeable person and generally 'good' but once her sexuality had been aroused it could not be contained, she seemed to want sex solely for pleasure and entered into a torrid adulterous affair with a past boyfriend; 'he had awakened in her a swift, unceasing hunger that, perhaps, might have been satisfied with marriage.'[65] As if to explain her infidelity we are told that Leila comes from a family where madness is rife; we are also informed that her husband is paralysed from the waist downwards following an accident so that she could not have children with him nor, it is implied, a 'normal' marital sex life. It is never made clear in the story whether Leila's sexuality would have been satisfied by her husband if he had not been paralysed or whether she was sexually over-active. It is also possible that her affair with her past boyfriend was inevitable because he had been her first, and therefore true, love. This last situation was often alluded to by psychologists who argued that once a girl fell in love and was aroused by a man she would always remain his, and she would only be fulfilled in marriage and motherhood. The safety catches in this story, for example the hint that Leila may be mad and therefore unlike normal passively sexual women, suggest that all three factors were involved.

Two important themes emerge from this analysis of magazine presentations of female sexuality, these are control and maternity. Girls either had a passive sexuality controlled by men and/or their sexuality was family and child orientated. Both denied women a sexuality in their own right reducing it to a controllable form which served capitalist needs for the reproduction of the labour force and male requirements for monogamous, heterosexual, subordinate females. These ways of understanding female sexuality were reinforced and mystified by the widely held belief that males and females experienced love and sex differently. Boys, according to the expert Cyril Burt, had relatively stronger aggressive instincts, while girls had the stronger maternal/protective and self-subjective instincts.[66] This reasoning lay behind discussions of female sexuality throughout the period 1920 to 1950; surprisingly, attitudes changed very little over these years. Judge Lindsey employed this idea in the twenties in his widely read study of female sexual delinquency:

all normal women are monogamous by instinct. By this I mean, not that she would be incapable of enjoying sex relations with more than one man, but that her maternal instinct, with an eye to the interests of herself and her potential children, is a check. Men, because their biological relations with their offspring are less close, do not experience this check to the same degree.[67]

Mace reiterated this argument in 1948:

A man can take his pleasure from one woman, forget about it, and go on to another woman ... A woman takes the personal side of the relationship more seriously. Besides she doesn't just want sex. That's only part of her need. She wants a home and children. And that means a steady relationship with one man.[68]

Interlinked with this, as we have seen, was the idea of a pro-active male sexuality and a passive female sexuality. This neatly packaged argument rationalised female monogamy and women's domestic and maternal roles; it also justified a double standard in sexual relationships.

In contrast to the treatment of the heroine's sexuality, male heroes had an active, even aggressive sexuality: there was 'nothing small, nothing tender about this love of his. It was a fierce desire, the passion of a lion for his lioness, a tiger for his mate.'[69] This aggressive sexuality was bestowed upon him by 'nature' and 'instinct': 'Instinctively he knew it [that he had her] and the knowledge surged through his veins, made his pulses race, rousing not the better part of him, but the primitive brute that lurks in every man, hidden, sleeping, waiting for the spark of passion to kindle it into flaming activity.'[70] When women were depicted as possessing an active sexuality they were also, with few exceptions, portrayed as evil. Unlike the hero, the active sexuality of bad women was promiscuous and unrelated to feelings of love. Louise, for example, 'liked men of any age, as long as they were men . . . her desires never lost fire'.[71] The 'bewitching' Carla Jenson who issued 'poisoned kisses' to unsuspecting men was another sexually active character.[72] The evil woman posed a threat to patriarchal relations in a number of ways. Her attempts to improve her social and economic position through remarriage, adultery and divorce show that she was trying to exert power over men; her active, independent sexuality defied male control; and her dismissal of marital and maternal roles and responsibilities threatened the family which represented an institutionalised form of patriarchal relations. It was for these reasons that the sexually active woman was always drawn as promiscuous and as evil. However, the introduction of characters like Cora Cripen, Carla Jenson and Sadie Bracken into romance magazines, did represent an attempt by editors to compromise readers' power fantasies with patriarchal expectations of girls.

Fowler has suggested that these evil female characters should be understood in terms of bourgeois morality. The femme fatale, she explains, 'exhibits in condensed form the stereotypes of the evil capitalist': her sexual excesses infringe Puritan sexual asceticism while her unbridled consumption, avoidance of work and love of luxury were anathema to the Protestant work ethic.[73] These motifs were indeed recurring and important aspects of the fictional representation of the evil woman. More generally the dislike of excess and the promotion of the work ethic pervaded both the fiction and non-fiction elements of these magazines. The work ethic which magazines promoted so unremittingly was not exclusively concerned with paid labour or indeed unpaid domestic labour, it also applied to the servicing of men as we saw in chapter 5 and the promotion of heterosexual body work.

Mirroring the depiction of the evil woman, the villain was similarly work shy and sexually unrestrained. Interestingly the villain also reveals traces of a foreign identity; he was usually dark and swarthy conveying a middle-eastern, mediterranean or gypsy parentage. Although bad women were often related in some way to the devil it was also common to suggest that they too were not pure (white) English girls or that they associated with 'foreigners'. The linking of race and sexuality was common in the interwar years. The presence of black men in major British ports was high on the media's agenda during 1919 when race riots broke out in Tyneside, Glasgow, Liverpool, London, Cardiff and Newport spurred by fears about the shortage of housing and jobs. These riots resulted in a number of deaths; a black man in Liverpool was thrown into the docks and stoned until he drowned; three men were killed in Cardiff.[74] These economic dimensions of race conflict were not mentioned in girls' magazines which focused exclusively on the sexual threat which foreign men posed to white English girls, a threat no doubt fuelled by the drug panics which caught the media's attention in the 1920s. The significance of these lies in their equation of foreign men with drugs and the seduction of innocent white girls, especially Chinese and Jamaicans, the notable Brilliant (Billie) Chang and Edgar Manning.[75] Not surprisingly, these dangerous drug dealers were popularly portrayed as living in luxury paid for by the labours of others. Magazine fiction utilised these racist stereotypes and the drug motif to accentuate the evil of many of their male and also female villains. Carla Jenson, for example, was equipped with a secret Indian narcotic which enabled her to take control of men: 'love dreams for them – power for Carla'.

Racist suspicions also surfaced in the occasional features which explicitly addressed race. The article which we looked at in chapter 4 which cautioned girls against taking posts abroad is one such example of racist zenophobia. Another way in which this racism appeared was in the rare references to mixed-race marriages. The writer of the following 'true story' in 1932 explained how at 18 she had married a black man and after two years of marital happiness when she was expecting their first child they went to live in India: 'My first shock was to find he had five other wives as well as me, and that I was expected to live with them.' After she gave birth to a girl her husband started to neglect her so she returned to England. Her suffering was not over as the child of her marriage was the focus of considerable prejudice.[76] The treatment of this topic and the warning which this tale conveyed was not surprising in the context of attitudes during this period; it is nevertheless deeply racist and suggests that 'white' men were deeply threatened by sexual competition from other racial groups.

As race was clearly a component of fiction villains, so too was social class. Both the wayward girl and the sexually active evil woman were always working class; middle-class characters were never presented in this way and middle-class magazines avoided these types of characters. It has not been possible to discover whether this was a conscious policy of magazine editors but it would appear that magazine fiction was reflecting a widely held belief that working-class girls reached sexual maturity at an earlier age than their middle-class peers. As we have seen, during the twenties attention was directed to female sex delinquents by the work of Cyril Burt and Judge Lindsey. Judge Lindsey attempted to explain the apparently early sexual maturation of working-class girls in terms of nutrition: 'it is my opinion that well-nourished children, other things being equal, are likely to mature more slowly and normally than ill-nourished children; and that since early maturity is likely to bring with it a tendency to easily aroused sexual activity, and so-called immorality: the whole problem of malnutrition has a direct bearing on that of sexual continence in the young.'[77] According to Griffith, children from secondary modern schools matured earlier than their grammar school counterparts. Unfortunately, he lamented, those children who matured early were also those who were deprived of ethical guidance at an early age due to their expulsion from school into the labour market.[78]

Whatever the reasons for the alleged differential rates of sexual maturity, the important issue was the gulf which existed in modern times for the working-class girl between the attainment of sexual maturity and the age at which she could marry and legitimately express her sexuality.[79] Whilst this was a concern throughout the interwar period it reached new heights during the Second World War amidst fears that young working-class girls were 'running wild' and engaging in pre-marital sex. Increases in VD and pregnancy outside wedlock amongst young women were cited as evidence of this. As we have already seen, the moral panic in wartime did not lead to an opening up of discussion of body matters in schoolgirl or working girls' magazines, nor did it lead to a significant change in the treatment of female sexuality except in the mother-daughter magazines. One exception to this which emerged after the war was the occasional discussion in the *Girls' Own Paper* of young women's exploratory heterosexual activities. In the following article entitled 'Teenagers and Petting' the author addresses the question of how far a 'nice' girl should go with petting. The author reassures readers that it is quite natural that there should come a time when they are interested in boys; this 'change in attitude is a very important point in the life of the teenager. It is the first step towards a mature relationship; it is the first step in the selection of a future mate.'[80] While an occasional kiss, some hugging and holding of hands was quite acceptable the author warned girls not to drift into unwholesome relationships which could lead to unhappiness: 'Petting is biological and psychological, but when it becomes too extensive or incessant it is extremely bad for both parties', causing frustration and physical damage.[81] The author advised that teenagers who become attracted to each other should join a youth club, pursue mutual hobbies and take an interest in each other's work and family.

Romance magazines presented heterosexuality as the only option for girls and women; homosexuality was never directly referred to or portrayed, and close female friendships and crushes were extremely rare in magazines after 1920. Although there were no direct references to homosexuality, correspondence editors did receive letters from girls who they regarded as 'perverts'.[82] My interviews indicate that these 'perverts' included girls who experienced a sexual attraction towards other women and those involved in lesbian relationships. The obvious horror with which these girls' confidences were received is probably symptomatic of the more widespread hostility towards close relationships between women.

Throughout the interwar years the term 'homosexual' was bandied around and used extremely loosely to refer to any woman who refused or could not get married, or who exhibited independence (a common characterisation in novels of the twenties and thirties), or who did not passively submit and enjoy sexual intercourse with a man, preferably her husband.[83] Basically all those women who were labelled 'homosexual' were regarded as posing a threat to heterosexuality, the family and male domination. Hence feminists, spinsters, 'bachelor-girls', 'man-haters' and lesbians were all encompassed under the same umbrella.[84] The sexual behaviour of single professional women, especially teachers, came under close scrutiny.[85] Women in the acting profession also received attention and in the twenties West End theatre managers refused to employ Edy Craig, a talented actress, because of her close relationships with women.[86] Sensitivity and hostility to lesbianism was further fuelled by a spate of anti-lesbian novels. (One of these was actually recommended to the readers of the *Girls' Own Paper* as offering a more realistic impression of school life than could be found in most school stories.) In view of the pervasiveness of this anti-lesbian feeling it seems likely that the editorial staff working on girls' magazines were influenced by debates concerning lesbianism and that they were sensitive to the anti-lesbian feelings of the period. Certainly the producers of magazines would have been aware of these cases given their close involvement in national news. Northcliffe's publishing empire, for example, embraced a range of schoolgirl and working girls' papers, as well as the *Daily Mail* and *Daily Mirror*.

In view of this extended understanding of the term homosexual it is not surprising, as Sheila Jeffreys points out, that the portrait of the twenties 'independent girl' was very similar to the model of the lesbian woman popularised by psychologists;[87] this similarity is also noticeable in girls' magazines. Stekel's description of a homosexual woman compares closely with many portraits of 'modern girls' in magazines from the 1920s. The homosexual woman according to Stekel

> wishes to dominate and is afraid to submit ... She plays the she-man, trying to imitate the habits, qualities, dress and sporting qualities and even the shortcomings of men, smoking, drinking, fighting and the like. She hates motherhood, she despises nursing.[88]

A similar tone and presentation is apparent in the magazine's description of Georgina Durham (1929) as independent, self sufficient and prone to wearing plain, practical and unfeminine clothes.[89] An equally good comparison could have been achieved by examining the presentation of the evil woman character against Stekel's characterisation. Both the modern girl and the evil woman exhibited independence, a disinclination towards marriage and motherhood, and traits which magazines regarded as masculine. Although sexuality was a key feature of the bad woman, the form it took was neither passive nor maternal; the evil woman's sexuality was not subordinate to a man's sexual needs, nor was it controlled by men. These women who came across as powerful and independent in the magazines were an illustration of the psychologists' theory that the lust for exercising power compensated for a woman's thwarted maternal instincts.[90]

Adult homosexuality was widely condemned except in liberal circles, but opinions were more divided concerning close friendships between girls. Two strands are apparent on this issue. There were those who argued that same-sex relationships, or 'pashes', were a natural stage of adolescent development with many positive aspects to recommend them. Phyllis Blanchard and Ira Wile, for example, both believed in the Victorian interpretation of crushes as a good preparation for wifely roles;[91] as Wile explained, they were invaluable

> because [their] existence is usually accompanied by the development of fine character trends involving loyalties, self-sacrifice, cooperation and willingness to work for social ends. This phase of homosexual attraction does not disturb society during the adolescent period, because society does not expect reproduction from the immature.[92]

In contrast, critics regarded such relationships as unhealthy and unnatural. Griffith argued that girls' crushes were 'ill founded and the energy expended on them is wasted in unproductive daydreams ... which have no relation to reality. There is a danger that they may persist into later life, when they become possessive and unhealthy.'[93] It is significant that Griffith was more casual about male homosexuality: boys' crushes he likened to an immature phase of 'mate love' which, if prolonged, could pose a hindrance in relations with the opposite sex. While the former argument embraced girls' relationships within heterosexual development, implicit in the latter stance was a fear of latent homosexuality. Both sets of arguments, however, justified their position with reference to the promotion of heterosexuality and the safe-guarding of the family; these were clearly the crucial factors determining the acceptance or rejection of girls' behaviour. Although some academics defended close relationships between schoolgirls it would appear that public opinion was generally suspicious. Lambs and Pickthorn have argued that schools were affected by the public's intolerance of close female friendships and responded by curbing emotions and sentimentality:

> The time honoured crush or pash came under suspicion ... close friendships were automatically broken up. Increased games instead of leisure time were ordered by heads ... there arose a new race of heroines to be worshipped for their muscles rather than their ladylike manners, dainty appearance and artistic talents of Brazil idols.[94]

Certainly headmistresses at Clapham High School and Cheltenham Ladies

College issued regular lectures to their girls following the trial of Radclyffe Hall, warning them of the moral dangers of crushes.[95]

Throughout the interwar and war years, schoolgirl magazines presented close but platonic relationships between girls. During the twenties schoolgirls loved and admired each other but this manifested itself in a very constrained form: crushes were not visible. Schoolgirls of the thirties were represented as more robust and any vestiges of sentimentality between girls were phased out of these stories. This may well have been a conscious policy on the part of the editors of schoolgirl papers who were mainly middle-class conservative men, the group which most heartily attacked lesbianism during this period. Schoolgirl novels by authors such as Elsie Oxenham, famous for the Abbey School books, changed more slowly in their depiction of close female friendships. As Auchmuty explains:

in the 1920s schoolgirl writers had a unique freedom to explore all dimensions of women's love for women. As the years passed this freedom was progressively curtailed, with writers becoming more and more confused by the new heterosexual demands and the negative image of lesbianism.[96]

That these novels were slower to respond than schoolgirl magazines can be explained partly by the fact that their authors were less in touch with the 'lesbian epidemic' and because the production of books was slower to respond to changes in popular opinion than magazines produced on a weekly basis by publishers involved in the making of news.

The only instance of a crush which I have located appeared in the fiction serial 'Mabel St John's Schooldays' which appeared in the business girls' magazine, *Girls' Friend* in 1920. Mabel attended a select school for young ladies and was befriended by Mistress Madeleine. Miss Madeleine had apparently been engaged to be married but her fiancé had been killed during the 1914–1918 war which probably explained her situation as a teacher. Mabel was sympathetic to Madeleine, she knew that Madeleine was

... hungry for love that she had never known. Her great big warm heart was aching for a tenant ... she gave her affection to me, and lying there, feeling comfortably drowsy and jolly glad to be back in bed again, I thought to myself what a wonderful wife she would make ... How happy she would make a man's home for him, and if she had children how they would worship her! What a pity it was that things were as they were, and she was only a maiden lady living in her sister's school.[97]

Madeleine, according to Mabel's description, had a 'pleasant face' and 'she loved me, and I returned her affection honestly, and after Helen, and of course, mother and father and Harry, I loved this dear, kind eyed woman better than anyone I had ever known.'[98] This relationship was not limited to just emotional support and comfort, it also had a physical aspect – 'I always kissed her when there was no-one else about. She liked it, so did I, and it did not harm anyone.'[99]

Two features are particularly significant in this story. Firstly the drama was set in Victorian England when schoolgirl crushes were regarded as quite normal. Secondly the author made a point of telling the reader that Miss Madeleine was heterosexual and that she had been intent upon marriage, and that Mabel respected and cared for her because she would make such an ideal wife. In this way the author avoided any implication that their relationship was threatening to heterosexuality and the family. However the author, through Mabel, made constant defensive remarks as if she was well aware of the castigation such love might receive. There are no clues as to why this story was published in 1920 when schoolgirl papers had moved far away from this type of scenario and nineteenth century romantic friendships between women were frowned upon.

The avoidance of lesbian relationships in schoolgirl and romance magazines probably accentuated girls' feelings of isolation, and perhaps shame and persecution. The correspondence *Girl* magazine received in the fifties concerning crushes gives the impression that close female friendships were common but they were either ridiculed or punished at school; girls wrote about the withdrawal of various privileges and harsh talks from the headmistress. Hemming concluded from these letters that 'adolescents who are caught up in a crush relationship may have their perplexities increased by a sense of guilt about their feelings and by lack of understanding upon the part of those to whom they should be able to turn for support and guidance.'[100] It seems likely that when schoolgirl papers ceased to recognise crushes in their fiction and in their letter columns, girls probably felt even more alone with their feelings and experiences. Readers who wrote to *Girl* about these matters were dealt with sympathetically although, in line with the views of Wile, Hemming treated these relationships as 'just a passing phase'. It is doubtful, however, whether such matters would have received even this heterosexualised understanding by a correspondence editor on an Amalgamated Press schoolgirl paper.

Conclusion

The body was central to modernity but it was also at the heart of the differentiation of the sexes so central to patriarchal relations. During periods when gender roles and relations were disrupted, as during the two World Wars, the body seems to have attained a particularly important role in articulating sexual and social difference, thereby rationalising the sexual division of labour.

It also justified, through its particular construction of the female body as passive and child-like, the naturalness of heterosexuality and female subordination to men. In these ways the body came to embody the heterosexual imperative. Given that this body was set up to be so vocal on sexual and social matters, it is not perhaps surprising that magazines devoted so much attention to the construction of a feminine look. Nevertheless, aspects of the body's exterior were constructed by magazines as private, as were various internal components and also sexuality, and magazines avoided overt discussion of these. This silence also contributed to the construction of femininity in that it excluded aspects of girls' bodies which problematised sexual difference, or which suggested girls were not sexually or socially dependent on men. It is testimony to the significance of the female body for patriarchal relations that this was an area in which magazines for young workers and also schoolgirls were least amenable to readers' needs and interests. Spaces were made in the correspondence features and the medical columns of mother-daughter magazines to address some readers' queries. But papers for schoolgirls and working girls encouraged their readers to seek personal responses on intimate body matters and issues of sexuality. This public avoidance of matters concerning the body and sexuality denied girls knowledge, and it also excluded their experiences.

The centrality of advice on appearance in most working girls' papers clearly conveys that the leisure of girls of this age should be concerned with feminine body work. The fact that magazines for working-class schoolgirls, aged 10–14 years, and middle-class schoolgirls, aged 12–18 years, were less attentive to this topic is evidence of the significance accorded to age, and the social-class dimension of this, for girls' position in the heterosexual career.

Notes

1 For example, Tinkler (1994a), pp.385–403; Tinkler (1995a); Summerfield (1987a) and (1987c), pp.19–31. Two general collections which offer a useful introduction to historical work in this area are Smart (1992); Summerfield and Tinkler (1992).
2 Matthews (1987), pp.17–34.
3 Scott and Morgan (1993), p.viii.
4 Thanks to David Morgan for drawing my attention to this point.
5 *Girls' Favourite*, 4 February 1922, p.12.
6 Matthews (1987) p.26.
7 *Schoolgirl*, 6 January 1940, p.13 and 8 August 1931.
8 Summerfield (1987a).
9 Brownmiller (1986), p.59.
10 On the 'backlash' see Beddoe (1989).
11 Coward (1984), p.30.
12 *Miss Modern*, November 1940, p.18.

13 Faderman (1985), p.339.
14 *Woman*, October 1940, p.17.
15 *Girls' World*, 7 March 1927.
16 *Poppy's Paper*, 2 February 1934, p.l0.
17 *Lucky Star*, 6 January 1940, p.l8.
18 *Girls' Weekly*, 3 January 1920, p.2.
19 *Woman*, 24 February 1945, pp.l8, 23.
20 Drawbell (1968), p.49.
21 *Girls' Favourite*, 4 February 1922.
22 *Miss Modern*, 25 February 1935.
23 This was most powerfully and overtly expressed in the new women's service magazines, *Woman* and *Woman's Own*. See for example, *Woman's Own*, 5 January 1935, p.449.
24 *Miss Modern*, October 1930, pp.22, 42.
25 *Girls' Friend*, 19 July 1930, p.32.
26 Cadogan and Craig (1986), p.246.
27 *Oracle*, 11 February 1933; *Secrets*, 5 November 1932.
28 *Girls' Weekly*, 3 January 1920.
29 Marwick (1991), p.151; Graves and Hodge (1991), p.39.
30 *Red Star Weekly*, 16 September 1950, p.31.
31 *Poppy's Paper*, 25 January 1930.
32 Cadogan and Craig (1986), p.244.
33 Hemming (1960), p.70–1; also pp.128–31.
34 *Schoolgirl's Weekly*, 21 October 1922.
35 Griffith (1947), p.28.
36 Rodaway (1985), p.77.
37 Rowbotham and McCrindle (1977), p.219.
38 *Woman's Own*, 15 October 1937, p.35.
39 *Peg's Paper*, 8 January 1940, p.26.
40 Spring Rice (1981), pp.57–61, cited in Beddoe (1989), p.110.
41 Powell (1924).
42 Lewis (1980).
43 *Lucky Star*, 14 September 1935, p.34; also *Fortune* 24 October 1936, p.2, 31 October 1936, p.31, 19 December 1936, p.2.
44 *Lucky Star*, 6 January 1940, p.ll and 12 March 1945, p.15.
45 Roberts (1984), p.104.
46 Griffith (1947), pp.9, 28; Calverton and Schmalhausen (1929).
47 Kent (1979), p.247.
48 *Peg's Paper*, 10 August 1940, p.27.
49 *Peg's Paper*, 10 April 1940, p.40.
50 *Lucky Star*, 7 September 1935, p.34.
51 This silence was inconsistent with schoolgirl experience, see Hemming (1960), ch.6.
52 *Girls' Weekly*, 3 January 1920, p.2; *Poppy's Paper*, 2 November 1929, p.7.
53 Coward (1984), makes a similar point.
54 *Girls' Own Paper*, July 1946, pp.12–13, 46.
55 Ibid.
56 *Woman*, 5 July 1937, p.25; also *Lucky Star* 1940, p.18.

57 *Silver Star*, 10 February 1950, p.19.
58 Lindsey and Evans (1928), p.84.
59 Ibid., p.88.
60 Russell (1940), p.28.
61 Lindsey and Evans (1928), p.186.
62 Jeffreys (1985), pp.166–7, 169.
63 *Lucky Star*, 12 October 1935, p.2.
64 Riley (1983).
65 *Lucky Star*, 5 October 1940, p.22.
66 Board of Education (1923), p.89.
67 Lindsey and Evans (1928), p.191.
68 Mace (1948), p.42.
69 *Poppy's Paper*, 2 February 1924.
70 *Peg's Paper*, 1930, p.3.
71 *Lucky Star*, 'The Girl Who Stole Their Men' 1940, p.7.
72 *Poppy's Paper*, 'The Passionate Kisses of Carla Jenson', January 1930.
73 Fowler (1991), ch.3 especially p.54.
74 Kohn (1992), p.148.
75 Ibid.
76 *Woman's Own*, 3 December 1932, p.271. A similar story is told in 'I Loved A Coloured Man', *Lucky Star*, 7 September 1935 in which a reader tells of how she loved Haj who is later revealed to have a harem back in India which he expects her to join.
77 Lindsey and Evans (1928), p.148.
78 Griffith (1947), p.96.
79 Jordan and Fisher (1955), p.107; Blanchard (1929), p.540; Griffith (1947), p.59; Lindsey and Evans (1928), p.54; Schwaab and Veeder (1929), pp.24–5, 100.
80 *Girls' Own Paper*, July 1948, pp.24, 56.
81 Ibid.
82 In my interviews with people who were involved in magazine publishing 1920–1950 I asked whether letters were received from lesbians or readers confused about their sexuality. I was told by one interviewee that some letters were received from 'sexual deviants', another informant referred to 'sex perverts at times'. In both these cases, further information was not forthcoming. Whilst these responses are ambiguous about the sexual identity of readers and their 'problems', these two replies nevertheless speak volumes about contemporary attitudes to women who strayed from the heterosexual norm.
83 Jeffreys (1985), ch.9; Faderman (1985), Pt III, ch.3.
84 Vicinus (1985), p.208.
85 Oram (1989).
86 Holledge (1981), p.155.
87 Jeffreys (1985), ch.9.
88 Ibid., p.170.
89 *Poppy's Paper*, 9 November 1929. Fiction invariably featured the heroine reverting to femininity.
90 Jeffreys (1985), ch.9.
91 Blanchard (1924), pp.136–7; Wile (1929).
92 Wile (1929), p.608.

93 Griffith (1947), p.183.
94 Lamb and Pickthorn (1968), p.71.
95 Humphreys (1991), p.200.
96 Auchmuty (1989), p.138.
97 *Girls' Friend*, 3 January 1920.
98 Ibid.
99 Ibid.
100 Hemming (1960), pp.78–9.

Chapter 7

Conclusion

Girlhood is a cultural construct, one which embodies the cross-cutting of gender by age. As with other social categories, girlhood is the product of social processes and is historically and also regionally variable. The cultural construction of girlhood between 1920 to 1950 has been the subject of this study. Focusing on popular girls' magazines and key themes which they addressed – school, work, relationships, the body and sexuality – we have explored some of the ways in which these papers mapped out what it was to be a 'girl' in this period, how this varied for different groups by age and social class, and how this changed over time. Editorial negotiation of the interests of readers, of patriarchy, and of capital, was central to this process of constructing 'girlhood'.

One of the most obvious ways in which publishers demarcated the boundaries of 'girlhood' was by launching magazines specifically and explicitly targeted at an audience of 'girls', for the most part aged between 12 and 20 years. The period 1920 to 1950 was, as we have seen, marked by a proliferation of periodicals for 'girls' including papers for elementary and secondary schoolgirls and magazines for working girls in manual and non-manual occupations. The middle-class and missionary *Girls' Own Paper* was the only 'girls'' magazine to embrace the whole of adolescence which it accomplished by treating all its readers as if they were sexually innocent schoolgirls. This construction of the intended reader was, however, inconsistent with the interests and concerns of many middle-class girls in this period who entered full-time paid employment and also sexual relationships during their teens. Commercial papers of the period 1920 to 1950 adopted a different approach and typically differentiated between two groups of 'girl' readers, the schoolgirl (10 to 14 years) and the young worker (15/16 to 20 years). Competition amongst publishers was perhaps the main reason for the segmentation of the 'girl' market. However, this was dependent on adolescent girls having access to disposable income. Publishers' initiatives also required that girls possessed, or could be persuaded to adopt, a specific

useful
Teenager

consumer identity; in this instance, an identity which hinged on two key variables, girls' occupation and their place in the heterosexual career.

Although the emergence of specifically teenage consumption has been located in the period after 1950, recent research suggests that generation-specific leisure practices and consumption were apparent prior to this.[1] Indeed, as the proliferation of popular magazines indicates, adolescent girls were courted as consumers throughout the period 1920 to 1950. The category 'girl' was not, however, homogeneous nor fixed. The *Girls' Own Paper*, for instance, was initially combined with *Woman's Magazine* suggesting that its publisher, the RTS, found it difficult to distinguish between adolescent 'girls' and 'women'. Elementary schoolgirl papers were, from the outset, clearer about the identity of their female readership which hinged on its schoolgirl status and its exclusion from romantic and sexual relationships. Magazines aimed at older working girls defined their audience both in terms of its occupation, in full-time paid or unpaid work, and its position in the heterosexual career, that is courting and preparing for future marriage. This category of 'girls' was less clearly demarcated than its schoolgirl counterpart. In the context of economic difficulties during the late 1920s and 1930s, first the business girls' papers and then the millgirl papers were amalgamated with magazines aimed at a broad audience of female readers. The fact that this rationalisation was deemed feasible indicates that working and courting 'girls' were seen to share interests with older and married women, namely an interest in racy fiction concerned with heterosexual relationships, either thrillers or passionate, and often tragic, romances. Although 'adolescence' was increasingly institutionalised in the first half of this century as a specific age category, developments in commercial publishing indicate that once girls reached an age when they were expected to be interested in the opposite sex, their identity as 'girls' became unstable and inclined to merge with that of older 'women'.

McRobbie, writing of *Jackie* magazine in the 1970s, describes how it 'introduces the girl to adolescence, outlining its landmarks and characteristics in detail and stressing the problematic features as well as the fun.'[2] Girls' magazines of the period 1920 to 1950 similarly mapped out the terrain of girlhood presenting different sets of issues and topics as the appropriate concerns of their readers. Most commercial magazines, especially those aimed at a working-class audience, focused on fiction suggesting that girls desired entertainment. This prioritised leisure as a key aspect of adolescent experience and identity. In contrast, magazines targeted at middle-class girls featured an extensive range of information and education features alongside stories and serials suggesting that the lives of these readers were broader than those of their working-class peers. A concern with the private sphere of relationships was a further characteristic of the world of girlhood as constructed by working-class magazines. The public world was excluded from elementary schoolgirl papers, except as a backdrop for the fiction, while magazines for working-class working girls confronted the public world of paid work but principally in terms of its implications for finding and securing a potential husband. The Second World War, for example, was featured as a context for romantic fiction and advertisements for beauty aids rather than as a subject in itself. Mother-daughter papers spoke more openly about the war but this was in terms of its domestic implications; the public sphere was introduced by way of the private and familial. Middle-class papers such as *Miss Modern* and *Girls' Own Paper* were more attentive to the world outside the home in their discussions of education, training, paid work and, during the Second World War, war work, youth organisations, reconstruction and community service.

The form and content of girls' magazines varied according to the age and social class of the intended reader. But whilst there were differences in the models of girls and girlhood which different magazines presented to their audiences, there was also a significant point of continuity. The 'girl' whom publishers targeted, and whom editors worked to please, was invariably white. The representation of English girlhood, indeed English society, was a white one. Girls from other racial groups were only occasionally represented. Schoolgirl magazines sometimes featured rather romantic characters such as the Indian schoolgirl princess, while working girls' papers incorporated references to 'foreigners' and other races in their construction of the bad or evil woman.

Absences, as the treatment of race suggests, were as important for defining girlhood as what was included in these magazines. Schoolgirl papers prioritised female friendships but they denied any form of sexual interest either between girls, or between the sexes. These papers also promoted their readers as physically child-like and denied the changes associated with puberty. While schooling was central to the readers' identity, employment prospects were not presented as a legitimate schoolgirl concern even if fantastic careers were featured in the fiction. These magazines suggest that schoolgirls occupied a distinct period between child and adult during which the concerns of paid work, marriage and motherhood were not yet relevant. Magazines for working girls were characterised by a different range of absences. Whereas heterosexual relationships were of paramount importance for defining the reader, these papers were silent on the subject of female friendships and the possibilities of lesbian relationships. Paid work was of key importance to their reader's identity but schooling was not. Appearance was also paramount, linked as it was to heterosexual success, but the external and also internal dimensions of the female body were cross-cut by a public/private division such that the breasts and genitalia, the changes of adolescence, menstruation and pregnancy were not publicly discussed.

Representations of femininity and girlhood were not reflections or distortions of girls' lived experience, nor were they merely the imposition of dominant ideologies. Magazine representations of education, work, relationships, the body and sexuality were all products of negotiation. At one level this involved the editor mediating between a range of needs and interests. These included publishers' objectives, codes and cultures; readers' interests, needs and fantasies; the concerns of parents and teachers (which were an important consideration for editors producing magazines to be purchased by adults for girls); and the requirements of the government, particularly during the Second World War and post-war reconstruction. Discourses on adolescence and prevailing ideals of femininity and of girlhood also impinged on decisions as to what constituted the concerns of girls from different social groups and how these matters should be representationally managed. At another level, the articulation of the interests of patriarchy and of capital were at the heart of magazine production processes and central to the construction of girlhood. Whilst editorial negotiation often involved addressing the often discordant relations between patriarchy and capital it could also entail the management of tensions within these different sets of relations. The interests of capital, for instance, were often split between the promotion of motherhood and encouragement to girls to consume, while patriarchal relations were sometimes bedevilled by the often diverse preoccupations of fathers, boyfriends and husbands. Most importantly, however, the world of girlhood which was represented in different magazines was the product of attempts to address readers' interests, a need motivated by the commercial imperative, whilst avoiding a challenge to patriarchal interests in girls as future wives, domestics, emotional and sexual servicers.

The articulation of the interests of capital and of patriarchy was an on-going feature of the construction of girlhood in girls' magazines because the conditions which shaped readers' lives, and the context of magazine production, were not static. The period between 1920 and 1950 was characterised by considerable social, political and economic upheaval which did have implications for the organisation and experiences of adolescent girlhood. Magazines for working girls in factories, mills and offices and papers for middle-class schoolgirls were more responsive to socio-economic changes than the working-class schoolgirl papers. For middle-class papers, attention to social change represented one aspect of a wider concern with the public sphere as a legitimate interest of middle-class girls. In contrast, most working girls' magazines were usually attentive to change in terms of its significance for heterosexual relations. Letter pages, editorials, and articles broached various changes and 'fashions' from this perspective. So too did the fiction which, because of its rapid production under editorial direction, often addressed current issues and controversies. Editors of these magazines offered readers ways of understanding current trends and guidance on how to respond to these.

Representations of the 'modern girl', which were one outcome of editorial processes, embodied the articulation of prevailing interests within, and between, patriarchy and capital (readers' interests were fundamental to the commercial interests of capital). The 'modern girl' also embodied a dialogue with past idealisations of girlhood and femininity. Gorham discovered that late nineteenth-century ideals of girlhood incorporated aspects of the mid-Victorian ideal of the 'sunbeam', in particular her domestic and nurturant femininity. Constructions of 'modern' girlhood in the period 1920 to 1950 were similarly characterised by continuity with pre-established, 'old-fashioned', conceptions of girlhood which were the product of past attempts to culturally manage gender and social change, and negotiate the interests of capital and of patriarchy. This incorporation of the old with the new served to diminish the perceived implications of modernity by establishing its continuity with more established ideals of femininity. Whilst this strategy may have softened opposition to the 'modern girl', it also undermined the possible independence and resistance of many girls and women whose actions and beliefs were redefined in ways which did not challenge prevailing gender relations.

Auchmuty, in her study of schoolgirl novels, argues that changes in the representation of relationships between girls and between women constitutes evidence of the imposition of compulsory heterosexuality in twentieth-century Britain.[3] The form and content of popular girls' magazines offers further evidence of this and the often convoluted negotiations through which this was achieved. Indeed, the promotion of a domesticated heterosexuality, organised according to a specific career progression, was central to the cultural management and representation of biographical and also historical change within girls' magazines throughout the period 1920 to 1950. This is not to argue that girls were manipulated or duped by their reading of magazines, rather that, given the organisation and experiences of adolescent girlhood, many readers would have recognised the 'preferred meanings' embedded in girls' magazines and would have learned the feminine lessons conveyed in their weekly and monthly papers, even if they subsequently rejected them. To ignore this, is to deny readers their cultural 'know how'. It is also to dismiss the concerns which preoccupied many girls who grew up in England between 1920 and 1950.

Notes

1   Davies (1992) addresses this point.
2   McRobbie (1991), p.83.
3   Auchmuty (1989).

Bibliography

I Archival Sources

British Library (Papers consulted and range of years examined).
Betty's Paper, 1922–41.
Butterfly, 1930.
Children's Newspaper, 1919–40.
Every Girls' Paper, 1923–24.
Fortune, 1934–36.
Girl, 1951.
Girls' Cinema, 1920.
Girls' (Best) Friend, 1920–31.
(Girls') Crystal, 1935–50.
Girls' Own Paper and Woman's Magazine, 1920–30, Girls' Own Annual, 1931–41, Girls' Own Paper, 1941–46, Heiress, 1947–50.
Girls' Favourite, 1922–27.
Girls' Weekly, 1920–22.
Girls' World, 1927.
Lucky Star, 1935–50.
Mabs Weekly 1931–35.
Merry and Bright, 1930.
Miracle, 1935–58.
Miss Modern, 1930–40.
My Favourite, 1928.
My Weekly, 1930.
Pam's Paper, 1923–27.
Peg's Paper, 1919–40.
Polly's Paper, 1919–24.
Poppy's Paper, 1924–34.

Red Letter,1930.
Red Star Weekly, 1929–50.
School Friend, 1919–29.
School-Days, 1928–29.
Schoolgirl, 1929–40.
Schoolgirls' Own 1921–36.
Schoolgirls' Pictorial, 1924–25.
Schoolgirls' Weekly, 1929–39.
Silver Star, 1937–40.
The Oracle, 1933–50.
The Playbox, 1930.
Woman, 1937–50.
Woman's Own, 1932–50.

Mass-Observation Archive, University of Sussex.
File Report 3150 (August 1949), *A Report On Teenage Girls*.
File Report 1422/1355 (July 1942), *The Service of Youth – Survey of Board of Education Youth Welfare Scheme as it Operates in North Town*.
File Report 1567 (12 January 1943), *Report On Girls Between School Leaving Age and Registration Age*.
File Report 3012 (June 1948), *Children Out Of School: an enquiry into the leisure interests and activities of children out of school hours carried out by J.C. Ward for the Central Advisory Council for Education, Nov–Dec 1941* (Social Survey).

Institute of Practitioners in Advertising, Belgrave Square, London.
Institute of Incorporated Practitioners in Advertising (1939) *Survey of Press Readership*, vol. I and II.
Institute of Incorporated Practitioners in Advertising (1947) *Survey of Press Readership*, London.
Hulton Press (1948) *Hulton Press Readership Survey*, compiled by Hobson, J.W. and Henry, H., London.
Attwood (1947) *The Attwood National Publications Readership Survey*, Part I and II (March), London.

USCL/Religious Tract Society Archives, SOAS Library, London.
USCL/RTS, Minutes of Executive Committee, Boxes 99–121, 6 January 1920–20 March 1951.
USCL/RTS, Ledgers and Accounts, Boxes 223–228, 1920–1950.

Interviews and correspondence with the author
Mary Grieve, correspondence 18 March 1986.

James Hemming, interview 2 November 1985.

Pat Lamburn, interview 23 July 1985; correspondence 6 November 1986, 19 February 1987.

Mrs Jean Lee, interview 9 July 1985.

W.O.G. Lofts, correspondence 17 February 1987.

Marcus Morris, interview 22 November 1985.

Lorrie Purden, interview 23 July 1985.

SG 1 A, interview 18 November 1985.

SG 2 B, interview 18 November 1985.

II Books, Articles and Theses

ABRAMS, M. (1961) *Teenage Consumer Spending in 1959. Middle Class and Working Class Boys and Girls*, London, London Press Exchange.

ADLEY, D.J. and LOFTS, W.O.G. (1970) *The Men Behind Boys' Fiction*, London, Howard Baker.

ALDERSON, C. (1968) *Magazines Teenagers Read With Special Reference to Trend, Jackie and Valentine*, London, Pergammon Press.

ALEXANDER, S. (1989) 'Becoming a woman in London in the 1920s and 1930s', in FELDMAN, D. and STEDMAN JONES, G. (Eds) *Metropolis, London: Histories and representations since 1800*, London, Routledge.

ALTHUSSER, L. (1970) 'From Capital to Marx's Philosophy', in ALTHUSSER, L. and BALIBAR, E. *Reading 'Capital'*, (translated by Ben Brewster), London, Francais Maspero.

ANG, I. (1985) *Watching Dallas. Soap Opera and the Melodramatic Imagination*, London, Methuen.

APPLEBEE, A. (1978) *The Child's Concept of Story: ages two to seventeen*, Chicago, University of Chicago Press.

ARMSTRONG, W.A. (1972) 'The Use of Information About Occupation', in WRIGLEY, E.A. (Ed.) *Nineteenth-Century Society: Essays in the use of quantitative methods for the study of social data*, Cambridge, Cambridge University Press.

AUCHMUTY, R. (1989) '"You're A Dyke, Angela!" Elsie J. Oxenham and the rise and fall of the schoolgirl story', in LESBIAN HISTORY GROUP (Ed.) *Not A Passing Phase. Reclaiming Lesbians in History 1840–1985*, London, The Women's Press.

AUCHMUTY, R. (1992) *A World of Girls: The Appeal of the Girls' School Story*, London, Women's Press.

AVERY, G. (1991) *The Best Type of Girl: A History of Girls' Independent Schools*, London, Andre Deutsch.

BALLASTER, R., BEETHAM, M., FRAZER, E., and HEBRON, S. (1991) *Women's*

Worlds. Ideology, Femininity and the Woman's Magazine, London, Macmillan.

BARTHES, R. (1972) 'Myth Today' in *Mythologies*, translated by Annette Lavers, London, Cape.

BEAUCHAMP, J. (1937) *Women Who Work*, London, Lawrence & Wishart.

BEAUMAN, N. (1983) *A Very Great Profession: The Woman's Novel 1914–1939*, London, Virago.

BEDDOE, D. (1989) *Back To Home and Duty: Women between the Wars*, London, Pandora.

BETTERTON, K. (1982) 'White Pinnies, Black Aprons', in BURNETT, J. (Ed.) *Destiny Obscure: Autobiographies of childhood, education and family from the 1820s to the 1920s*, London, Allen Lane.

BEVERIDGE, W. *et al.* (1932) *Changes in Family Life*, London, Allen & Unwin.

BLANCHARD, P. (1929) 'Sex in the Adolescent Girl', in CALVERTON, V.F. and SCHMALHAUSEN, D.S. (Eds), *Sex In Civilization*, London, Allen and Unwin.

BLOOM, U. (1944) *Me-After The War. A book for girls considering the future*, London, Gifford.

BOARD OF EDUCATION (1923) *Report of the Consultative Committee on the Differentiation of the Curriculum for Boys and Girls Respectively in Secondary Schools*, London, HMSO.

BOARD OF EDUCATION (1926) *Report of the Consultative Committee on the Education of the Adolescent*, London, HMSO.

BOARD OF EDUCATION (1931) *Report of The Consultative Committee on The Primary School*, London, HMSO.

BOARD OF EDUCATION (1933) *Yearbook Of Education*, London, HMSO.

BOARD OF EDUCATION (1938) *Report On The Secondary School*, London, HMSO.

BOARD OF EDUCATION (1943a) *Sex Education in Schools and Youth Organisations*, London, HMSO.

BOARD OF EDUCATION (1943b) *Youth In A City*, London, HMSO.

BONNER, F. *et al.* (1992) (Eds) *Imagining Women. Cultural Representations and Gender*, Cambridge, Polity Press, in association with The Open University.

BOWEN, E. (1984) 'The Mulberry Tree', in GREENE, G. (Ed.) *The Old School*, Oxford, Oxford University Press.

BRANSON, N. and HEINEMANN, M. (1971) *Britain in the Nineteen Thirties*, Herts, Panther/Granada.

BRANSON, N. (1977) *Britain In The Nineteen Twenties*, London, Weidenfeld and Nicholson.

BRATTON, J.S. (1981) *The Impact of Victorian Children's Fiction*, London, Croom Helm.

BRAYBON, G. (1981) *Women Workers in the First World War: The British Experience*, London, Croom Helm.

BREW, J.M. (1943) *In The Service of Youth. A practical manual of work among adolescents*, London, Faber & Faber.

BRITTAIN, V. (1928) *Women's Work In Modern Britain*, London, Noel Douglas.

BROWNMILLER, S. (1986) *Femininity*, London, Paladin.

CADOGAN, M. and CRAIG, P. (1986) *You're A Brick, Angela!: The Girls' Story 1839–1985*, London, Gollancz.

CALVERTON, V.F. and SCHMALHAUSEN, D.S. (Eds) (1929) *Sex In Civilization*, London, Allen and Unwin.

CENSUS OF ENGLAND AND WALES (1921) Occupation Tables, London.

CENSUS OF ENGLAND AND WALES (1931) Occupation Tables, London.

CENSUS OF ENGLAND AND WALES (1951) Occupational Tables, London.

CENSUS OF ENGLAND AND WALES (1951) General Report, London.

(charles), Helen (1992) '"Whiteness" – The Relevance of Politically Colouring the "Non"', in HINDS, H., PHOENIX, A., and STACEY, J. (Eds) *Working Out: new directions for women's studies*, Lewes, Falmer Press.

CONSTANTINE, S. (1980) *Unemployment In Britain Between The Wars*, London, Longman.

COWARD, R. (1984) *Female Desire. Women's Sexuality Today*, London, Paladin.

CROOK, R. (1982) 'Tidy Women – Women in the Rhondda Valley Between the Wars', in *Oral History*, vol.10, no.2, (Autumn), pp.40–46.

CROSTHWAIT, E. (1986) 'The Girl Behind the Man Behind The Gun: The Women's Army Auxillary Corps, 1914–18', in DAVIDOFF, L. and WESTOVER, B. (Eds) *Our Work, Our Lives, Our Words*, London, Macmillan.

DAVIDSON, C. (1982) *A Woman's Work Is Never Done: A history of housework in the British Isles 1650–1950*, London, Chatto & Windus.

DAVIES, A. (1992) *Leisure, Gender and Poverty: working-class culture in Salford and Manchester*, Buckingham, Open University Press.

DAVY, T. (1986) '"A Cissy Job For Men: A Nice Job For Girls": Women Shorthand Typists In London 1930–39', in DAVIDOFF, L. and WESTOVER, B. (Eds) *Our Work, Our Lives, Our Words*, London, Macmillan.

DELAMONT, S. (1978) 'The Contradictions in Ladies' Education', in DELAMONT, S. and DUFFIN, L. (Eds) *The Nineteenth-Century Woman: Her Cultural and Physical World*, London, Croom Helm.

DELPHY, C. and LEONARD, D. (1992) *Familiar Exploitation. A New Analysis of Marriage in Contemporary Western Societies*, London, Polity.

DICKENS, M. (1980) *An Open Book*, Harmondsworth, Penguin.

DIXON, J. (1987) 'Fantasy Unlimited. The World of Mills and Boon', *Women's Review*, vol. 1, (July).

DORE, R. (1976) *The Diploma Disease: Education, Qualification and Development*, London, Allen and Unwin.

DOUIE, V. (1949) *Daughters of Britain*, London, Women's Service Library.

DRAWBELL, J. (1968) *Time On My Hands*, London, Macdonald.

DROTNER, K. (1988) *English Children and their Magazines, 1751–1945*, New Haven and London, Yale University Press.

DURANT, H. (1938) *The Problem of Leisure*, London, G. Routledge & Sons.

DYHOUSE, C. (1978) 'Towards a "feminine" curriculum for English Schoolgirls: the demands of Ideology 1870–1963', *Women's Studies International Quarterly*, vol.1, pp.297–312.

DYHOUSE, C. (1981) *Girls Growing Up in Late Victorian and Edwardian England*, London, Routledge & Kegan Paul.

DYHOUSE, C. (1987) 'Miss Buss and Miss Beale: Gender and Authority in the history of education', in HUNT, F. (Ed.) *Lessons For Life. The Schooling of Girls and Women, 1850–1950*, Oxford, Basil Blackwell.

DYHOUSE, C. (1989) *Feminism and the Family in England 1880–1939*, Oxford, Basil Blackwell.

FADERMAN, L. (1985) *Surpassing The Love Of Men*, London, The Women's Press.

FENWICK, L. (1953) 'Periodicals and Adolescent Girls', in *Studies in Education* (University College, Hull), vol.2, pt. l, pp.27–45.

FERGUSON, M. (1983) *Forever Feminine. Women's Magazines and the Cult of Femininity*, London, Heinemann.

FOAKES, G. (1972) *Between High Walls: A London childhood*, London, Shepheard-Walwyn.

FOLEY, W. (1977) *A Child In The Forest*, London, Futura.

FORRESTER, H. (1981) *Twopence To Cross The Mersey*, Glasgow, Fontana/ Collins.

FORRESTER, H. (1982) *Liverpool Miss*, Glasgow, Fontana/Collins.

FOWLER, B. (1991) *The Alienated Reader. Women and Popular Romantic Literature in the Twentieth Century*, Hemel Hempstead, Harvester Wheatsheaf.

FREEMAN, G. (1976) *The Schoolgirl Ethic. The Life and Work of Angela Brazil*, London, Allen Lane.

FRITH, G. (1985) 'The Time Of Your Life: The Meaning of the School Story', in STEEDMAN, C. *et al.* (Eds) *Language, Gender and Childhood*, London, Routledge.

GAMBLE, R. (1982) *Chelsea Child*, London, Ariel Books/BBC.

GARSIDE, W.R. (1980) *The Measurement of Unemployment: Methods and Sources in Great Britain 1850–1979*, Oxford, Basil Blackwell.

GATHORNE-HARDY, J. (1977) *The Public School Phenomenon*, London, Hodder and Stoughton.

GILLIS, J. (1974) *Youth and History: Tradition and Change in European Age Relations 1770 – present*, New York and London, Academy Press.

GITTENS, D. (1982) *Fair Sex, Family Size and Structure 1900–39*, London, Hutchinson.

GLUCKSMANN, M. (1990) *Women Assemble: women workers and the new industries in inter-war Britain*, London, Routledge.

GLYNN, S. and OXBORROW, J. (1976) *Inter-war Britain: A Social and Economic History*, London, Allen and Unwin.

GORHAM, D. (1982) *The Victorian Girl and the Feminine Ideal*, London, Croom Helm.

GORHAM, D. (1987) 'The Ideology of Femininity and Reading for Girls, 1850–1914', in HUNT, F. (Ed.) *Lessons for Life: The schooling of girls and women, 1850–1950*, Oxford, Basil Blackwell.

GRAVES, R. and HODGE, A. (1991) *The Long Weekend. A Social History of Great Britain 1918–1939*, London, Cardinal/Sphere (1st published 1940).

GRIEVE, M. (1960) *Millions Made My Story*, London, Gollanz.

GRIFFIN, C. (1985) *Typical Girls? Young Women From School to the Job Market*, London, Routledge and Kegan Paul.

GRIFFIN, C. (1993) *Representations of Youth. The Study of Youth and Adolescence in Britain and America*, Cambridge, Polity Press.

GRIFFITH, E.F. (Ed.) (1947) *The Road To Maturity*, London, Methuen.

HADDON, C. (1977) *Great Days and Jolly Days: The Story of Girls' School Songs*, London, Hodder and Stoughton.

HALL, E. (1977) *Canary Girls and Stockpots*, Luton, WEA.

HALL, S. (1980) 'Encoding/Decoding', in HALL, S. *et al.* (Eds) *Culture, Media, Language: Working papers in cultural studies*, London, Hutchinson.

HALL CARPENTER ARCHIVES LESBIAN ORAL HISTORY GROUP (1989) (Eds) *Inventing Ourselves. Lesbian Life Stories*, London, Routledge.

HALSEY, A.H. (1972) *Trends In British Society Since 1900. A guide to the changing social structure of Britain*, London, Macmillan.

HAWKINS, A.D. (1943) 'Some Investigations Concerning The Work In A Central School in Relation To The Future Occupations Of Its Pupils', *Journal of Educational Psychology*, vol. xiii, Pt. ii.

HEMMING, J. (1969) *Problems Of Adolescent Girls*, London, Heinemann.

HOGGART, R. (1958) *The Uses of Literacy. Aspects of working-class life with special reference to publications and entertainments*, Harmondsworth, Penguin.

HOLLEDGE, J. (1981) *Innocent Flowers: Women in the Edwardian Theatre*, London, Virago.

HOLTBY, W. (1983) *South Riding*, Glasgow, Fontana/Collins.

HUDSON, B. (1984) 'Femininity and Adolescence', in MCROBBIE, A. and NAVA, M. (Eds) *Gender and Generation*, London, Macmillan.

HUMPHREYS, S. (1981) *Hooligans and Rebels? An oral history of working-class childhood and youth 1889–1939*, Oxford, Oxford University Press.

HUMPHREYS, S. (1991) *A Secret World of Sex. Forbidden Fruit: The British Experience 1900–1950*, London, Sidgewick and Jackson.

HUNT, F. (1985) 'Social Class and The Grading Of Schools: Realities In Girls' Secondary Education 1880–1940', in PURVIS, J. (Ed) (History of Education Society) *The Education of Girls and Women*.

HUNT, F. (1991) *Gender & Policy in English Education: schooling for girls,1902–1944*, Hemel Hempstead, Harvester Wheatsheaf.

JAMES, H.E.O. and MOORE, F.T. (1940) 'Adolescent Leisure in a Working-Class District', *Occupational Psychology*, vol. xiv, no.3, (July) pp.132–45.

JAMES, H.E.O. and MOORE, F.T. (1944) 'Adolescent Leisure in a Working-Class District II', *Occupational Psychology*, vol. xviii, no.1 (January) pp.24–34.

JAMIESON, L. (1986) 'Limited Resources and Limiting Conventions: Working-class Mothers and Daughters in Urban Scotland c. 1890–1925', in LEWIS, J. (Ed.) *Labour and Love. Women's Experience of Home and Family, 1850–1940*, Oxford, Basil Blackwell.

JEFFREYS, S. (1985) *The Spinster and her Enemies: Feminism and Sexuality 1880–1930*, London, Pandora.

JEFFREYS, S. (1989) 'Does it Matter If They Did It?' in LESBIAN HISTORY GROUP (Ed.) *Not A Passing Phase. Reclaiming Lesbians in History 1840–1985*, London, The Women's Press.

JENKINSON, A.J. (1940) *What Do Boys and Girls Read?*, London, Methuen.

JEPHCOTT, P. (1942) *Girls Growing Up*, London, Faber & Faber.

JEPHCOTT, P. (1948) *Rising Twenty: notes on some ordinary girls*, London, Faber.

JOHANSSON, S. R. (1980) 'Sex and Death in Victorian England. An Examination of Sex-Specific Death Rates 1840–1910', in VICINUS, M. (Ed.) *A Widening Sphere: changing roles of Victorian women*, London, Methuen.

JORDAN, G.W. and FISHER, E.M. (1955) *Self Portrait of Youth: or, the urban adolescent*, London, Heinemann.

KENT, R. (1979) *Aunt Agony Advises: problem pages through the ages*, London, W.H. Allen.

KING, S. (1990) 'Technical and vocational education for girls. A study of the central schools of London, 1918–1939', in SUMMERFIELD, P. and EVANS, E. (Eds) *Technical Education and the State Since 1850: historical and contemporary perspectives*, Manchester, Manchester University Press.

KOHN, M. (1992) *Dope Girls. The Birth of the British Drug Underground*, London, Lawrence & Wishart.

LAMB, F. and PICKTHORN, H. (1968) *Locked-Up Daughters. A parents' look at girls' education and schools*, London, Hodder & Stoughton.

LAST, N. (1983) *Nella Last's War; A Mother's Diary 1939–1945*, London, Sphere.

LEMAN, J. (1980) '"The Advice of a Real Friend": codes of intimacy and oppression in women's magazines 1937–1955, *Women's Studies Inter-*

national Quarterly, vol. 3, no.1, pp.63–78.

LEWENHAK, S. (1977) *Women and Trade Unions: An outline of Women in the British Trade Union Movement*, London, Ernest Benn.

LEWIS, J. (1980) *The Politics of Motherhood: child and maternal welfare in England, 1900–1979*, London, Croom Helm.

LEWIS, J. (1984) *Women In England 1870–1950: Sexual Divisions and Social Change*, Sussex, Wheatsheaf.

LINDSAY, K. (1926) *Social Progress And Educational Waste: being a study of the 'free place' and scholarship systems*, London, G. Routledge & Sons.

LINDSEY, B.B. and EVANS, W. (1928) *The Revolt of Modern Youth*, London, Brentano's.

LINGWOOD, J. (1941) 'The Vocational Information Possessed By Secondary School Girls', *Occupational Psychology*, vol. xv, no.4, (October), pp.185–97.

LOFTS, W.O.G. (1978) 'Why did men write for girls?', *Collectors Digest Annual*.

MACE, D. (1948) *Marriage Crisis*, London, Delisle.

MACNICOL, J. (1980) *The Movement For Family Allowances, 1918–1945: a study in social policy development*, London, Heinemann.

MADGE, C. (1943) *War-Time Patterns of Spending And Saving*, Cambridge, Cambridge University Press.

MARTINDALE, H. (1938) *Women Servants Of The State, 1870–1938: a history of women in the Civil Service*, London, Allen & Unwin.

MARWICK, A. (1991, 2nd edition) *The Deluge: British Society and the First World War*, London, Macmillan.

MATTHEWS, J.J. (1987) 'Building The Body Beautiful', *Australian Feminist Studies*, vol.5 (Summer), pp.17–34.

MCROBBIE, A. (1981) 'Just Like A *Jackie* Story', in MCROBBIE, A. and MCCABE,T. (Eds) *Feminism For Girls. An Adventure Story*, London, Routledge & Kegan Paul.

MCROBBIE, A. (1991) '*Jackie* Magazine: Romantic Individualism and the Teenage Girl', in *Feminism and Youth Culture: from 'Jackie' to 'Just Seventeen'*, London, Macmillan.

MERCER, E. (1940) 'Some Occupational Attitudes of Girls', in *Occupational Psychology*, vol. xiv, no. 1, (January), pp.14–25.

MINISTRY OF EDUCATION (1947) *School and Life: A First Enquiry Into The Transition From School To Independent Life*, London, HMSO.

MINISTRY OF EDUCATION (1954) *Early Leaving. A Report of the Central Advisory Council for Education (England)*, London, HMSO.

MINISTRY OF LABOUR AND NATIONAL SERVICE (1945) *Report On The Committee On The Juvenile Employment Service*, London, HMSO.

MYERS, C. (1939) 'The Servant Problem', *Occupational Psychology*, vol.

xiii, no.2, (April), pp.77–88.

NATIONAL PANEL MEMBER (1984) 'Rats in the NAAFI', in CALDER, A. and SHERIDAN, D. (Eds) (1984) *Speak For Yourself: A Mass Observation Anthology 1937–49*, London, Jonathon Cape.

NAVA, M. (1992) *Changing Cultures: Feminism, Youth and Consumerism*, London, Sage.

NOAKES, D. (1980, 2nd edition) *The Town Beehive – A Young Girl's Lot, Brighton 1910–1934*, Brighton, Queen Spark Books.

ODDY, D. (1982) 'The Health Of The People', in BARKER, T. and DRAKE, M. (Eds) *Population and Society in Great Britain, 1850–1980*, London, Batsford.

OKELY, J. (1978) 'Privileged Schooled and Finished: Boarding School Education for Girls', in ARDENER, S. (Ed.) *Defining Females: The Nature of Women in Society*, New York, John Wiley.

ORAM, A. (1987) 'Inequalities in the Teaching Profession: the Effect on Teachers and Pupils, 1910–39' in HUNT, F. (Ed.) *Lessons for Life. The Schooling of Girls and Women, 1850–1950*, Oxford, Basil Blackwell.

ORAM, A. (1989) '"Embittered, Sexless or Homosexual": Attacks on Spinster Teachers 1918–1939', in LESBIAN HISTORY GROUP (Ed.) *Not A Passing Phase: Reclaiming Lesbians in History 1840–1985*, London, The Women's Press.

ORAM, A. (1992) 'Repressed and Thwarted, or Bearer of the New World? The Spinster in Inter-War Feminist Discourse', in SUMMERFIELD, P. and TINKLER, P. (Ed.) *Women's Sexualities: contest and control, Women's History Review*, Special Issue, vol.1, no.3, pp.413–34.

ORWELL, G. (1982a) *The Road To Wigan Pier*, Harmondsworth, Penguin (1st published 1937).

ORWELL, G. (1982b) 'Boy's Weeklies' (1940), in OWEN, S. and ANGUS, I. (Eds) *The Collected Essays, Journalism and Letters of George Orwell*, vol. 1, Harmondsworth, Penguin.

OWEN, L. (1974) 'The Welfare of Women In Labouring Families: England, 1860–1950', in HARTMANN, M. and BANNER, C. (Eds) *Clio's Consciousness Raised: New Perspectives on the History of Women*, Harper and Row.

PELLING, H. (1976, 3rd edition) *A History of British Trade Unionism*, Harmondsworth, Penguin.

PHILLIPS, A. (1987) *Divided Loyalties: Dilemmas of Sex and Class*, London, Virago Press.

PILGRIM TRUST (1938) *Men Without Work*, A Report Made To the Pilgrim Trust, Cambridge, Cambridge University Press.

POLLERT, A. (1981) *Girls, Wives, Factory Lives*, London, Macmillan.

POUND, R. and HARMSWORTH, G. (1959) *Northcliffe*, London, Cassell.

POWELL, H. (1924) 'The Problem of the Adolescent Girl ', in SCHARLIEB, M.

(Ed.) *Sexual Problems Of Today*, London, Williams and Norgate.

PRATT, M. (1934) 'Reflections Of A Headmistress On Vocational Guidance', *Journal Of Occupational Psychology*, vol. xiii, no.4, pp.285–94.

RADWAY, J. (1987) *Reading The Romance: Women, Patriarchy and Popular Literature*, London, Verso.

RAPHAEL, W., WHITE, I.H.B., HEARNSHAW, L.S. and MUNRO FRASER, J.H. (1938) 'An Inquiry Into Labour Turnover In The Leeds District', *Occupational Psychology*, vol. xii, no.4, pp.257–70.

RATHBONE, E. (1940) *The Case For Family Allowances*, Harmondsworth, Penguin.

REED, B. (1950) *Eighty Thousand Adolescents. A study of young people in the city of Birmingham ... for the Edward Cadbury Charitable Trust*, London, George Allen & Unwin.

REYNOLDS, K. (1990) *Girls Only? Gender and Popular Children's Fiction in Britain, 1880–1910*, Hemel Hempstead, Harvester Wheatsheaf.

RICH, A. (1980) 'Compulsory Heterosexuality and Lesbian Existence', *Signs*, vol.5, no.4, pp.631–60.

RICHARDS, F. (1982) 'Frank Richards Replies to George Orwell' (1940) in OWEN, S. and ANGUS, I. (Eds) *The Collected Essays, Journalism and Letters of George Orwell*, vol. 1, Harmondsworth, Penguin.

RILEY, D. (1983) *War In The Nursery: Theories of the Child and Mother*, London, Virago.

ROBERTS, E. (1984) *A Woman's Place. An Oral History of Working-Class Wives 1890–1940*, Oxford, Basil Blackwell.

ROBERTS, R. (1980) *The Classic Slum*, Harmondsworth, Penguin.

ROBERTSON, E.A. (1984) 'Potting Shed Of The English Rose', in GREENE, G. (Ed.) *The Old School*, Oxford, Oxford University Press.

RODAWAY, A. (1985) *A London Childhood*, London, Virago.

ROOFF, M. (1935) *Youth and Leisure. A Survey of Girls' Organizations in England and Wales*, Edinburgh, Constable.

ROSEN, M. (1973) *Popcorn Venus: Women, Movies and the American Dream*, New York, Avon.

ROUTH, G. (1965) *Occupation and Pay in Great Britain, 1906–60*, London, Cambridge University Press.

ROWBOTHAM, J. (1989) *Good Girls Make Good Wives: Guidance for Girls in Victorian Fiction*, Oxford, Basil Blackwell.

ROWBOTHAM, S. and McCRINDLE, J. (Eds) (1977) *Dutiful Daughters*, London, Allen Lane.

ROWNTREE, B.S. (1941) *Poverty and Progress, A Second Social Survey Of York*, London, Longmans, Green & Co.

RUSSELL, G.L. (1940) *Sex Problems In Wartime*, London, Student Christian Movement Press.

SAVE THE CHILDREN FUND (1933) *Unemployment and the Child. Being the Report on an Enquiry... into the effects of unemployment on the Children of the Unemployed and on Unemployed Young Workers of Great Britain*, London, Longmans.

SAYWELL, E. (1922) *The Growing Girl, her Development and Training*, London, Methuen.

SCHARLIEB, M. (Ed.) (1924) *Sexual Problems Of To-day*, London, Williams & Norgate.

SCHWAAB, S.I. and VEEDER, B.D. (1929) *The Adolescent: his conflicts and escapes*, New York and London, D. Appleton & Co.

SCOTT, J. (1990) *A Matter of Record: Documentary Sources in Social Research*, Cambridge, Polity Press.

SCOTT, S. and MORGAN, D. (Eds) (1993) *Body Matters: Essays on the Sociology of the Body*, Lewes, Falmer Press.

SHERRATT, N. (1983) 'Girls, Jobs and Glamour', *Feminist Review*, 15 (winter), pp.47–61.

SMART, C. (Ed.) (1992) *Regulating Womanhood; Historical essays on marriage, motherhood and sexuality*, London, Routledge.

SPRING RICE, M. (1981) *Working-Class Wives, their health and condition*, London, Virago.

SPRINGHALL, J. (1986) *Coming of Age: Adolescence in Britain 1860–1960*, London, Gill & Macmillan.

STACEY, J. (1993) *Star Gazing. Hollywood Cinema and Female Spectatorship*, London, Routledge.

STOTT, M.B. (1939) 'Some Differences Between Boys and Girls In Vocational Guidance', *Human Factor*, vol. xi, pp.121–31.

SUMMERFIELD, P. (1984) *Women Workers In The Second World War: Production and Patriarchy in Conflict*, London, Croom Helm.

SUMMERFIELD, P. (1987a) 'Cultural Reproduction in the Education of Girls: a Study of Girls' Secondary Schooling in Two Lancashire Towns, 1900–1950', in HUNT, F. (Ed.) *Lessons for Life. The Schooling of Girls and Women, 1850–1950*, Oxford, Basil Blackwell.

SUMMERFIELD, P. (1987b) 'Women In The Professional Labour Market 1900–1950: the case of the secondary schoolmistress', in SUMMERFIELD, P. (Ed.) *Women, Education and Professions*, History of Education Society, Occasional Publication no.8, pp.37–52.

SUMMERFIELD, P. (1987c) 'An Oral History Of Schooling in Lancashire 1900–1950: Gender, Class and Education', in *Oral History*, vol. 5, no.2, (Autumn), pp.19–31.

SUMMERFIELD, P. (1988) 'Gender and Class in Lancashire Schools', paper presented to the Women's Studies Research Seminar, Lancaster University, January.

SUMMERFIELD, P. and BRAYBON, G. (1987) *Out of the Cage: Women's Experiences In Two World Wars*, London, Pandora.

SUMMERFIELD, P. and CROCKETT, N. (1992) '"You weren't taught that with the welding": lessons in sexuality in the Second World War', in SUMMERFIELD, P. and TINKLER, P. (Eds) *Women's Sexualities: contest and control, Women's History Review*, Special Issue, vol. 1, no.3, pp.435–54.

TAWNEY, R.H. (1922) *Secondary Education For All: a policy for Labour*, London, Labour Party.

THOM, D. (1987) 'Better A Teacher than a Hairdresser? "A Mad Passion for Equality" or, Keeping Molly and Betty Down', in HUNT, F. (Ed.) *Lessons for Life. The Schooling of Girls and Women, 1850–1950*, Oxford, Basil Blackwell.

TINKLER, P. (1987) 'Learning Through Leisure: feminine ideology in girls' magazines, 1920–50' in HUNT, F. (Ed.) *Lessons For Life. The Schooling of Girls and Women, 1850–1950*, Oxford, Basil Blackwell.

TINKLER, P. (1994a) 'An All Round Education: The Board of Education's Policy for the Leisure-Time Training of Girls, 1939–1950', *History of Education*, vol. 23, no. 4, pp.385–403.

TINKLER, P. (1994b) 'Contested Terrain: Citizenship, Adolescence and the County College Proposals', paper presented at the History of Education Conference, Birmingham, 5 December 1995.

TINKLER, P. (1995a) 'Sexuality and Citizenship; the state and girls' leisure provision, 1939–1950', *Women's History Review*, (June).

TINKLER, P. (1995b) 'Introducing Miss Modern: popular literature and the cultural management of difference and change', in PURVIS, J. (Ed.) *Women's History: Britain, 1850–1945*, London, UCL.

TOWNSEND, J.R. (1983) *Written For Children. An Outline of English-Language Children's Literature*, Harmondsworth, Penguin.

TREASE, G. (1948) *Tales Out Of School*, Surrey, Windmill Press.

VICINUS, M. (1985) *Independent Women: Work and Community for Single Women, 1850–1920*, London, Virago.

WALBY, S. (1986) *Patriarchy At Work: Patriarchal and Capitalist Relations in Employment*, Cambridge, Polity Press.

WALBY, S. (1987) *'Theorising Patriarchy'*, paper presented to the Women's Studies Research Seminar', Lancaster University, October.

WALBY, S. (1990) *Theorising Patriarchy*, Oxford, Basil Blackwell.

WALL, W.D. (1948) *The Adolescent Child*, London, Methuen.

WARD, J.C. (1948) *Children Out of School: an enquiry into the leisure interests and activities of children out of school hours carried out by J.C. Ward for the Central Advisory Council for Education, Nov–Dec 1941* (see Mass-Observation Archive).

WARE, V. (1992) *Beyond The Pale: White Women, Racism and History*, London, Verso.

WELLS, R. (1993) An Investigation into Representations of Girlhood in Girls' Popular Magazines and School Texts 1900–1930, Unpublished PhD Thesis, Cambridge University.

WHITE, C. (1970) *Women's Magazines 1963–1968*, London, Michael Joseph.

WHITE, C. (1977) *Royal Commission on the Press. The Women's Periodical Press in Britain, 1946–1977*, Working Paper 4, London, HMSO.

WILE, I.S. (1929) 'Sex and Normal Human Nature', in CALVERTON, V.F. and SCHMALHAUSEN, D.S. *Sex in Civilisation*, London, Allen and Unwin.

WILLIAMS, G. (1945) *Women and Work*, London, Nicholson & Watson.

WILSON, E. (1980) *Halfway To Paradise, Women In PostWar Britain 1945–1968*, London, Tavistock.

WINSHIP, J. (1987) *Inside Women's Magazines*, London, Pandora.

WOMEN'S GROUP ON PUBLIC WELFARE (1943) *Our Towns: A Close Up*, London, Oxford University Press.

YOUNG, M. and WILMOTT, P. (1990) *Family and Kinship in East London*, Harmondsworth, Penguin (1st published 1957).

Subject index